MW00580612

The Walking Dead

Pat Holliday, PhD

Agapepublishers
2011

The Walking Dead

Copyright © 2011 by Pat Holliday, PhD
ISBN 978-1-884785-02-3

Published by Agapepublishers
9252 San Jose Blvd., 2804
Jacksonville, Florida 32257
904-733-8318
Web page: http://patholliday.com
E mail: holliday.pat@gmail.com

This book is dedicated to Vadim Holliday

With the exception of my immediate family or well-known religious leaders, the names used are fictitious.

Thank you Tom McGonegal PhD cfi@graceba.net for your suggestions concerning the manuscript.

All rights reserved. No part of this copyright protected material may be reproduced or unitized in any form or by any means, electronic or mechanical without written permission from the copyright owner. Printed in the United States of America.

Contents

Introduction

OCCULT PROBLEM

This book was not produced to lionize the powers of darkness but rather to expose the all-encompassing rise and social acceptance of witchcraft and Satanism in the world. The New Age supernatural age of progressive interest and involvement in the occult have arrived to get a harvest of souls for hell through witchcraft and Satanic worship, coupled with human sacrifices is widespread and happening now!

Satan's ambassadors are very successful and extremely evangelistic, capturing spiritual slaves. It is sad indeed in many instances that God's people are choosing spiritual blindness and for it is a terrible thing to see the demonstration of the powers of darkness upon human beings. The occult is not a passing fad. Thousands find themselves bound by the powers of witchcraft and are seeking a way out of the darkness, CHRIST IS THE ONLY WAY OUT and the workers in the Churches are few.

My phone rang at 4:00 A. M. "Are you Pat Holliday," a dead sounding voice asked?

"Yes." I replied.

"I have just escaped from a satanic group. They will kill me if they find me. I heard that you could help me," she sounded fearful and very desperate.

I told her that I could deliver the demons out with the power of Jesus and she would have to receive Jesus Christ because He was the only way to get out of Satanism, she flatly replied no! Then she hung up and I never heard from her again.

RETURN TO BIBLICAL BASICS

Christian ministers must return to the preaching the foundations of the Bible. "But we preach Christ crucified, unto the Jews a stumbling block, and unto the Greeks foolishness; 24 But unto them which are called, both Jews and Greeks, Christ the power of God, and the wisdom of God. 25 Because the foolishness of God is wiser than men; and the weakness of God is stronger than men," (1 Cor. 1:23-24).

We must reproduce Jesus' ministry of saving, healing the sick and releasing the captives from the bondages of darkness and leading souls into the gateway of salvation. Churches have filled with strange doctrines of devils. Playtime Christianity leaving its participants shipwrecked as many leaders walk as spiritually blind, deaf and spiritually ignorant false leaders who have forgotten the simple instructions of Jesus save the lost, heal the sick and set the captives free. Witchcraft powers are rising and Satan does have power to strike those who are ignorant of his devices. History affirms the reality of the destructive horrors that witchcraft produces. Most Christian Churches simply ignore the power of demons that ensnare people with the evil bonds of witchcraft.

DEMONOLOGY A BASIC PROBLEM

A basic problem in the Christian Church today is the indwelling demons which have not been dealt with in deliverance and uncommitted Christians are filled with rebellion, sexual perversion, adultery, lust, incest, fornication, oral sex, whoredom, homosexuality, gossip, hate, bitterness and bondage. There are two terms that refer to demon possession in the New Testament. First, the Greek word, *daimonizomai* is usually translated "to be

5

possessed by a demon." Or when it refers to a person, it is translated, "demoniac." The word is found thirteen times in the Gospels and is sometimes translated, "to be demonized." The second term, *daimonion echein* means "to have a demon". This term is used eight times.[1]

Reverend James Robison, television evangelist and author, shocked his audience years ago with his testimony of deliverance from the power of an evil spirit in his life. He confessed that he was delivered from a spirit of lust and by Robison's own account, he was often a "dark-visage, angry preacher," railing against other preachers whom he considered too liberal, too greedy, or too lustful.

In 1979, he was put off the air for strident anti-gay rhetoric. He came to attribute his much-criticized, angry demeanor, as well as turmoil in his personal life, to the activity of demons. After undergoing what he regarded as a successful exorcism performed by lay exorcist Milton Green, a kinder, gentler James Robison emerged. "Deliverance" or demon exorcism became part of his stock-in-trade.[2] Mr. Robison said that Mr. Green was just a carpet cleaner when he prayed over him. He said that he was so proud at that time he didn't want a carpet cleaner praying over him because he was afraid somebody would overhear him. It was funny when he explained how it all happened.[3]

Truthfully, demons attack every believer. Unfortunately, Christians are not taught how to defend themselves.

---

[1] [Thomas Ice and Robert Dean, Jr., *Overrun By Demons*, (Eugene, OR: Harvest House, 1990), p. 116].
[2] http://www.secularhumanism.org/library/fi/cohen_24_4.htm
[3] http://www.sermonindex.net/modules/mydownloads/viewcat.php?cid=521&min=20&orderby=titleA&show=20 Rev. Milton Green, Sermons.

Demon possession simply means that a demon resides within a person and is controlling that person. There are no other variations of demons indwelling a person. Demons can oppress, attack, and tempt from the outside. According to Robison, "Evil powers in the realm of darkness can affect and even control the actions of people." The Bible refers to these powers as evil spirits, tormenting spirits, unclean spirits, seducing spirits, deceiving spirits, spirits of bondage and murder and destruction. It is important to realize that not all destructive spirits are as obvious and despicable as those responsible for the tragedy of September 11 and other atrocities. Seducing spirits are often subtle, sophisticated, and in some ways attractive. They can control professors, politicians, artists, and even religious leaders including Jesus' own disciples . . . . *The entertainer, teacher or leader who undermines the relevance of absolute principles is no less demonically manipulated than the terrorist.* [Italics added.] [4] (Robison (commands "death" to the growth on his daughter's lip). Believes that he has authority from God to cast-out demons, as do all Christians who really believe that they are "to do the ministry of Jesus ... You have total authority over demonic powers. You can cast them out."

JESUS DELIVERS

Jesus clearly showed that His deliverance power was for the believer when the Greek woman brought her daughter to Him to be delivered. (Mk. 7:26-27), "The woman was a Greek, a

---

[4] Robison's "Absolutes" are nothing but mainstream American civic values: "People Matter Most," "Greed Destroys," "Character Counts," etc. The chapter on "People Matter Most" (*The Absolutes*, pp. 83–99) could pass for a discussion of secular humanism! Robison finesses the question of how these "Absolutes" arise from the Bible. (They are, for the most part, at odds with what I understand the Bible to be teaching.)

Syrophenician by nation; and she besought him that he would cast forth the devil out of her daughter. 27 But Jesus said unto her, Let the children first be filled: for it is not meet to take the children's bread, and to cast it unto the dogs."

It was so sad concerning the Satanist who wanted to be free apart from receiving Jesus turn from Him; He is the one way to freedom. Jesus once said, "I am the way, the truth, and the life: no man cometh unto the Father, but by me" (Jn. 14:6). His apostles preached, "Neither is there salvation in any other: for there is none other name under heaven given among men, whereby we must be saved" (Acts 4:12).

The Bible clearly teaches that Christ alone is the Savior of the world and He is the world's only hope of salvation and deliverance. Apart from Christ, "there is no Savior" (Isa. 43:11; Hos. 13:4). His disciples preached repentance and receiving Jesus Who died on the cross. "Then Peter said unto them, Repent, and be baptized every one of you in the name of Jesus Christ for the remission of sins, and ye shall receive the gift of the Holy Ghost. 39 For the promise is unto you, and to your children, and to all that are afar off, even as many as the Lord our God shall call," (Acts 2:38-39).

Jesus revealed Himself as God the Savior and deliverer, (Luke 4:18). He works in the heart is a grace of healing, deliverance; which causes them to pass from sickness to health, from slavery to liberty, from darkness to light, and from the lowest degrees of misery to supreme eternal happiness. He came for those who feel their spiritual poverty, whose hearts are broken through a sense of their sins, who see themselves tied and bound with the chains of many evil habits, who sit in the darkness of guilt and misery, without a friendly hand to lead them in the way in which they should go-to these, the Gospel of the grace of Christ is a pleasing sound, because a present and full salvation is proclaimed by it. [5]

THE NAME OF NAME OF JESUS

The battle goes on. The Bible instructs us to "call upon the name of the Lord" for salvation (Rom. 10:13). Have you ever wondered why we are not instructed to simply call upon the Lord? Why are we to specifically call upon the name of the Lord rather than just upon the Lord Himself?

The name "Jesus" means "the salvation of Jehovah." The salvation of God is found only in Him. There is therefore no other name that can save us. "Allah" can't do it, neither will "Mohammed," "Buddha," "Brahma," or "Krishna." Only Jesus can save us from our sins!

The Lord's name is Jesus—the "name which is above every name" (Phil. 2:9-11). According to the Apostle Paul, the name Jesus will ultimately be universally bowed to and confessed by "things in heaven, and things on earth, and things under the earth." The only question is: When will you bow to Jesus Christ and confess Him as Lord? You can freely do so now for salvation or wait till later when you are forced to do so in condemnation. The choice is yours."

To be truly saved we must trust Christ and Christ alone for salvation. We must give up all notions of being saved by our own works and believe that Christ's atoning work on our behalf is sufficient in and of itself for our salvation.

---

[5] From Adam Clarke's Commentary, Electronic Database. Copyright © 1996, 2003, 2005, 2006 by Biblesoft, Inc. All rights reserved.)

True salvation is only available for those who believe that all faiths apart from the Christian faith are spiritual dead-ends, leading only to destruction (Prov. 14:12). No matter how sincere their adherents, false religions can no more save us from our sins than a sincere belief that strychnine is milk can save us if we drink it. There is simply no way that a false faith can lead anybody to the one and only true God. [6]

Multitudes are being ensnared by Satan through dabbling in the occult and many Christians may be included in this number. There is one way out, Jesus! He called sickness Bondage and every bound person is commanded to be loosed to be set free. Jesus' ministry was made up of both healing and deliverance according to the Bible Mark. 1: 32-34 which summarizes the healing and deliverance side by side. They brought to him all the sick and demon possessed for ministry. The Word says, "And he healed many who were sick and various diseases and drove out many demons and he did not permit the demons to speak, for they knew him." Sickness and demon possession are here closely associated, yet kept distinct. The same is true of Mark 3: 10-12.

Jesus calls sickness BONDAGE IN Luke. 13:16, "...ought not this woman' whom Satan Hath bound . . . be loosed from this BONDAGE?" God's will is never to use bondage because Jesus' ministry was designed to "set at LIBERTY THEM THOSE ARE BRUISED," (Lk. 4:18). As prophesied of His divine ministry, "It would lose the bands . . . undo heavy burdens. . . And . . . break every yoke," (Isa. 58:6).

The word bondage means oppression and Jesus said, "Woman thou art loosed from thine infirmity in verse 12. The Word infirmity means: ill-health, illness, sickness, frailty, medical

---

[6] http://www.forgottenword.org/naming-names.html

condition. What in the world do preacher teach when they say that "Christians cannot have a devil? I know many Christians that Jesus loosed from the BONDAGES, of all sorts of medical conditions. If Jesus said, SATAN HAD BOUND HER, I believe Jesus. God does not bind people, Satan binds them but Jesus loosens them. Jesus did not say that this condition existed in this woman to keep her humble or that it was a mysterious way God had of working out His will in her life. SATAN HAD BOUND HER.

"For he had healed many; insomuch that they pressed upon him for to touch him, as many as had plagues. And unclean spirits, when they saw him, fell down before him, and cried, saying, Thou art the Son of God. And he straightly charged them that they should not make him known," (Mk. 3:10-12).

"Even so we, when we were children, were in bondage under the elements of the world: But when the fullness of the time was come, God sent forth his Son, made of a woman, made under the law, to redeem them that were under the law, that we might receive the adoption of sons. And because ye are sons, God hath sent forth the Spirit of his Son into your hearts, crying, Abba, Father, wherefore thou art no more a servant, but a son; and if a son, then an heir of God through Christ," (Gal. 4:3-7).

Millions of Christians are content to live with attacking demonic powers controlling their lives, minds and their families. Sin has become a companion and they do not resist temptation; they do not want to resist attractions. In fact many pastors have changed their churches into civic center's by removing Jesus and His Bible from their pulpits and have brought in worldly movies; ball room dancing; Karate; Yogi exercises; sports; while pastors play the role of circus masters and life coaches.

"For the weapons of our warfare are not carnal (fleshly) but mighty through God to the pulling down of strongholds: casting

11

down imaginations and every high thing that exalted itself against the knowledge of God, and bringing into captivity every thought to the obedience of Christ," (II Cor.10:4).

Pastor Eni' book, *Delivered from the Powers of Darkness,* Satan's agents are freely infiltrating Christian Churches and working powers of darkness while the shepherds are spiritually sound asleep. Look at this testimony from a former African wizard. After becoming born again, Pastor Eni, former wizard from Nigeria, Africa wrote a warning to the Christian Church. After the command by Lucifer to fight the Christians we then sat and mapped out ways of fighting them as follows: [7]

Causing sickness
Causing barrenness
Causing a slumber in the church
Causing confusion in the church
Causing church to be cold
Making them ignorant of the word of God
Fashion and emulation
Fighting them physically.

FIGHTING PHYSICALLY

Pastor Eni goes on to write, "The powers of darkness that lives under the sea gave me a (supernatural) television. I could see through this television the born again Christians that Satan had assigned to me to defeat. (We do not fight hypocrites because they belong to us already). The wizards would SEND OUR GIRLS (Satan's agents) into the big churches to work against Christians.

---

[7] http://www.divinerevelations.info/dreams_and_visions/Dilivered_from_the_powers_of_Darkness_by_Emmanuel_Eni.htm

Once the girls were inside the church, they would chew gum. They would cause a child to cry. They would do anything to distract the people from hearing the Word of God. These witches may spiritually cause the people to sleep while the preaching is going on."[8]

Many Christians are like spiritually starving concentration camps; there is a Word famine in our churches. Blinded leaders are taking the church into secular transformations and blinded preachers and blinded congregations will fall into the ditch.

Many Christians are satisfied to live with doctrines of devils.

AUTHORITY

Christians receive their authority from Jesus Christ and all authority is vested in Him. Jesus' power is always greater. "Who is the image of the invisible God, the firstborn of every creature: For by him were all things created, that are in heaven, and that are in earth, visible and invisible, whether they be thrones, or dominions, or principalities, or powers: all things were created by him, and for him: And he is before all things, and by him all things consist," (Col. 1:15-17). This scripture shows Him victorious over Satan. However Christians must use their power that Jesus gives to them. It's catch-up time for the western church.

The modern Church has not even begun to touch the fringes of the knowledge of the supernatural power of God. Let me encourage your hearts as the coming of Christ approaches; that coming which I believe a multitude of Christian hearts are looking for in these days, I believe that the consciousness of Jesus Christ, Son of God, will take possession of His Body with His power, and strength and might. We shall see a great conquering spiritual army

---

[8] ibid, http://www.divinerevelations...

13

boldly pour forth to show the world His glory everywhere! The captives will go free as the blessed Spirit of God reveals the mighty power of the living Christ in the souls of men and women and we shall have a great awakening; a time of triumph when many shall acknowledge that Jesus is the King of Kings!

Pat Holliday, PhD
August 20, 2010

Chapter One
A Family's Journey into Mystical Darkness

The most publicized psychic activities in America and the one which people in great numbers are embracing today is divination. This goes under the names of: telepathy, ESP, clairvoyance, a hypnotic trance, spiritualism, psychic research, etc. Although the term "psychic research" has a respectable sound, it involves the same old witchcraft referred to many times in the Bible. Sorcery or traffic in familiar spirits is strictly forbidden in the Scriptures, (see Lev. 20:6; Lev. 20:27; Isa. 8:19). Many know that the present Christian religious system, whether traditional or spirit-filled has become a distorted caricature of what Christ left us.

EFFECTS OF WITCHCRAFT

Rita was a typical housewife, the girl next door. She was dressed in a long plaid skirt. Her face was bright as she stood before a group of interdenominational Christian women. She was a small lady, four feet, eleven inches. The absence of makeup, warm hazel eyes and hair tied back into a ponytail gave her the appearance of being much younger than forty. Actually, looking at her that day, it was hard to conceive that she had a most unusual story to share. The women knew that she had an experience with witchcraft and they were stirring anxiously as she took the microphone.

"My name is Rita Lamb. First of all, I want to be sure that God's Word is spoken and only God's Word is honored. Please turn with me to the Word of God 'For I am persuaded that neither death, nor life, nor angels, nor principalities, nor powers, nor things present, nor things to come can separate me from the love of God,' (Rom.8: 38). "Please bow your heads with me and ask the Lord to bless the message." She raised her head after the 'Amen' and gave the crowd a huge smile. She seemed very relaxed as her mind began to work on her testimony. "This time last year, I was in the hospital with what they thought was a heart attack. Really, it was a broken heart. I was living under the curse of a witch. I will reveal some things regarding the beliefs and doctrines of witchcraft. "

A CURSE FROM A WITCH!

Now Rita had the attention of everyone sitting in the room. Her soft, eyes swept the room, trying to measure the group's reaction to words that had immediately stripped her soul bare but the ladies sat wide-eyed (but willing to continue to listen). No one believed that witches were real in America. They were just figments of fairy stories or Walt Disney's fantasies. Many of the women present were regular churchgoing housewives who had never heard such deep spiritual exposures.

It is an interesting thing in America that many people think they are Christians because they attended church when they were young; however, they actually have never been born again. The next part of Rita's testimony bears this out.

Rita went on to say, "At the time of the heart attack, my teenage son had completely changed. He was not the same boy. He had been a good, Christian boy, not saved, but a good, traditional Christian, as far as going to church. He suddenly started being disobedient and disrespectful. He was just failing in many ways. It was breaking my heart. Although, I did not know then, it was due to a demon that came from a curse put on him by a witch!"

You could see the doubt on the faces of women. They were hearing something new. Many did not believe her story, imagine, a demon that she thought was causing her problems. As Rita stood, clutching her new Bible tightly before women who truly felt compassion for her, you could feel it in the air. They are ready, I thought, to hear the reality of the deeper things of God . . . We just can't afford to mollycoddle Christians anymore. They must have their spiritual eyes and ears opened to what Christ is saying to the Church at this time.

Rita stopped for a moment and picked up her story again. "A woman from our church, Cindy Bowen, brought us a book, Holliday for the King, by Pat Holliday. "Rita, you especially must read this chapter," Mrs. Bowen said. "I tried to read it but it was too heavy for my heart at that time. I thought: "This is science fiction" . . . so, I just sort of put it down.

"Pat had been in our town and had ministered powerfully in miracles. She really impressed Mrs. Bowen, who had the spiritual understanding that I really needed her particular book, Holliday for the King. She could see that the heart attack was a spiritual problem. She believed that it because demons that were causing my physical problems."

"It was Pat Holliday's book that gave my family the first clue as to what was wrong with me. It was through her book that God reached me. I was going to hell and was being killed by Satan and I would have been lost . . . Praise the Lord, He saved me, my husband, my daughter, my seven and nineteen-year-old sons. They are all filled with the Holy Spirit! Praise You, Jesus." Rita raised her hands and began to worship the Lord, caught up in the emotion of the moment. Tears of joy gently washed her cheeks; she quickly brushed them away and continued in a low composed voice.

"Since April," she said, "three people, who were under satanic possession, have been saved and filled with the Holy Spirit. We have gone out and we bring them to people who have been exposed to books like Pat's, people who have spiritual knowledge. It is so important to get these books into people's hands. Share with them. Don't treat satanic possession and oppression as though it was VD. If it happens to you or a friend, share the answers with them. Only Jesus can free them. The worse you are, the more you should share; for it just shows the glory of Jesus and how great a miracle He can bring forth."

Yes, it does show His glory to heal and deliver, I thought, looking again at Rita. It is really hard to believe that she was once crippled physically and mentally by Satan's powers. Today she's so strong and alert, by the deliverance of Christ.

". . . I was saved at age fourteen, lost at fifteen . . . I remember experiencing a real encounter with Christ when I was young. I always yearned to have it back. But I didn't know how to get Him back into my life. My family has heard all these years, if only I could have that feeling back. Satan put me through a lot and took me to hell twice during two years of physical and mental torture. In getting out, I feel the Lord said to me, 'Hey, I've been watching over you all these years and getting you out of all kinds of messes: now you had better come to Me all the Way' . . . and I did. I've completely committed my life to Jesus."

Rita says that she was saved at age fourteen and then lost at fifteen. She had made a confession of faith in Jesus Christ. Evidently, when she got into sin, she felt lost, or separated from Jesus. However, the question is this, can a Christian have demons?

No one can dabble in the occult and walk away unshackled. It is not really fun and games. Occult involvement is forbidden by God. Even if a person is ignorant of the prohibited by the scriptures, they will still be possessed by demons. When they ignore God's Word, they will pay a price.

Once the author ministered to a pastor who was a pastor of a very large Christian church that considered himself a Christian, but he was not born again. He said that his church did not believe that doctrine. He said that he had the biggest church in his town. A group of people within his church was following spirit guides to contact the dead. The pastor was drawn into these occult practices. Eventually, he lost his mind and was placed into an insane institution. The doctors put him on heavy psychological drugs. He lost his wife and friends. His life was being destroyed by devils.

Someone brought him to me for deliverance and at the time he was doing odd jobs in a Christian community. Although he had asked Jesus to save him, demons were actually speaking through this man's lips. When I laid my hands upon him, he became extremely agitated. His eyes became glazed. He spoke in a deep religious voice, "I am God the father, god the son and god the holy spirit I hate your guts." After I prayed for him, he renounced, his occult activity, and with commanding prayer authority in the name of Jesus, he was released by the power of God.

Rita continued to testify. "Seven years ago we moved to Summer Place, (fictitious name) a very small and quaint town, thinking we were getting away from the bad things of the big cities. We were wrong. The Devil is everywhere these days and he's even active in the Bible belt. Witchcraft and the occult powers are on the rise. The Boat People from Haiti and Cuba have brought both witchcraft and voodoo into our country. It's everywhere."

"What is the occult," Rita asked? "Briefly stated, it is involvement in any way with fortune telling, magic practices, witchcraft and Satan worship. The Word of God warns a great increase in occult activity will occur in the last days."

Multitudes of people, Christians and non-Christians alike, find themselves suffering physical, mental and spiritual oppression and possession. Few realize that they have become ensnared by Satan through occult, which is under control of the powers of darkness. Ignorance of these powers furnishes no protection. You may not believe it but participation can entrap you by these evil powers. The people still perish for a lack of knowledge.

Rita said, "I have discovered that by resisting Satan through the Name of Jesus is the only protection." She pushed a loose hair from her brow and continued talking in a matter-of-fact voice. "We came into contact with a woman in town called Della. She told me that she was a 'white witch'. I really felt sorry for her, of course, I did not believe in witches. I thought that she had a mental problem. Imagine her thinking that I would believe that she was a white witch. Why there are no such things as witches, except maybe in fairy stories such as The Wizard of Oz or, Snow White and the Seven Dwarfs. I thought that she felt that she had envisioned powers that did not really exist. She told me that she could do many supernatural things. 'Well, I thought, poor thing, she's in her fifties, perhaps going through the menopause'. I really did not believe that there could be real witches. It was a fictional, just imagination, nonsensicality stupid . . . Of course, I was to find the reality of her evil power and its source, because it almost cost me my family and life."

Witchcraft power such as, fortune telling (divination), spiritualism (calling back the dead), and omens, are abominable to God. He hates such practices, according to the Word, because the

20

Lord knows the source and the reasons behind it. God knows the spiritual destruction and the psychological and physical damage these grotesque demons can achieve in humans who are open to them. He gives us many warnings in the Bible to stay clear of the occult. Ignorance of it does not protect us.

God tells us, "There shall not be found among you anyone who makes his son or his daughter pass through the fire (an ancient pagan rite), one who uses divination, one who practices witchcraft, or one who interprets omens, or a sorcerer, or one who casts a spell, or a medium, or a spiritualist, or one who calls up the dead. For whoever does these things is detestable to the Lord; and because of these things the Lord your God will drive them out before you," (Deut. 18:10-12).

The mind has a protective wall about it, provided by the will, man's ability to say "No" to what is wrong and "Yes" to what is right. When one gives up his will, the door is opened for the demonic to invade the person's psyche. The person may become partially or even completely controlled by the demonic. Rita, through association with the witch and unbelief in her supernatural powers, simply was not operating her "no" will to protect herself! Supernatural powers are real and unbelief does not protect a person from them. The person can only be protected by the Name of Jesus Christ!

Rita described her friendship with Della, the witch. "She told me that witches do not believe in Satan. The first thing that is taught to an apprentice witch is that there is a "force," and that has two sides of good and evil. This malevolent force can be controlled by magic spells, words, potions, incantations, rope magic, rings, amulets, and so on. Witches believe that there is good witchcraft (white) and bad witchcraft (black). The good always triumphs over evil! (Rita's testimony will prove this theory wrong). Witches also

21

teach that battles are fought in the Middle Earth and in the astral plane causing upheavals both above and below. Thus, witches emphasize that good must triumph over evil. The Bible tells us it is all witchcraft. Jesus is the only supernatural power that can win over these evil powers."

Rita had the attention of the group. It was an astonishing testimony. She was actually telling them that witches were real. Also, she claimed that they had power to harm Christians. Although she had been raised in the Christian Church, she had not attended for years. She was vulnerable because she was not born again or spiritually enlightened. Protection from demonic spirits comes from a person committed to Jesus. "My heart rejoices in the Lord; in the Lord my horn is lifted high. My mouth boasts over my enemies, for I delight in your deliverance, there is no one Holy like the Lord; There is no one besides You; There is no rock like our God, For the foundations, of the earth are the Lord's upon them he has set the world," (1 Sam. 2:1,2).

Rita continued her testimony. "She gave me many objects, books with her name and hex sign on them. Her hex sign was a five-pointed star with a snake twisted around the bottom point, and flying owl at the top. It was only later, after I was healed, when the Lord led me to clean these things out of my home that I realized how much she had filtered into my house. She even sent things in through my children."

A witch wants to get objects into your home. There are great spiritual repercussions because demons are attached to these objects. A witch can control a person from a distance through these objects. Her ability is attributable to a divine power, or demon. This is why the Bible warns us to, "Wherefore, my dearly beloved, flee from idolatry," (1Cor. 10:14).

A witch can work her spells when she uses a Talisman (charm) that she has worked demonic rituals for demonic power. You can compare this in Christianity when a Christian prays over an item to bless it. As Rita's story shows, the demonic article will accomplish it purposes.

Rita seemed to be disturbed as she continued to remember her awful ordeal. Small drops of sweat appeared on her forehead. "One particular thing that she brought me when I was in the hospital was a talisman (a small amulet or charm used to carry curse powers). The talisman was made of beads. These beads were made in the image of a little purple snowman with two little, rolling eyes. I really did get worse after she brought me that thing. She gave my son, John a little round medal with a breastplate on it and snake curled around it that had written on it: 'This, we will defend.' It was also a talisman. She cursed the medal and gave it to him on his eighteenth birthday and that's when he started to change so drastically."

Think about this. She and her son were placed under a curse by a white witch. We, as Christians, must know scripturally, if this is possible. A curse is a prayer or invocation for injury, disease, ill-success, desolation, death, etc. or the opposite of a "blessing." In ancient times, when a curse was pronounced, it was not considered simply as a wish for misfortune to befall an individual or group, but thought to have inherent power to convey itself into effect. The term is also used in reference to the penalty for disobedience of God's law, depicted in (Deut. 21:22-33). Human cursing is also forbidden in the Bible. (See Num. 22:6).

DESTROY ALL OCCULT OBJECTS

The Bible clearly informs believers' to destroy all pagan objects. In 1982, Reverend, James Robison befriended Texas millionaire T. Cullen Davis. Davis had been acquitted of the murder of his wife's lover and his stepdaughter in 1977. In 1979, Davis was acquitted again, this time of attempting to procure the murder for hire of fifteen people, including the judge who had presided in his divorce case. Davis owned over one million dollars worth of Asian religious art treasures made of jade, ivory, and gold. He wanted to contribute them to Robison's ministry. Robison opined that the objects were idols and had to be destroyed in obedience to Deuteronomy 7:25, "The graven images of their gods shall ye burn with fire: thou shalt not desire the silver or gold that is on them, nor take it unto thee, lest thou be snared therein: for it is an abomination to the Lord thy God." Davis and Robison broke the art objects to pieces with hammers and dumped the shards into a lake. [9]

Rita continued her testimony of her bondage to a witch that had devastated her life. "Della did not seem to have many friends. She had a cold air about her. She stood about five feet nine. Thin. Not attractive. Jet black hair, eyes so brown they, at times, looked black. She looked sixty instead of fifty. Her voice was very deep and when she spoke each word was precisely enunciated. She seemed honest at times. I did not understand her when she'd say things such as, 'I burned brown candles for so and so and he stopped doing such and such. It's a good thing I did not burn black candles.' Rita did not know that burning different colored candles represented to the witch, her ability of performing different acts

---

[9] http://www.secularhumanism.org/library/fi/cohen_24_4.htm

that was intended to be carried out, for instance, green candles represented money and Black Death!"

"This witch would constantly weasel her way into our lives. We really felt sorry for her, but she had become very close to our children. They even called her Aunt Della. She was a very strange person, but it was hard to believe that she actually trafficked with evil spirits or that anything harmful could come from our relationship with her. She never hid her interest in witchcraft from us but, as I said before, we just didn't believe in it. We just thought she was a little different."

Suddenly, Rita put her hands over her eyes for a moment as if trying to chase the memories from her mind. An indescribable oppression filled her with anguish from the dark memories. The women listening immediately went into prayer to lift away the dark clouds that seemed to just sit over Rita's head. She regained her composure. "The witch was certainly a mysterious lady; but I still thought that she was imagining these things or just taking circumstances and applying to what she was doing. It was only after I received deliverance that I began to understand Della and her evil powers over my life as well as others."

"We heard about a man and his wife had a deliverance ministry. They helped me by casting out the demons that had possessed me. Although they lived more than two hours away from me, they told us the about thirty other families from our town at that time. These people had come to them seeking deliverance. (There are more now). They explained the occult spirit of witchcraft and malignant influences over people's lives. Envision this. We whose lives had been touched by the evil powers of the witch all lived in the same town! We were not living close to each other. We did not all go to the same church. There was absolutely no common denominator - except that we all had contact with this same witch, Della!"

"Mr. White, the deliverance minister, is a quiet spoken person and he has a knack for converting scoffers into believers. He explained to us, 'Witches have familiar spirits that work through them and uses their power to bring people under the evil spirit's power and influence. However, Christians, have the protection of the Blood of Jesus when they are obedient to His Word.' "I've discovered that we do have superior power to break all curses if we just use it! That's exactly what Jesus told us to do, cast out devils."

She stopped talking for a moment took a deep breath. "The witch put my family through much torture by putting this demonic curse on us. I'd rather have died, at times because I was under great emotional strain and my head throbbed with ever-increasing pressure. I was exhausted and overwhelmed with constant thoughts of dying as I dropped deeper and deeper into a shell as destructive evil forces controlled and infected my life. Finally, I could no longer clearly think nor walk and became totally bedridden. I resented my family having to do everything for me. I became uncontrollably enraged and my husband and children could not hold me down. Eventually, they had to tie me to the bed and could not even feed myself. I felt like a captured animal. I was living in a nightmare."

Rita swabbed her forehead with a handkerchief. Her eyes were filled with tears and pain as she told the horrors of the memories in her mind. "Without my family, I would not be standing here . . . but, they loved me and the Lord was working in my family. He touched each one of us. The Devil meant to kill me and destroy them, but Christ saved me and my entire family. I will always appreciate the prayers and support of the Christian community toward my family in our crisis. It's very important for you to pray for people because God does listen. It's not popular to talk about the reality of witches and the fact that they do have supernatural power, but I must warn people . . . THEY ARE REAL, THE BIBLE SAYS SO!"

Failure to recognize Satan's ability to work through human instruments can be a fatal spiritual mistake. The Devil's greatest weapon today is pretending not to exist. Demons, in their constant harassment, overcome and occupy when there is a yielding, no resistance, even in ignorance to them. Their chief purpose is to capture people, then draw them away from the reality of Jesus Christ's blood atonement. They do this by blinding the mind to spiritual things. The goal is to bring humans down into the pit of hell. Rita's closet full of unpleasant memories continued to open words that seemed unbelievable.

WITCHES COVENS

"There are three witches' covens in our town. They all belong to the local Humane Society because that's where they get their animals for sacrificing! They kill them. Each animal represents a particular person they are working curses against. They bury them and sometimes they'll dig the animals up again. I don't know why they are doing these things, but they do it. They also plant the sacrificed animals under the sign of the churches in our area. They do this to have power over the church. "

It's hard to imagine that right here in America these primitive ceremonies are occurring. Christians tend to think of these things in terms of remote, uncivilized lands, places to send missionaries to confront backward people with the gospel of Jesus

Christ. But Rita was pointing her finger at devilry right here, in the most advanced civilized country in the world!

Rita fingered her Bible for a moment. Silence, but the women were quiet, alert and interested. Finally, she broke the silence again. "The Lord has opened my spiritual eyes to see things. I not only saw demons, but saw and felt the fires of hell. Just when I thought I would break and could no longer bear the horrors, there would be a peace and beauty, a vision from the Lord . . . someone praying and singing. These things helped me to hold on. He gave me a goal to see my children educated - showing me how much I was needed in spite of what Satan was doing and saying . . . "Her voice trailed off. Memories were still raw in her mind and too deep. Without words, it was plain to see that Christ had made her whole. She could think, talk and function normally. What more needed to be said!

Rita had told us in her testimony that she was saved at fourteen years old and lost at fifteen-years-old. What she was actually trying to say was she did not seem to have the power to live without sinning, so she gave up the idea of being a Christian. She also said her son was a good boy who attended church, a "traditional Christian" who was not saved. Unfortunately, churches are filled with "Christians" who are in the same boat as was Rita's family. We know that Christianity is an experience with Christ, a new life with provisions made by Christ for His people to live victoriously. Sometimes people walk through much tragedy before they can learn to live spiritually with Christ, instead of living in the flesh.

The interesting thing that Rita said was that she was saved at age fourteen years old and lost at fifteen years old. How can it be that she became so demonized through the curse of a witch? We must understand the answers to this question, because so many are in danger due to the rise and boldness of witchcraft in our age. It is possible that "Christians can be demonized." This is one of the most controversial subjects in the Church today. Many arguments occur and churches actually split over this question. Both sides can point to their text in the Bible. Both can talk eloquently on the subject. But, how can we explain a situation like Rita's? Some teach that once saved, always saved. While others teach by the power of the person's will, he or she can decide to fall away. While many people are being tortured in our churches by oppression from demons, it seems to be more important to most of the theorists to prove their particular doctrine than to help the spiritually sick.

THE TRUE SALVATION

Jesus once said, "I am the way, the truth, and the life: no man cometh unto the Father, but by me" (Jn. 14:6). His apostles preached, "Neither is there salvation in any other: for there is none other name under heaven given among men, whereby we must be saved" (Acts 4:12). The Bible clearly teaches that Christ alone is the Savior of the world and the worlds only hope of salvation. Apart from Christ, "there is no Savior" (Isa. 43:11; Hos. 13:4).

The Bible instructs us to "call upon the name of the Lord" for salvation (Rom. 10:13). Have you ever wondered why we are not instructed to simply call upon the Lord? Why are we to specifically call upon the name of the Lord rather than just upon the Lord Himself?

The Lord's name is Jesus—the "name which is above every name" (Phil. 2:9-11). According to the Apostle Paul, the name Jesus will ultimately be universally bowed to and confessed by

"things in heaven, and things on earth, and things under the earth."
The only question is: "When will you bow to Jesus Christ and
confess Him as Lord?" You can freely do so now for salvation or
wait till later when you are forced to do so in condemnation. The
choice is yours.

The name "Jesus" means "the salvation of Jehovah." The
salvation of God is found only in Him. There is therefore no other
name that can save us. "Allah" won't do, neither will
"Mohammed," "Buddha," "Brahma," or "Krishna." Only Jesus can
save us from our sins!

To be truly saved we must trust Christ and Christ alone for
salvation. We must give up any notion of being saved by our own
works and believe that Christ's atoning work on our behalf is
sufficient in and of itself for our salvation.

Two thousand years ago the apostle Paul was greatly
concerned about Christian discernment, he wrote, "And this I pray,
that your love may abound yet more and more in knowledge and in
all judgment; 10 That ye may approve things that are excellent;
that ye may be sincere and without offence till the day of Christ;11
Being filled with the fruits of righteousness, which are by Jesus
Christ, unto the glory and praise of God." (Phil. 1:9-11).

Paul shows in this Scripture the need for the Saints to have
the quickness to sense the true spiritual situation which exists. In
these latter days, it is imperative that they have the ability to make
wise choices among all the correct Biblical alternatives. Christian
discernment means the ability to distinguish evil and good.

There are many voices crying, "Follow me, I have the way to
truth." Among these voices are the true ministers of God who
have been anointed by the Holy Spirit to lead His people into all
truth. While there are also many false prophets who main desire is
to gather a following to led them into the Big Lie. Yes, it is very

important for every Christian to be able to distinguish between the things that differ.

NEW AGE MOVEMENT

This is the most deceptive, damaging philosophy around today. It is entwined not only in witchcraft and Satanism but also prevalent in all branches of Christianity and political movements. Some belief systems have become deeply intermixed and rooted in eastern mysticism. Followers are told "you are a god," awakening their God consciousness thru Transcendental Meditation, Yoga, Hypnosis, visualization etc. What most people do not understand is this is the same thing Satan said in the Garden of Eden to Eve, "You will be as Gods" (Gen. 3: 4, 5). [10]

No one is a god but Jesus Christ and accepting yourself as a god, puts you on the list of those going to hell. Big old fat Buddha was demon possessed. Hinduism, Taoism and all the eastern philosophies are a result of demons talking to those who would allow them through the demon of Kundalini; faith comes by hearing the Word of God, not through Gurus, meditative practices, rituals or methods, "Take heed therefore that the light which is in thee be not darkness," (Luke 11:35).

Sadly, many Christians are falling into the traps of Satan through their trust of wealthy, prominent, so-called religious men and women who no longer preach the redemption of Jesus Christ or the Bible but they serve the god Mammon. Countless Christians have not had their mind renewed through the Word of God. They have not been sanctified through the washing of the blood of Jesus. Their faith centers all-around Christian icons or stars instead of Jesus Christ as God and His purpose of giving them salvation for

---

[10] http://www.miracleinternetchurch.com Dr. Pat Holliday, articles

them to enter into His Kingdom. He never taught us to seek a kingdom on this earth to take dominion over world government or that calls all religions to come into religious unity.

The Christian Church has become cold and lukewarm and some have given their minds over to forms of Better Homes and Garden or Disney World, Star Trek and Friendly Seekers-sin-filled-bloodless, Christianity. Some are seeking after material things or emotional experiences. Jesus is rarely preached, (Rom. 10:17), "So then faith cometh by hearing, and hearing by the word of God."

Many of these "prosperity preachers" are living sumptuously like kings and queens in multimillion dollar homes while you are overwhelmed by debt. I'm telling you that you are NOT listening to the real gospel. Repent for seeking after God the Father as a sugar daddy in the sky instead of seeking the God that sent His Divine Son Jesus to save you from your sins and give you eternal life. Rededicate your life to Jesus and ask Him where you can go to receive the true Gospel. "And be not conformed to this world: but be ye transformed by the renewing of your mind, that ye may prove what [is] that good, and acceptable, and perfect, will of God," (Rom. 12:2).

How greatly we need wisdom. We must turn from the great spiritual slumber, material worldliness, entertainment church centers and following all religious pathways in the Church and see our true spiritual condition. Let Christ awaken our souls in deep compassion for the trapped spiritual slaves of Satan's kingdom using Christ's power to set them free. The Church is facing its most significant, final battle which is Satan's ultimate conflict. We pray for willing Christian warriors who will seek the Holy Spirit's anointing to vanquish this satanic rise to power. The Holy Spirit's anointing is the energy to wield the victory over this vast satanic invasion aimed at the destruction of man's souls.

The future belongs to those who prepare for it and that preparation should include biblical spiritual knowledge concerning the rise of witchcraft and its effect upon our land. I believe a person's judgment can be no better than his information. Given good information in sufficient quantity, most people have the capacity to make intelligent decisions.

The future belongs to those who prepare for it and that preparation should include spiritual knowledge concerning the rise of witchcraft and its effect upon our land. I believe a person's judgment can be no better than his information. Given good information in sufficient quantity, most people have the capacity to make intelligent decisions.

THE RISE OF WITCHCRAFT

The following testimonies describe the explosion of witchcraft often cloaked in glamour for acceptance in American life. Witchcraft is the vehicle the Devil uses that causes the destruction that will send millions to hell. I have looked at the implications for the world and the media promotion. Also, I noted the willful ignorance of Christ's Church that sits (in general) on the mighty power of Christ delegated to it. Only a few are willing to answer the call to set the captives free. The Bible says, "For your hands are defiled with blood, and your fingers with iniquity; your lips have spoken lies, your tongue hath muttered perverseness," (Isa. 59:3).

Fiendish devil-worshiping cultists are on the verge of spawning an insane bloodbath of murder and terror in cities and towns across the country. Recently, while the author was

33

evangelizing in Miami, a young girl who had escaped from a group of Satan worshipers told a frightening tale of human sacrifice and kidnapping. She said, "They find old people who have no relatives and put them in cages. They torture them with hot irons and within three days their hair will actually turn snow white from terror! They tie them to a pentagram table (a table with a five-pointed star, a witchcraft symbol, on the top). Then they sacrifice them to Satan! This Satanist temple is located in a very elite section."

In 1982, a bewitching message appeared newspapers across America and Salem, Massachusetts is no longer trying to hide its past as the witch-burning capital. As the director of Salem's Witch Museum put it, "We have the image anyway, why fight it? The city was hoping to capitalize on its reputation that Halloween with a series of Halloween events - a psychic festival, a magic and juggling show, a parade and a costume ball." A Great Pumpkin hot-air balloon will rise from a "pumpkin patch" on a waterfront wharf. Old Town Hall will be turned into a haunted house and there will even be a Monster Mash record dance. But, there would also be serious lectures and exhibits on the hysteria of 1692, when colonists executed 20 women believed to be witches and imprisoned 150 others have not even begun to touch the fringes of the knowledge of the power of God. Let me encourage your hearts as the coming of Christ approaches which I believe a multitude of Christian hearts are looking for in these days; I believe that the consciousness of Jesus Christ, Son of God, will take possession of His Body (His Church) with His power, and strength and might. We shall see a great conquering army boldly pour forth to show the world His glory everywhere! The captives shall go free as the blessed Spirit of God keeps on revealing the mighty power of the living Christ in the souls of men and women, we shall have a great move of God; a time of triumph, when many shall acknowledge that Jesus is the King of Kings!

Something very strange is going on in the United States, and the spirits that are hard at work are now bringing a power that is designed to captivate the entire world. We shall examine the real effects of Voodooist/witchcraft as it was practiced on the Lamb family, and also Louise Carl, a young girl (name fictitious) living somewhere in Florida.

Through these testimonies, you will discover curses placed on Rita Lamb and her family and Della, a witch who openly expressed that she practiced "white witchcraft." I know that to people who do not live in the same world as we do, these experiences will seem impossible. You should remember Napoleon's words: "Impossible" is a word only to be found in the dictionary of fools. This is a true story about the deliverance of Rita who was a hopeless cripple and suffering a complete mental breakdown. She was delivered and healed through the Christian faith in the power of the Name of Jesus.

Witchcraft works by spells, curses and personal control over a person' life and it is never the will of God for one person to dominate another person. Anytime a person tries to control another. It is evil; the force behind that is witchcraft. The psychic or witch does have supernatural power. We must correctly assess and recognize the extent of that power. Many battles have been lost because of underrating the strength of the enemy. Ignoring the devil's power, hoping it will go away, does not work. Many battles also have been lost because of lack of knowledge and a lack of spiritual assistance by the church of Jesus Christ.

REBELLION

We are going to see the darkest force of the horrors of witchcraft in the following pages. Once entrapped in witchcraft, it is not easy to get out. There is one way out and that's through receiving Jesus Christ as Lord and His blood sacrifice as His covering for our sins.

Deliverance is having the power to set the captives free. It is never done ritualistically. It must be done by the teaching and anointing of the Holy Spirit. Deliverance works with love, the Compassion of Jesus Christ Himself operating through the deliverance minister, then the love of the deliverance minister to the one who is possessed. We have the advantage of having learned the repugnance with which demons regard genuine love and compassion to a bound and helpless individual. True Christian Love is a powerful spiritual weapon in warfare with Satan. A person filled with the Holy Spirit who allows the love of Jesus to flow through them can cause the demons to be in torment by embracing the bound individual and letting that holy love flow through them. Evil spirits react with hatred, rage revulsion, often screaming and sobbing to be left alone.

First is the personal experience of Coni, a 24-year-old ex-Satanist from Berkeley, California.

Coni says, "My involvement in a "witch thing', came partly as a result of trying to get off drugs. I started reading a book about the devil. I already believed in supernatural forces, and Satan seemed like a powerful being to me. The book made sense; I thought what it had to offer would take the place of drugs, and maybe even straighten out my head.

"The dude I was living with knew a witch who had been into it for a long time. She was enthusiastic about my background . . .

felt I could become a "familiar," under her. Since she was responsible to Elji, a demon of destruction, she was going to teach me to destroy.

"At first it was all memory work. We weren't allowed to get any books on our own. The whole spiritual thing seemed real and exciting. I got insights into why man does the things that he does. I began to develop what seemed like a close relationship to Satan. I had a feeling of power to do what he wanted me to do. I wasn't afraid at all. I dug it."

"And besides that, I was off drugs! There were still temptations, but concentration on the new things that I was learning kept me from "turning on."

"Then came the day of my first Black Mass and I discovered it was a mockery of the Roman Catholic Mass. The priest, called the goat, led the assembly in chants and meditations. People performed perverted sexual acts. A girl named Jan who had sacrificed her baby, burning it alive. As for me, I was one of six up for approval by Satan and the requirement was for a week we had a special herb diet designed to "dry us out." Before the Mass, there was a big dinner of selected foods which made my whole body tingle."

"The whole thing was a big deal and I wondered would we make it or not? How I wanted to work for Satan! I was told that when I died, I would be a demon to possess people. The giving of this gift really excited me, and I wanted to die so I could become a demon right away. While I lived, my job was to literally blow people's minds. My witch taught me that the best tool is to get people stoned on drugs and play games with their heads. She also taught me to hurt people deliberately. I succeeded with one guy named Steve. He's still in a mental hospital."

"It was also my job to get more people into Satan worship. I was the favorite of my witch supervisor and she got me deep into her craft. She laid on me lots of subtle ways to get into people's heads. It was exciting to feel Satan's power."

"Then suddenly one morning everything in my head flashed back to the beautiful people I had known in high school and college. Why was I now trying to destroy people? Suddenly, Satan's power was something I hated. This wasn't it. I took to heroin, a new drug for me, and began riding with the Gypsy Jokers. What I dug about them was their beating up people, raping girls. There lingered a sense of being under Satan's power. I was sort of a backslidden demon."

"It was an old high school friend and her husband who caught me off-guard. They told me I didn't have to look all my life for new ways to get power. They said God had a much better life for me if I would just take it. The thought of Christianity turned me off, but they shared with me their personal experience with a Person . . . Jesus Christ wasn't distant and inaccessible like I'd thought. They talked as if they knew Him. From then on strange things began happening to me, and eventually, I asked Jesus to come into my life.

"I lost my appetite for drugs. Two months later reality began to replace fantasy. I felt a new inner strength which enabled me to face life in a way I never had before. God was healing my mind. The hardest thing is to keep from trying to use God's power to meet my own needs. I still have a long way to go."

WITCH TERRORIZES LAMB FAMILY

In order for a person to be released from the shackles of the clutches witchcraft, it is crucial for the believer to trust the gospel and everything it teaches, (2 Tim. 3:16-17). The first step required is repentance, confession and renunciation of all the occult, New Age, cult experiences and also all known sin according to the scriptures shown in Acts 26:18; 2 Cor. 6:17.

Obedience to God and His Holy Word is crucial to be freed and seeking for power of the Holy Spirit, (Lk. 11:13; 24:49; Acts 1:4-14; 2:38-39; 5:32).

Total submission to God, walk and live in the Spirit, (Rom. 8:1-2, 8:10, 13-16; Gal 5:16-26; Col. 3:17).

Pray in faith, (Jam. 1:5-8; Heb. 11:6). Know your position in Christ, (Eph. 2-6). See my books, *New Creation, from Curses to Blessings*, Vol. I and Vol. II. [11]

Learn to use the name of Jesus in accordance with the Word of God, (Acts 3:16; 4:12; Jn. 14: 12-15; 16:23-26; Col. 3:17; Jn .15:7-16; 13:35).

Rita Lamb declares, "I am now spending my life in a mission of exposing witchcraft and its forces of darkness. My message is. There is a great deceptive cloud of witchcraft that has descended upon our nation. Even many Christians are being pulled into the forbidden realm of the occult, because they are so unenlightened of Satan's devices."

Danny, Rita's husband stood by her throughout this awful ordeal, even though many "Friends" advised him to put her away in the mental institution. Despite the fact that it did look hopeless, he believed in his heart that somehow, someday, she would be healed. Many will not believe this testimony, but it is true. Only the names of the people and the name of the town have been changed for their privacy and protection from Satan's servants' retaliation.

---

[11] http://www.patholliday.com Pat Holliday, Ph.D.

All too often, the end of delving into the occult causes mental and physical breakdowns or complete demon-possession. Insane asylums are full of people who have dabbled in these powers of darkness. Such was the case of Rita Lamb, the next testimony showing how the malignant powers of a Voodoo witch affected her life and the lives of the members of her family.

Rita touched lightly her eyes, "Satan is real. There is no neutral force. Behind every inflow of power dwells a supernatural being, Satan does work through people. Spirits can work apart from the medium, but not as effectively as they can with a body to use. When a witch or psychic does a work such as, pronounce a curse, spell, and hex or charm . . . that work they do will remain standing until a stronger power supersedes it. Make no mistake about it: these people are children of the devil and they do only his bidding."

SUBJECT TO DEMONIC INFLUENCE

Hal Lindsay, probably one of the most widely read Christian writers in the 20th century, has summed up the position that we hold, in almost perfect wording: "The semantics of separating demon possession and demon influence seem important to people. A person who is demon-influenced is under the power of evil spirits which may result in anything from mental torment to extreme abnormal behavior. Both believers and unbelievers and can be subject to demonic influence.

A non-Christian can be totally controlled and manipulated by demon power, but a Christian rarely has the same degree of complete subjugation. This is my position; also . . . I've talked to many missionaries who have had to deal with these things personally. I must say that it seems to be possible for a Christian to have a certain degree of demon possession . . . Whenever we deliberately turn from depending on the Holy Spirit to resist temptation, and then knowingly plot to commit sin, we open ourselves up for the possibility of Satanic attack and even control."[12]

We will look into the complete invasion of Rita's body, and mind by evil spirits sent to her to a witch who was practicing Voodooist. Through her husband, Danny, and her daughter Jessica, we will see also the effect on the entire Lamb family.

[12] Hal Lindsay, Christian Minister, http://en.wikipedia.org/wiki/Hal_Lindsey

Chapter Two
Witch's Spell Casting

"That we henceforth be no more children, tossed to and fro, carried about with every wind of doctrine, by the sleight of men, and cunning craftiness, whereby they lie in wait to deceive." (Eph. 4:14).

TEENAGER DEALING WITH A WITCH'S CURSE

The deliverance ministry is as controversial today as it was when Jesus was alive. Religious people of His time charged that, **"He cast out devils by Beelzebub,"** Lk. 11:15. Jesus had compassion for the demon possessed, oppressed, peoples above peer pressure. It is terrible to see someone under the control and power of demons.

It is true that Jesus Christ left awesome spiritual power to His church. "And Jesus came and spake unto them, saying, All power is given to me in heaven and in earth. Go ye therefore, and teach all nations, baptizing them in the name of the Father, and of the Son, and of the Holy Ghost. Teaching them to observe all things whatsoever I have commanded you: I lo am with you alway, even unto the end of the world, Amen," (Matt. 28:18:20). This "Great Commission" is our marching order in evangelism. It is worldwide in its scope; sin-deep in its reach; heaven-high in his hope and eternity long in the duration of its results. Jesus said in Matt. 12: 23-33 that Satan is not going to let anyone destroy his house without putting up a strong fight. He must be neutralized before a Christian can release his captives, Jesus asks this penetrating question; "How can anyone enter a strongman's house and carry off his possession unless he first tie up the strongman?" Jesus told us that we could enter his house in the Word. "Or else how can one enter into a strong man's house, and spoil his goods, except he first bind the strongman and then he will spoil his house,"Matt. 12:29.

Many modern witches claim to be heirs to an unbroken religious tradition stretching back into primeval history. They worship the Great Mother, Gaia, the earth mother, the symbol of fertility and the oldest and most elemental of the ancient gods. White witchcraft insists that it is a religion and not an evil cult. [13]

White witches believe there is a distinction between white magic and black magic; but the source of power for white witchcraft, white magic is the same as that of black witchcraft and black magic. It is all from the same Devil. Remember any supernatural power that is not association with Jesus Christ and His Word is of Satan. Della, the white witch, had affected the entire Lamb family with spiritual pollution and her indelible mark of madness caused this family unbelievable pain.

Jessica Lamb, Rita Lamb's daughter moved to the platform to speak to the Christian women about her part of the Lamb testimony. Looking thin and fragile, dressed in a wool skirt and print blouse topped by a sweater, she nervously switched from one foot to the other. A pretty girl with dark brown eyes, yellowish-brown hair, she wore no make-up and her curly hair was pulled back in a pigtail tied with a scarf. A few wisps of hair had fallen loose and were in tendrils. She was wholesome looking rather than beautiful; quick and bright, she fixed her gaze on the group, and she cleared her throat nervously.

---

[13] Ibid, Pat Holliday...

43

"My name is Jessica. I'm seventeen and had to care for my mother, Rita, during the time of her sickness." Rita sat straight with a small smile on her face. Our teens are subjected to so much more than we were," I whispered to her. "It's as though childhood is lost forever in our age of sophistication." My impression of Jessica was she looked older than 17 years.

"Della (not her real name) the witch – my brother and I called her Aunt Della, was very close to us. We've known her for about seven years. Her book, *Woman Witchdoctor,* was put together on the table in our house. The name of the book was also her CB handle. It's a book that's filled with potions, herbs and spell casting formulas. It sells for about two dollars. She showed me how to do a spell to get my boyfriend back. Although she calls herself a white witch, she gives out potions even if you really want to hurt someone."

This is one of her witchcraft spells that she taught to me. "You have to kill a frog," Della told me, "put it on an anthill and when the ant eats it you sort through the bones. Then find a piece of clothing or picture of the boy and hook it and then bury it. She taught me a little chant to say over it and it was supposed to get your boyfriend back." Although Jessica seemed shy, she forced herself to talk. Her fingers were white as she clutched the tiny white Bible. She nervously worked her tongue around to moisten her mouth, obviously dry. Someone passed her a glass of water. She sipped the water while gazing over the rim of the glass at the people . . . Most people present had teenagers just like her. So they were very interested in what she had to say. "My shoulders became tense and my mind is cloudy, I feel as though whole sections of my body were missing, torn away by some unseen force. And my mind became confused and I could not remember things."

44

HISTORY

Jessica talked like she was giving a school paper to her classmates and cited a little history about witchcraft. "History shows that a person associated with witchcraft becomes the object of diabolic attack. In 1324, a witch of Coventry, England, stuck a pin into a doll image of Richard D. de Sowe. The pin pierced the doll's head and de Sowe immediately went out of his mind. Later, the pin was thrust into the heart of the effigy. Three days afterwards de Sowe died. Following his death, Robert le Mareschel of Leicaster turned himself into the King. His shocking confession revealed his part in a plot to kill the King and six others. Twenty seven customers were to pay the witch twenty pounds (and Robert le Mareschel fifteen pounds) to effect the deaths. They molded seven figures of wax and canvas to represent their enemies. But after de Sowe's death, the guilt was too much and Robert turned King's evidence. The customers escaped. The witch died in jail. Satan does have powers of darkness to kill."

"Pat Holliday told us that today, in America, Christians are not afraid of witchcraft. In fact, most do not believe that it is real and most pastors don't believe that witchcraft can have an effect on a Christian. However, if a person walks onto Satan's highways of evil, he has powers and will work them. Furthermore," she said, "the powers will work on the Christian because of the open doorways of sin. The Bible clearly declares that prior to the return of Jesus Christ to earth, Satan will use supernatural miracles to deceive masses of men and turn them away from God says, "And deceiveth them that dwell on the earth by the means of those miracles which he had power to do." (Rev. 13:14).

The mothers were listening. They had children and that faces where stamped with concern as Jessica continued to talk about her ordeal. We are living in the days of great delusions and every mother seemed to feel the dangers that our children were experiencing. We all must wake up and see that our children are exposed to so much deception every day. Jesus left no room for doubt about His enemy's miracles. Speaking of conditions before the end of the world, Christ said: "For there shall rise false Christ's and false prophets and shall show great signs and wonders; insomuch that, if it were possible, they shall deceive the very elect," (Matt. 24:24). As the Bible predicted, masses are being led astray by the miraculous signs and wonders of witchcraft by ministers working under the power of Angels of light.

Jessica described the diabolic attack on her own life as a result of associating with the witch: "About two years ago, I really started to have problems. I had a very good childhood with loving parents. I liked to go to Sunday school to play but I wasn't a Christian and didn't want to be. I thought if I become a Christian, I'd have to give something up. I didn't know what, but I just felt that if I have to give something up, I'd do it when I became older. I wanted to be like all the kids in my class. So, I refused to become a Christian. I went to Church for social purposes, you know, to meet boys."

Jessica resumed her report about the demonic assault as a result of fellowshipping with Della, the white witch: "As soon as I could, I got a job in a grocery store. I didn't know the woman who worked in the store was also a witch; we've got three covens in our town. She and her mother were Mexicans. Her name was Gracia and her mother's name was Marie and they told me they had power to do supernatural things. One day, Mom and Dad asked them to exorcize me because I was having so many problems. They told my parents that I did have a lot of spirits in me and they were going to exorcize me. They used holy water and prayers; but that's

46

still Satan working and it just brings more evil spirits into you. Of course, we didn't know it was Satan's power at the time; we would not have stood for that. We believed them when they told us that they had "good spirits" and they could get rid of our "bad spirits." Of course, we didn't know that Satan was a real supernatural being that was able to affect your life. Our pastor never mentioned him and my parents didn't believe in devils either. They thought it was a bunch of mumbo jumbo stuff."

Jesus said, " . . . Every kingdom divided against itself is brought to desolation; and every city or house divided against itself shall not stand: And if Satan cast out Satan, he is divided against himself; how shall then his kingdom stand?" (Matt. 12:25). These scriptures show that it is impossible for witches to cast out evil spirits! Witchcraft is a part of his kingdom and Satan does control witches, whether they realize it or not!

"My family believed Gracia would take the evil spirit into herself because that's what she told them. Then Garcia said that she would leave our presence and go off alone and put them in a bottle to get rid of them. Demons really do collect demons when they are cast out because the more demons they get, the more power they get."

"Pat Holliday told me that witches can't cast out demons. She said that only Jesus could make them leave."

"I worked in the store for about the rest of the summer and whenever Mom and Dad went on vacation. I stayed at the witch's house. I have no idea what she did to me while I was asleep. All I know is, she'd put me under a spell. I did care what Mom or Dad said because what the witch said was more important. When Mom had a heart attack, instead of wanting to be home with her, I wanted to be with Della, the witch! Mom and I always had a good relationship, but the witch placed me under spells like you can't believe. Whatever she said . . . I did. I was totally being controlled and corrupted by her. It did not matter if it went against Mom, Dad or anybody! I followed her like a slave."

Deep hurt and guilt appeared in Jessica's mother's eyes. She glanced over at her parents, seeing the color mount in her father's face. Checking herself, she changed the subject. I noticed her hands were now trembling.

"I began to hear voices in the back of my head. At first, it scared me. The voices always were nice to me and they even helped with my school work. Many of my friends later told me they had the same experience. Now, I know they were demons telling me to do things. Sometimes they are not really bad things . . . but, they're not good, either. I've always enjoyed reading. I'd read anything that I could get my hands on except my school books and the Bible. I wanted to read instead of doing housework or homework. When Mom wanted me to do something, I'd sneak off into the bathroom and read. Something kept drawing me to disobey her. One day, Mom threatened to kill herself if I didn't stop my rebellion. But, I couldn't stop. The demons inside of me were telling me to go ahead and do it. It wasn't such a big thing, but it was tearing me apart," she sniffed.

"I usually heard one voice in the back of my head. I know it wasn't my imagination because it was not telling me to do good things. At bedtime, it would talk to me and I'd talk back to it, inside me. Dad would ask me a question and the voice would tell me to answer him with something mean or hateful. It told me to say I just didn't care about him and hated him. Now, that's not how I felt at all. It was just a way for the demon to keep me in trouble. I didn't know what was going on. Maybe I was crazy . . . I wondered if anyone else ever had these kind of things happen."

Jessica looked down at her clenched hands. Little beads of sweat poured out of skin on her forehead and slid down her face.

Every parent in the room suddenly had new insight into teenage rebellion. Imagine: demons telling them to disobey their parents. Many probably had never even thought of that before today.

Jessica pushed on with her testimony. "At times when I'd really get into trouble, get depressed and I'd think about committing suicide. The witch told me that she could help, but she didn't help. She made everything worse! She gave me all kinds of magical drinks. Sometime they will affect me like drugs, I'd feel really lightheaded. Finally, I had to realize what she was." Jessica bit her bottom lip. "It was like she was my . . . mother. I even cared about her more than I did my mother! She just had me completely under her spell." How diabolical!

Silence, all eyes focused on Jessica, faces were clearly affected by her strange confession. One lady sat head down, hands folded in her lap, and eyes clouded and seemed to be in a world apart from the others and absolutely no reaction to the testimony. I'm certain Satan had captured her mind from hearing the story of his darkness being uncovered.

Breaking the silence, Jessica continued to share: "All my life my mother had been sick but never enough that I had to take complete care of her. It really gave me a lot of nurse's training though, and I had always wanted to be a nurse. Many times I wanted to run away from the responsibilities. Once, Mom was really mad and told me she did not love me. Usually I would retaliate; but this time, I was really hurt. It would hurt anyone to hear their mother say those awful things. She kicked me in the chest and knocked me against the wall. She didn't like depending on us carrying her around. She'd get really angry about it. I didn't realize that she was not herself but that demons were making her act like that."

I looked at Rita's face. Pain ran across her eyes from the recovered memory and public exposure. Her eyebrows knit tightly together as she turned the pages of her Bible. (A funny thing about her Bible, I noticed: Although she was a new Christian, many passages were already highlighted - she was already studying the Word, that's for sure).

"I really got tired of it. I'd come into the bedroom and she'd slap me. I know that I deserved it sometimes, because I'd lost my temper and all control, too. It's kind of hard for a kid six-years-old to realize that their mother is mentally ill. By this time, I realized that I was, too. I knew that once that she got help. I would need help, also. But I was just sick of it . . . she was constantly screaming and yelling. I thought: the heck with it; I don't need this. I've got one-hundred and twenty dollars from my income tax return. I'll just run away.

FINDING HOPE

"When I read Pat Holliday's Book, Holliday for the King, I realized what was causing Mom's problems. Their backgrounds were so much alike . . . both were in politics and had witchcraft involvement. I know that Mom was going through the very same things Pat described in her book. It helped me a great deal with my own problems and with dealing with Mom's possession. It helped me know that it wasn't her that was evil and ugly . . . it was something else in her that was driving her and controlling her."

Jessica became restless, her mind twisting and turning. "Mom was sick, really sick. I was worried and feared what was happening to her. There nothing that we could do. Next, I read

50

Deliver Us from Evil, by Don Basham, mentioned in Pat's book. I began trying to do deliverance on myself. It didn't work because I wasn't saved. Actually, I had confessed Jesus, but didn't mean it from my heart."

"Finally, after Mom recovered, "I was delivered by Mr. and Mrs. White, the same people who had ministered to my Mom. So grateful to them for what they had done for Mom, we invited them to dinner. I thought we were just going to have dinner but the Lord had already told the man that day I was to be delivered. We were sitting in the kitchen and he came over and gave me a big hug. He held onto me gently. He was very kind. I didn't know what was going on, except my stomach hurt a lot; that happens when you are about to be delivered because the spirits inside you get really stirred up. I was delivered by the power of Jesus. I had seven spirits inside of me and there was one that came out screaming. The Whites explained that it was a spirit of witchcraft. They told us that witchcraft demons always came out screaming and shrinking.

"Right after deliverance, I received the Baptism of the Holy Spirit but the gift of tongues was in my head, but somehow, I couldn't get the words out of my mouth! I still had doubts. Until yesterday actually, I was still really having a lot of problems renouncing Satan. Then my brother, John, was saved, delivered and received the Baptism of the Holy Spirit at Pat's house. I knew he couldn't be faking what had happened to him because he had not heard anything that had happened to us. He had been away in the Navy. When I saw it happen to him, I knew it had to be real. Then, I believed in my heart and there's no way that I can doubt it anymore."

"After Pat ministered to John last night, we were all so happy. We went swimming. I went into the sauna and began to sing in the Spirit. I received the gift from the Holy Ghost of tongues. I had never sung in the Spirit before. It was beautiful. A little while later, I went back in there and sang in the Spirit again. Wow, it is an incredible experience!"

Jessica did not realize it, but she was giving thanks to God in tongues. (1Cor. 14:15-17), tells us: "What is it then? I will pray with the spirit, and I will pray with the understanding also. I will sing with the spirit, and I will sing with the understanding also." Praise His Holy Name.

Some faces were radiant with the light of new hope. Still others had the tense, set features: reluctant about believing all that had entered into their ear gates that day. Her testimony moved many to tears. (I had cried). This young lady had been through a terrible experience with a practicing witch. At the same time, she had been victorious through faith in Jesus Christ.

Resist the Devil. Align yourself with Jesus Christ' invincible power, Satan and his demons will flee from you. It's scriptural . . . and God cannot lie!

DEMONIC SPELLS AND MAGIC

The invisible things are more important than the visible; Invisible things are constructed in the spiritual realms before they appear in the visible. Col. 1:15-(Jesus) Who is the image of the invisible God, the firstborn of every creature: 16 For by him were all things created, that are in heaven, and that are in earth, visible and invisible, whether they be thrones, or dominions, or principalities, or powers: all things were created by him, and for him: 17 And he is before all things, and by him all things consist." It is very important for you to in touch with Jesus and His power than the invisible demons and their powers. Your eternal life is dependent upon what you receive and believe.

Why are housewives, business executives and other Americans stepped into the powers of darkness and becoming so obsessed with the occult? Is it really "just for kicks" or "fun and games" as some suggest or is there a terrible fear of the future and what is "beyond? Perhaps they are looking for God." How does it all begin? What are the results? [14]

In a popular TV show, the heroine calls upon spirits, spells, and magic to overcome demonic beings. In another show, teen-age witches use their white magic to defeat evil warlocks and spirits. Such popular shows deal with the world of the occult. The occult has thrived since the beginning of civilization. Throughout the Old and New Testaments, the prophets of God confronted the problem of the occult.

The term occult is derived from the Latin word *"occultus,"* which means to cover up, hide, or those things which are hidden or secret. A brief definition of the occult is the practice of attaining supernatural knowledge or powers apart from the God of the Bible. The first is disillusionment with the church and organized religion. The second factor is curiosity. There is an attraction to the occult that appeals to our interest in the unseen. Many begin with "harmless" dabbling, but this can often lead to more. Third, there is the quest for power. People want control over the future, spirits, or over other individuals. [15]

There are three primary categories of the occult world: divination, (magic, Satanist and witches spelling) and spiritualism. Divination is the attempt to foretell the future and thereby shape

---

[14] Christians and the Occult, Pat Holliday, Ph.D
http://www.miracleinternetchurch.com/ebooks
[15] Christians and the Occult

our lives accordingly. The divination arts include astrology, zodiac charts, crystal balls, tarot cards, palm reading, psychics, numerology, and horoscopes. [16]

The second category is magic or paganism; those in magic attempt to control the present by ceremonies, charms, and spells. The magic arts include witchcraft, white magic, black magic, sorcery, Satanism, black mass, and witch doctors. Then there is spiritualism. Those involved in spiritualism attempts to communicate with the dead and receive information or help from them. Spiritualism involves Ouija boards, séances, necromancy, and ghosts. [17]

The world of the occult not only brings a false message, but a dangerous one as well. Experiences with the occult drive us away from God and bring us into contact with the demonic realm. Jesus said the Devil is "a liar and the father of lies." (Jn. 8:44) In dealing with the demonic, you cannot expect them to deal in truth. The Devil and his legion only seek to "steal, kill, and destroy." (Jn. 10:10) For this reason, (Deut. 18), labels the practices of witchcraft, sorcery, divination, and necromancy as detestable to the Lord. It was these practices that brought judgment on the Canaanites and expelled them from the land. God did not want such teachings to infiltrate any culture. The church must not only present the danger of the occult, but the message of life and victory found in Jesus Christ over the principalities of darkness. [18]

---

[16] ibid
[17] ibid
[18] Roberta Blankenship, *http://www.amazon.com/Escape-Witchcraft-Paperback-Roberta-Blankenship/dp/B000V77IIY*

THE GREAT COUNTERFEITER

We know that in the same way as God uses the human vessel to do His work; Satan does likewise. Satan will try to counterfeit even God's own methods by starting with the human vessel first. He cannot create anything so he will try to imitate God. Many are fooled by his cheap copy of God because they refuse to receive Jesus. His demons work undercover to engender a feeling of his enslaved followers to believe that it is their power that they tap into; however if the victim crosses the demons, they will show the true evil colors.

The story of Roberta Blankenship, former witch, recalled in her book *Escape from Witchcraft* shows the power of demonic control over his victims. She had been raped and emotionally hurt and her damaged spirit wanted revenge. Roberta cried ". . . Why did this happen to me . . . me of all people . . . with powers like mine? If that man that molested me in the park knew what I could do, he would have been afraid to abuse, afraid to touch me. He will pay! He will pay! [19]

"I called my friend Josie and told her that I planned to put a hex on him. I returned to the park to look for anything which might belong to him. I found a carton of cigarettes and the brick with which he'd tried to hit me. Then, I went home to prepare and perform the incantation.

"I dressed myself in black, cursing like a madwoman: He will die for that. I'll destroy him. He'll suffer the wrath of hell!" I ran around the house chanting: Give me power. Draw it up out of my soul from the very roots of hell."

"Suddenly I fell on my knees. Realization poured over me. The powers that I had thought were my own gifts were really the

---

[19] ibid

55

devious tricks of the Devil. Tricks used to trap me. My powers were produced by, and rooted in, evil. For almost three years I had blindly claimed these powers as my own, never realizing whose puppet I became."

"A scary sound of thunder echoed within the walls of my mind and a voice crackled, "You stupid fool. Where did you think you got your power from?' It laughed and snarled, "not you, Roberta' and laughed again, "I'm not through with you.' I screamed aloud, hoping I could hear my own voice above the other. 'I'm crazy. I'm crazy. Kill me, I'm crazy.' I ran to the kitchen and grabbed a butcher knife, ready to slash my wrists.

Suddenly I froze, standing in terror as the voice continued: "I'm not through with you. You've just begun. So do as I say. Bow your knees to your master!" The next thing I knew, I, Roberta Blankenship, bowed down on my knees, raised my arms into the air, and said: "Satan, you are my master and prince. I know you are my source of power. Use me as you will. I am yours." With that, I fell flat on the floor crying, "The devil is real."

Hell is real, at the same time, I tell you that the Bible is real, Satan is transforming himself into an Angel of Light; therefore, it is no great thing if his ministers also are transforming themselves as ministers of righteousness. "For such are false apostles, deceitful workers, transforming themselves into the apostles of Christ. 14 And no marvel; for Satan himself is transformed into an angel of light. 15 Therefore it is no great thing if his ministers also be transformed as the ministers of righteousness; whose end shall be according to their works," (2 Cor 11:13-15).

His method is to imitate God's method. These false spirits are teachers, representing themselves as men or women of God, but energized by Satan. [20]

"And I say unto you my friends, Be not afraid of them that kill the body, and after that have no more that they can do. 5 But I will forewarn you whom ye shall fear: Fear him, which after he hath killed hath power to cast into hell; yea, I say unto you, Fear him. Fear him," (Lk. 12:5).

Many Churches no longer preach the basics of the Bible and Jesus as its center. People live for today and have absolutely no concern for their eternal souls. Popular new self-styled Christian teachers are inspiring new agendas to transform the Christian faith to shift it into just another religion. Jesus becomes presently another god-avatar that sits alongside all the gods of the world.

The New World Religion is here and you may follow any religion that you want and the Devil will answer. You may worship any false god, including yourself and it will be fine as long as you don't say that Jesus is the only way back to God.

"Jesus saith unto him, I am the way, the truth, and the life: no man cometh unto the Father, but by me," (Jn. 14:6).

The religious pathways to the gods will only lead people into the valley of hell.

"Enter ye in at the strait gate: for wide is the gate, and broad is the way, that leadeth to destruction, and many there be which go in there at: 14 Because strait is the gate, and narrow is the way, which leadeth unto life, and few there be that find it," (Matt. 7:13-14).

---

[20] ibid

SIN IS A TIE THAT ONLY JESUS CAN BREAK

Satan is destroying the foundation of Christianity in America. "If the foundations are destroyed, what can the righteous do," (Ps 11: 3)? God is judging the raging sins of America and the nations. He is allowing Satan to destroy the biblical foundations many false Churches. Many seeking cravings after marvels were symptoms of the sickly state of men's minds in our Lord's Day; they refused solid nourishment, and pined after mere wonder. The gospel which they so greatly needed they would not have; the miracles which Jesus did not always choose to give them eagerly demanded. Many nowadays must see signs and wonders, or they will not believe. Some have said in their heart, "I must feel deep horror of soul, or I never will believe in Jesus."[21] "Except ye see signs and wonders, ye will not believe," (Jn. 4:48).

The prophet Jeremiah pleaded with wicked Israel, "And they said, There is no hope: but we will walk after our own devices, and we will every one do the imagination of his evil heart," (Jer. 18:11-12) God is devising a catastrophe against you and designing a plan against you. The Prophet pleaded with them to turn back each of you from your evil way, and reform your ways and deeds. But they say, It's impossible; for we are going to follow our own plans, and each of us will act according to the stubbornness of his evil heart .

In Psalm 11:6, David warns, "Upon the wicked he shall rain snares, fire and brimstone, (coals of fire) and an horrible tempest (burning wind): this shall be the portion of their cup. 7 For the righteous Lord loveth righteousness; his countenance doth behold

---

[21] Charles Spurgeon, Spurgeon's Daily Devotional

the upright." Why? David answered, "Because the Lord is righteous" (v. 7).

"But I fear lest by any means, as the serpent beguiled Eve through his subtlety, so your minds should be corrupted from the simplicity that is in Christ. For it he that cometh preacheth another Jesus, whom, we have not preached, or if ye receive another spirit, which ye have not accepted, ye might well bear with him," (2 Cor. 11: 3-4).

Run for your lives and leave these friendly seeker churches where they do not teach about the pitfalls of sin. Your eternal life depends upon your receiving the truth. You must strive to live holy and dedicated to Jesus. "Jesus answered them, Verily, verily, I say unto you, whosoever committeth sin is the servant of sin," (Jn. 8:34).

The Holy Spirit will convict your heart. If you do not listen to the Word of conviction He will send the prophets (ministers) to deliver you through the Word. If you continue to indulge yourself in your hidden sins; spousal abuse, child abuse, self-abuse; verbal abuse, bitterness; rioting; raging; argument; anger, judging, sexual perversions, pornography, etc.; then judgment will fall in the form of curses on your finances; your job situation; etc. The tormentors (evil spirits) will come to nest in your life, after that religious spirits will prevail instead of the Holy Spirit. We must return to the Lord and repent, we are losing our Christian Church, County and this generation to the powers of darkness.

Chapter Three
Love Overcomes Witchcraft

"Husbands, love your wives, even as Christ also loved the church, and gave Himself for it," (Eph. 5:25).

MAGICAL ARTS

Could it be happening because America has left its faithful trail of seeking the one true God and is going after other gods? For sure, there has been a steady descent toward witchcraft which is known as the "Old Religion" which is an ancient practice dating back to biblical times. Witchcraft can be defined as the performance of magic, forbidden by God, used for non- biblical ends. The word witchcraft is related to the old English word Wiccan, which means, "practice of magical arts." You must separate yourself from the powers of darkness.

"And what concord hath Christ with Belial or what part hath he that believeth with an infidel? And what agreement hath the temple of God with idols? For ye are the temple of the living God; as God hath said, I will dwell in them, and walk in them; and I will be their God, and they shall be my people; Wherefore come out from among them, and be ye separate," (2 Cor. 6:15-17).

LOVE CONQUERS WITCHCRAFT

Danny Lamb was exactly the husband that Ephesians chapter Five describes. Husbands are supposed to love their wives as Jesus loves His church and He died for her. Many men would have given up on Rita's condition. However, despite the odds, Danny believed that she would be healed. His eyes sparkled as he kissed his daughter, Jessica and took the microphone. She bowed her head looking drained.

Danny went directly to the meat of the matter. "How many of you believe in witches? Do you believe they are real and have supernatural powers?" He stopped mouth opened, flushing deeply. You could almost see the effort he was making a point to insure getting his message across to the group. Almost everyone raised their hands, or shook their heads "yes." A few chose to sit in unbelief waiting to see what else would be said.

"Believe me," Danny continued, "I know that witches are real from personal experiences and they are very powerful. You may not believe this but they can hurt and even kill you even if you don't believe me. My wife Rita and I know a person in our town that died through drugs given by the witch, Della. Also, three teenage girls were killed in an automobile accident. They did everything together, worked at the same place and had even attended a séance and associated with the witch, Della! The weirdest thing happened when they died, their bodies mysteriously turned green and swelled and the doctors had no explanation! We knew it was caused from the spells of the witches. It's easy to understand why God warned us in the Bible to stay away from witches, when you've been touched by these evil powers as we have. (Lev. 19:31), says: "Regard not them that have familiar spirits (mediums), neither seek after wizards to be defiled by them. I am the Lord your God."

Danny took a sip of water waiting for that to sink into their minds. "Many people begin with "harmless," dabbling into the occult playing with the powers of darkness. However, we can warn you that this occult activity can often lead to capture by the devils possessing them. We've seen the victims become driven for a quest for power. People want control over the future, spirits, or over other individuals. Satan leads them deeper and deeper into witchcraft.

After a witch becomes involved with the Devil's power, she becomes a willing instrument to do his work. Satan blinds their minds and they actually believe that they are controlling the magic forces. However, if a witch ever wakes up, they discover that they are spiritual slaves.

Witchcraft can mean many different things: curses, hexes, talisman, séances, Ouija boards, psychics, palmists, automatic writing, and levitation, mineral divining," said Danny. "There are many other ways that we can be contaminated with evil spirits. With parents actively engaged in the occult, children may suffer as well. It's a spiritual law." He quoted the Bible 2 Chronicles 33:6, tells us that "And he caused his children to pass through the fire in the valley of the son of Hinnom: also he observed times and used enchantments and used witchcraft, and dealt with a familiar spirit, and with wizards: he wrought much evil in the sight of the Lord, to provoke him to anger."

He shuffled the pages of his Bible as he continued, "Also, turn with me to Deuteronomy 28:10-12, "There shall not be found among you anyone that maketh his son or his daughter to pass through the fire, or that useth divination, or an observer of times, or an enchanter, or a witch, or a charmer, or a consulter with familiar spirits, or a wizard or a necromancer. For all that do these things are an abominations to the Lord thy God, and because of these abominations, the Lord thy God doth drive them out from before thee." These Scriptures show us that want His people to be aware of the dangers of Witchcraft."

Danny pointed to a Christian author, Johanna Michaelsen, *The Beautiful Side of Evil* that captures the satanic essence of meditation and Guiding Spirits (demons) in her book. [22] *She* reveals how deception works when a person becomes involved with witchcraft. "She says, 'The person who is involved (in the occult) is truly deceived into thinking they have just discovered THE one, true way to actually come into contact with God. In reality, they have just come into contact with a satanic demon, who has temporarily transformed himself into a being appearing very kind, gentle, and wise. The stage is set for these demonic beings to manipulate and mislead their human victims. These people have become demonically possessed.'"

This happened in 1982 and witchcraft powers were just beginning creep out of the alleyways of darkness of Satan and appearing in books, newspapers, television and radio talk programs. Most Christians and certainly very few preachers talked about demons and devils. Danny had their attention. Looking at the faces of the women some looked fearful while others were full of unbelief.

Danny He cleaned his black rimmed glasses and turned to look out the window and he leaned back, trying to relax. His mind continued to run in many directions and then he warned the group to stay away from Ouija boards. "We have had many friends that have tried to burn them and found that they burn with great difficulty. Some had to soak them in gasoline. If you just throw them in the fire, they just won't burn. This is true, even though they are only made out of cardboard. These "games" are powerful satanic tools to entrap people into the occult; when they finally do burn, people report that they will make weird noises . . . enough to make the hair on the back of the neck stand up."

As Danny shared this testimony, a few of the women got strange looks on their faces. You could tell that they had these

---

[22] http://www.amazon.com/Beautiful-Side-Evil-Johanna-Michaelsen/dp/0890813221

"games" in their homes. "It's every bit as harmful to consult the Ouija board as it is to worship Satan or practice black magic," Danny pushed on with the dangers of having the occult games in the home. "It's just as demonic to read tea leaves or have one's palms read as it is to go to séances and 'call the dead back'. He explained that demons familiar with the deceased that impersonate their dead relatives in a séance. "All these practices are occult; all pave the way for the one practicing them to become demon possessed!"

When Danny was exposing these things, many Christians had never thought of things before. Our country was a Christian country and most people were just beginning to beginning to be exposed through the media and movies. However, these powers were being glamorized, heralded as great and particular good supernatural gifts. No one feared them. This was the beginning of time of Satan's taking our country church by church and block by block into the powers of darkness.

DESTROYING IDOLATRY OBJECTS

Danny went on to say, "First and foremost, Christians should never seek information from a witch, fortune teller, psychic or read their occult books. Satan lies! Always remember, that God never intended that his people be ignorant of the Devil's devices. God has Saints who are trained by Him to expose the wiles of Satan. You may find many books concerning the subject and exposing witchcraft written concerning the powers of darkness from God's point of view in many Christian book stores. Be careful!"

"If you have these occult items in your home," Danny pointed to his Bible, "the Word of God clearly instructs His people to destroy all things related to these occult items by burning them with fire or breaking them. Furthermore, it tells us not to desire any silver or gold that is on them. God commands that the believer is not to desire, or take for personal reasons, or to give to any other individual under any circumstances. In this respect, God was very strict and commanded that there should not be even any "desire" for the item or any part of it. There should also be no emotional attachment to the objects. This includes articles that are inherited from family members, and friends. Of course, these articles also can include objects that are inherited from family members in the Masons, cult religions such as Bibles, religious articles and statues from the Catholic faith such as, Jesus, Mary, Joseph, and dead saints."

Since Danny's family greatly suffered by the powers inflicted upon them from a practicing "white witch," he was driven to get his warnings to God's people. "It's important to get rid of all occult books and materials in your home. When Rita was delivered, the Lord led us to get all the things Della, the witch had given us. We got them out of our house. I discovered her contact objects where places for the demons to indwell. When we decided to burn her occult object, we had heard about the Ouija boards and decided we'd take our tape recorder in case something made sounds. I soaked the stuff in gasoline. It was a beautiful clear night with a full moon and we started the fire and listened for about ten minutes. Nothing happened. We were disappointed. The tape recorder was still going and we were having a good time, joking around. Everybody was feeling better."

The audience got the look, this is absolutely insane, and of course nothing happened.

Danny picked his theme of disposing of the witchcraft articles that they had collected from Della. He said, "Suddenly there was a feeling of evil in the air. It was like a cloud of darkness dropped from the sky. Yet, it was still bright and the fire flickered brightly, but there was a black was cloud coming over us. We all felt it. The fire was still smoldering and a feeling of fear filled the atmosphere and we all looked up. Suddenly a giant bird came out of the fire and flew south. It made a bloodcurdling screech was a large solid black bird, with a wing span of three or four feet. I know every bird in the state of Florida, but this was not a bird that I had ever seen before. The only way I can describe it is, like when you see "prehistoric movies"; they have a bird with claws on its wings, a long beak. This thing flew right over the fire and hovered a little bit higher than the roof of the house. When it got absolutely overhead, then we heard another penetrating, piercing screech. It sent goose bumps up and down my spine and my hair stood up on the nape of my neck. A black shadow of something lifted out of the fire soaring up to the bird!

"We have that piercing scream on our tape recorder and have played it many times! It's perfectly clear. I've never heard another bird make a sound like that." Danny cleared his throat. The people looked a little bewildered as he divulged this eerie information. "It was unbelievable. Much evil is being fed through the TV networks . . . witchcraft, séances, etc. And it's possible to become involved in witchcraft by simply watching TV. Unnerving, but true . . . Satan's the god of the air. In a popular TV show, the heroine calls upon spells, and magic to change whatever is going on. Such popular shows deal with the world of the occult. These type shows will open you to put your guards down. Don't be duped by the Devil. He knows what he is doing."

"The majority of Christians today are almost totally ignorant of the nature, tactics and presence of evil spirits. As a result, multitudes are needlessly living in torment. The Bible says, *"Lest Satan should get advantage of us: for we are not ignorant of his*

66

devices," (2Cor. 2:11). Unfortunately, during our ordeal of trying to find release for Rita we found today's Christians mostly ignorant concerning the powers of demons! We have learned that many diseases and physical infirmities are due to spirits of infirmity, unclean spirits or evil spirits to torment and ancestral bloodlines. Pat told us that God created us as three-part beings. We have bodies that are physical and spiritual, and then we have our eternal soul. At death, the physical and the spiritual [personality] die and cease to exist. However, the eternal soul goes back to God."

The Apostle Paul gives us some special insight on this matter. Each person has a physical and spiritual Body. "There is a natural body, and there is a spiritual body," (1 Cor. 15:44). In the next passage, Paul tells us that the physical body itself consists of two parts, body and spirit. He tells us that we are temples for God to dwell. "What? Know ye not that your body is the temple of the Holy Ghost which is in you, which ye have of God, and ye are not your own?" (1 Cor. 6:19). This Scripture reveals a three-part construction of each human being!"

"In our case, Rita became open to demon possession because of our association with a witch. Even though we didn't believe in her demonic powers, they still worked on our family. The devils were working and because they were invisible, we just thought that these destructive things that happened to my wife were caused by a medical problem but doctors could not cure her. After Rita's deliverance, we discovered that the problem for Satan is that he cannot just come in, without invitation or speaking in legal terms, he must be given "legal authority" to come into the inner soul of a person, by some action or inaction on the part of that person. Demons cannot just hop into people whenever they want. There is a spiritual wall placed there by God so that demons cannot get it unless we break down the wall of God's protection." Danny closed his Bible to finish his talk.

THE OCCULT IS EXPLODING WORLDWIDE

Ignorance is not bliss. Every time that a Christian disobeys the Word of God, opens the person to become subject to demonic spiritual attack. These satanic articles are doorways for Satan and his demons to captivate and enslave the minds of people that open the door by accepting these images into their homes.

The Bible gives a clear warning regarding graven images of these creatures. These images include drawings, imprints, diagrams, engravings, carvings, figurines, paintings, computer printouts, photographs, trinkets', artwork, jewelry and any other representation of mythological creatures.

The Bible says, "The graven images of their gods shall ye burn with fire: thou shalt not desire the silver or gold that is on them, nor take it unto thee, lest thou be snared therein: for it is an abomination to the LORD thy God. 26 Neither shalt thou bring an abomination into thine house, lest thou be a cursed thing like it: but thou shalt utterly detest it, and thou shalt utterly abhor it; for it is a cursed thing," (Deut. 7:25, 26).

Due to the growth of occultism in our society, people are now forced to notice things that were previously not mentioned. Although many Christians want to avoid discussion of these things ("too controversial"), we must face facts . . . only the Name of Jesus puts the Devil to flight. How amazing it is that the Lord has to use baby Christians to teach His people the importance of getting back to the Bible and using scriptural principles to fight spiritual warfare, Danny was such a Christian . . . although young in the spirit, willing to pay the price for victory in Christ, he was standing up because the powers of darkness almost destroyed his wife and children. He was on a mission. He wanted to warn everyone that witches and witchcraft is very destructive and is capable of killing whether you believe in it or not!

Americans are getting a steady diet of witchcraft. Even Christian Churches are diving into the promotion of fantasy movies and spiritual blindness is everywhere.

FAMOUS WITCH FROM THE IMMEDIATE PAST

Famous witch, the Late Sybil Leak exploded on the scene in the seventies. She is responsible for the explosion of witchcraft on the college campuses. A front line person spreading the powers of witchcraft worldwide, Mrs. Leek, also popularized the hunger for witchcraft in America visiting the television and radio talk shows and interviewed for featured articles in leading magazines. Her books are still taught in universities and colleges as courses. She became so successful that many said that she forgot how to cast a spell.

Did Ms. Leak become a Christian? Many Christians from Melbourne, Florida testify of first-hand knowledge of America's most famous witch, Sybil Leek's profession of repentance and confession of faith in Jesus Christ.

Rev. Arlene Coulter, Resurrection Ranch, Melbourne told me Mrs. Leek was on her death bed at a local hospital, fifty Christians linked arms outside and prayed for her soul and two women prayed for Ms. Leek. Coulter said, "Ms. Leek received Jesus as her personal Savior."

Former witch, the late Rev. Irene Park, *The Witch That Switched*, confirmed to me that a woman from Melbourne called her out of a meeting in Texas speaking to her about Sybil Leek.

The world's most famous witch, Sybil Leek and Florida's famous witch, Irene Park, were transformed out of the kingdom of darkness into His wonderful light. Both women both were most despicable women of the recent history are rejoicing around the throne of Jesus Christ.

Irene A. Park, author, the *Witch That Switched* grew up in the world of witchcraft, familiar spirits, voodoo, drugs and pornography. In the realm of satanic power, she rose to the position of High Priestess for the State of Florida only to see herself being destroyed by the very demons that she had faithfully served. Her amazing story that spans 40 years of every evil imaginable but ends in victory in Jesus! Given up to die by doctors and her own Satanic clan; her salvation, deliverance and healing is a mighty testimony to the power of Christian love and prayer. Left for dead at age 43 Irene Park calls out to God and He brings in the intercessors. In her book, *The Witch That Switched*, Rev. Park shares the moving and forceful story of Jesus' victory in her life. "The Lord told two bold Christian women to fast and pray for a woman called Irene Park. They obeyed Jesus and believed for her conversion by praying and fasting 40 days for her soul!

The bible tells us that 'she, who has been forgiven much, loves much'. Irene knows the lies of the evil one and took a stand for God every day of her life. Irene knew that the enemy of our faith will use any means possible to deceive those that are enticed to learn about any mystical powers, through board games, roll playing, or witchcraft. Irene found out that even at the early age of 3 that a seemingly innocent 'imaginary friend' can bring a lifetime of demonic influence if not brought under the blood of Jesus Christ. Irene knew that it was not a game. The enemy only comes to steal, kill, and destroy.

Reverend Park dedicated her life to following in the footsteps of Jesus. Jesus Himself said that "you will do the works that I do". Jesus told His followers that He came to 'Undo the works of the devil. She was definitely 'Special Forces' in the army of God. [23]

JESUS CHRIST OR SATAN

There are only two sources for supernatural power: Jesus or Satan. Seeking power beyond the Word of God and Jesus Christ finds one stepping into the world of the Occult.

The term *occult* is derived from the Latin word *occultus,* which means to cover up, hide, or those things which are hidden or secret; a brief definition of the occult is the practice of attaining supernatural knowledge or powers apart from the God of the Bible.

Through these practices' occultists seek to influence the present or future circumstances, of their lives or the lives of others. No one can dabble in the occult and come away unshackled. It is not harmless games and fun. Occult involvement whether done innocently or not, is disobedience to God's Word. When people ignore God's warning and enter a forbidden realm, they witness spiritual phenomenon.

The Devil does have supernatural power. However, everything he does for people, he requires payment. The result of occult involvement causes oppression, depression, confusion, delusion, and physical ailments of all sorts. We are warned not to be ignorant of Satan's devices in 11 Corinthians 2:11.

Christians should never seek service, direction or healing from an occultist or psychic. When any Christian pursues healing

---

[23] http://cdmin.com/IrenePark.htm Irene Parks books...

from these demons, they will be bewitched and guided by the devils. Many have discovered to their surprise and horror that Satan is the one who is willing to divulge supernatural affairs and give them momentary assistance. Often too late, they find that the real source of their advice and supernatural ability is demonic. Confusion results and many end up going into insane asylums and never return! Occult powers come from Satan. When one uses occult power, he or she opens a door for the devil to enter into their spirit. Once the door is opened, very few victims ever get it to shut again.

However, Jesus came to set the captives free and He sent His believers to release His powers and gave us our power of authority to represent Him on this earth. He said that we could overcome the power of the Satan if we could believe His Word.

The Bible shows His disciples failing that He personally taught and demonstrated His power over demons. In Mark 9:23 a certain man had a demoniac son who was afflicted with a dumb spirit. The father found the futility of the disciples to heal the child. He took his son to Jesus and the boy was healed. *If thou canst believe,* all things are possible to him that believeth." The man's trust was strengthened, he offered a humble prayer for an increase of faith, and instantly Jesus spoke the word, and the devil was cast out, with an injunction never to return. Then Jesus spoke to His disciples, Mark 9:28-29 "And when he was come into the house, his disciples asked him privately, why not we could cast him out? And he said unto them, this kind can come forth by nothing, but by prayer and fasting."Resist the Devil. Align yourself with Jesus Christ's invincible power, fast and pray and Satan and his demons will flee from you. It's scriptural . . . and God cannot lie!

Chapter Four
Medicine Cannot Cure a Witch's Curse

"But unto you that fear my name shall the Sun of righteousness arise with healing in his wings; and ye shall go forth, and grow up as calves of the stall," (Mal. 4:2).

Our Ministry has prayed for many Christians who were bound by demonic powers and seen the find freedom in Jesus Christ. If they are seeking religious experiences to feel good, instead of repenting and seeking Jesus Christ, they will be open to pick up evil spirits; only Jesus can free Satan's captives. If they live double lives, unholy, without true commitments to the Lord, they will be demonized. If they find themselves involved with a religious cult, they will need deliverance. If they are following a person instead of being led by Jesus Christ and His Word, they will receive spirits such as; religious confusion, Antichrist, rebellion, idolatry, and many others. These people will be led a away from Jesus. The Bible tells us, "Now the Spirit speaketh expressly, that in the latter times some shall depart from the faith, giving heed to seducing spirits, and doctrines of devils; 2 Speaking lies in hypocrisy; having their conscience seared with a hot iron," (1 Tim. 4:1-2).

MYSTERIOUS SICKNESS

Danny began to describe his wife's illness that was inflicted on her from the witch called Della who had worked witchcraft's curse against Rita. "Last year we spent $13,000 trying to find out what was wrong with Rita my wife. She had fuzzy double vision, black outs and seizures. She'd be sitting and suddenly, without warning, pass out sometimes for several minutes but, as time went on, this increased for a couple of hours; later at the hospital, it could last ten hours or more and these attacks just kept becoming more intense. The doctors ran every test you could name but found nothing. The Eye Institute confirmed that she had double vision. They said, 'there are two things that will cause this, but neither one of these things were present in Rita's case and they could not explain it'."

Danny leaned on the pulpit. His pale face was intense and frozen. He cleared his throat and continued "According to doctors, she had a rheumatic fever condition, diabetes, a bad heart valve. She also had kidney and bladder infections for years. She was allergic to almost all drugs and couldn't wear her wedding band or Medical Alert bracelet because she broke out with sores. The doctors said it's chronic this and chronic that and they started saying its psychosomatic means you're just imagining things in your mind but causing the actual symptoms to appear in your body. Some doctors came to the conclusion that she was crazy!"

Danny dutifully pushed his memory, searching to uncover the violations Satan had heaped on them as a defenseless family without Christ."

The diagnosis seemed hopeless but Danny determined to stand with his wife because he believed beyond faith that somehow she would be restored to health. "Finally, we ran out of doctors. They completely threw their hands up and said: We don't know what to do: there's no more medication to give her. 'Just keep her home.' But she kept on blacking out and we were left standing alone trying to daily muddle through her totally helpless reliance on me and the children to care for her."

CRIPPLED BY A WITCH'S CURSE

There are reasons that God warn his people to beware of witches and wizards; their powers of darkness are very real and damaging to a victim physical and spiritual well being. In the Old Testament, God told us in Exodus 32: 19, "Thou shall not suffer a witch to live." There is a great deep of our depravity involved in witchcraft and it is impossible for the people being inspired by evil spirits to give safety to God's people or people lacking belief or expressing disbelief about God. The malicious evil spirits will drive their captives, witches and wizards, to kill their victims. Witchcraft works in the mind. For instance, a witch may take complete possession of the victim's mind, leaving them with neither power of understanding nor wellbeing and can establish "possession" or "insanity." Witchcraft powers can refer either to divination (prediction, forecast, foretelling,) or sorcery, (use of magic and drugs ~ "the word pharmacy" is derived from the Greek *[pharmakeia-Strong's 5331]* and means sorcery.) the practice of the magician's art. Those who practice witchcraft also have paranormal connections with evil spirits which give them powers over humans and objects as well. There powers of darkness can be devastating and even kill their victims.

Meanwhile, Danny went on to describe the after effects of the curse that the so-called "white witch" called Della had placed upon his wife. "Della had a tremendous influence over my family. Rita needed twenty-four hour-a-day care or we feared that she would have hurt herself or kill us. Now when she'd black out she could be unconscious up to five and six days. Totally debilitated, she could not breathe, talk clearly, unable to walk, feed herself. Sometimes she'd get excited trying to walk and raise her arm in the air and it would stay there! I worked for twenty or thirty minutes to get the arm down. She'd take a bit of food while I was at work and when I came home I'd have to pry her jaws apart to get the food out... It had been there three or four hours since she took a bite and the food would still be there. She fell down many times and hurt herself." She'd make unintelligible noises and her eyes rolled back into her head with only the whites showing. She was being tortured day and night by an unseen force. See how Satan can destroy many lives by just attacking one person!

"It was it was really bizarre that the witch, Della, was still very active in our lives. I once received a bill from the drug store. It was quite large. When I checked, I discovered Della had received prescriptions from a local doctor (also involved with the covens). "This is unbelievable! She got the prescriptions in my wife's name, charging the drugs to me. She was getting the drugs in 100's while the prescription order called for one pill every four hours, giving Rita five at a time that was poisoning her! Something was exploding on the inside like a red light going off but I still let her come to our home. I decided that in our modern world that it was definitely not smart to believe in that witch stuff about Della was true. Matter of fact, it was totally beyond my power to even imagine that the Devil might be real.

Pat taught us that the word, "pharmacy" is derived from the Greek *[pharmakeia,-Strong's 5331]* and means sorcery. Historically, the definition primarily signified the use of medicine, drugs, spells, poisoning and witchcraft. In sorcery, the use of drugs whether weak or strong was generally accompanied by chants, spells and appeals to occult powers used with various charms, amulets, and prayers. The witch will use them to summons demons to work her designs. Sometimes these objects are professedly created to keep victims from the attention and power of more destructive demons; but, actually were used to impress the person with the mysterious resources and powers of the devil.

Danny's entire family was involved in care giving for Rita. They were determined to bring her back to sanity through their love. Danny said, "Our lives spun around taking care of Rita twenty-four hours a day. We had to watch her every move and we all took turns trying to look after her. Even our eight-year-old son, Mike, was involved in her problem. When she'd try to get up, he'd run over and push her back in the bed. He was like a policeman and she hated him for it. Sometimes she'd scream at him and try to fight him. We were all drained physically and emotionally from our unfailing task. There existed a constant state of anger and bickering and our lives were miserable, but we loved Rita and we had to remember her as she was before she got dreadfully sick; hopefully, thinking of the day when she'd be well again and although she seemed doomed to failure, but still we hoped.

"Her physical appearance had changed drastically. It was incredible Rita no longer looked human and deteriorated into a skeleton deathlike figure. The smell of death filled her room and at this point she became a chemical vegetable and was 95 percent of the time incoherent babbling about nothing for hours; sometimes with this kind of childlike drunken stupor yelling and screaming. Her eyes rolled back into her head with only the whites showing, and spittle dripping from her mouth, muscle twitches, cramps or spasms, itching, vibrating, prickling, tingling, stinging or crawling sensations, Intense heat or cold involuntary bodily movements, jerking, tremors, shaking; feeling an inner force pushing one into postures or moving one's body in unusual ways, just gyrating and pulsating like she was being ravaged from behind from some unseen force. And other times she'd become drunken uncontrollable laughter. Racing heartbeat, pains in the chest,

Digestive system problems, Numbness or pain in the limbs (particularly the left foot and leg),Pains and blockages anywhere, often in the back and neck, Emotional outbursts; rapid mood shifts; seemingly unprovoked or excessive episodes of grief, fear, rage, depression.

We still held onto her as best we could. Sometime we'd tape her during these times and get some interesting tapes, to say the least. She looked much older now. Every movement was that of a very old person on the edge of death. Sometimes, she exhibited great strength and I'd have to restrain her to keep her from hurting herself or someone else. Other times, she was extremely sick and weak falling into a great sleep. Going to the restroom was a major task and could take as much as two hours. Just as I'd get her back to bed, she'd have to go again. It became a very nerve racking process."

Some Christians advised Danny to take Rita to church and God was her only hope and even though she could not physically hear the Word of God but her spirit would hear and would respond to God's Word! "We took her to church even though she was deep in a loss of consciousness. We'd dress here and I'd throw her over my shoulders like a bag of salt, then prop her in the van, strap her in, drive her there. I had to get someone to help me . . . We'd hold her in the pew and she'd go through the entire service like that. However, little by little, they realized that God and prayer were truly the only answers to her problem. Imagine this, I wasn't even saved but the Lord told me that Rita was going to be healed! In my heart, I knew it and my daughter Jessica can confirm this.

Jessica was ready to leave at one point and I don't blame her. She took a lot of abuse from her mother actually it was really the demons working through her mother during this time.

"A Christian gave me Pat Holliday's book, *Holliday for the King* was given to us... and that sort of led to a clue as to what was actually wrong with Rita. A second book mentioned in Pat's book . . . *Deliver Us from Evil,* by Don Basham, gave us the final clue. It came to a head one night. I had been picking up Basham's book for about four weeks. Every time, Rita had protested, "Honey, that book is no good! I've read it. It's no good!" Of course, I know now that wasn't Rita talking to me, it was the evil spirit using her voice! It didn't want me to have light that might expose its presence."

"That night, I was determined to read Basham's book. I picked it up and began to finger through it, and then I turned to the back and began to read it. There were appendices A and B. 'A' was about Satan: where he came from, how he got here, about demons and evil spirits. I had heard about demons but didn't know too much about them."

Danny alleged, "Appendix B listed people in deliverance ministry, then Basham made a reference to chapter 17, so I turned there. I read the page about an elderly couple who had attended Don Basham's meeting and after they went home the wife was confronted by an evil spirit inside of her. Her husband came in and chased the thing out. As I read this, I thought at that moment I got faith and I knew it was a key for my wife to be healed. Rita, listen to this," and I read it to her. As I read the first page, she began having trouble breathing and was actually turning blue. Gasping for air, she just couldn't seem to breathe. This had never happened before and fear attacked me, so I put the book down because I didn't know what to do with Rita. Then she calmed down and wanted to go the bathroom. I helped her there and took the Basham book with me. Sitting on the sink, I again began to read it to her. The same thing happened; she turned blue and lost her breath.

Suddenly, I felt the Lord told me what to do! I know it was Him because I just didn't know what to do. I put my hands on her head to pray for her and God put the words in my mouth! "I rebuke you in Jesus' Name." Then, unexpectedly, her head rolled back, mouth opened and only the whites were showing in her eyes and something left her screaming. A wonderful peace came on her face and it was so dramatic and amazing because I wasn't even saved by Jesus at the time. I just read a page of a book that was all!"

Look at this my Christian friends, incredible! Although Danny was not saved at this time, he read the words of deliverance written by a born-again Christian, Don Basham, and God transferred His authority to overcome the power of the Devil to move devils out of Danny's wife and release her! Divine Knowledge is power! This was the first impression that Danny had that his wife could really be healed.

Danny continued his amazing testimony, "I felt excited and began to read another page and within minutes, the same thing happened. So, I did the same thing and she started gagging, choking and vomit started uncontrollably rushing out of mouth. At first my own stomach felt sick at the sight of this mess but I struggled for control. Then something else manifested a loud screeching and screaming sounds and she seemed to have a sudden immense, powerful, unnatural strength. I struggled to hold her down. She told me later that at this time, I was just a blur to her. After the demon left her, she was unable to talk, except maybe an occasional slurred word and too weak to walk. I continued to press the demons for a third time and she blurted out: 'My God, they are trying to kill me' and gave another high-pitched sidesplitting yell. She told me later that she could see into another spiritual dimension and saw a black band around her head. Rita described that as I prayed for her, it tightened and closed in on her. As the band obstructed her wind pipe, she was unable to breathe. At this moment, she was also seeing little black things that were running up and down her arms. She said they were about two inches high."

There was a great battle going on for Rita's freedom. Danny continued to relate this most unbelievable description of her deliverance. "I repeated the command for her to be set free and another demon left and she returned to normal and color came back into her face. Her pale gray face of death changed and suddenly she looked different. Immediately, I knew that a big change had occurred within her. So, I turned the book around, saying to her, 'here, honey, read this'. She was actually able to read it! Her eyesight was back and she was then able to walk to her bed without help! She could talk normally for the first time in several years. Sadly, this miracle didn't last, because she still had other spirits inside her and she did not get saved and now I know, without receiving Jesus, she could stay free. I guess the original ones did come back. However this experience gave us an insight as to what was going on. I continued to read until my eyes were hooded and droopy because for the first time since Rita got sick, I'd found a ray of hope. Within the next few weeks, I took her to a healing service and she was dramatically healed and was able to walk. It was a great miracle but, Rita was still not delivered."

AMERICA FALLEN INTO RELIGIOUS MIXTURE

The deceivers work with a mixture of dark and light in the shadows and through paranormal mysteries, witches that weave power and lore known only to them. Walking the border between esoteric and arcane, witches forge pacts with demons, draw blood from animals for strange rituals to call spirits out of the lands of the forbidden. To many people they are figures of fear to be persecuted; to others, they are venerated keepers of an ancient tradition of wisdom, healing, and home-brewed sorcery. And maybe some do go mad under the strain of their black and white magic or cackle at the moon to seduce young men with love potions, or turn fools and princes into toads; such is the price one may have to pay when dabbling in forbidden arts. [24]

Are they real? Do they have powers? Are they simple fairy stories? We can find them in movies, magazines, newspapers, toy stores and television programs. However, almost no one takes them seriously. Yes it is true that Walt Disney taught us there were white witches who nice and helpful and then black witches who deserved nothing better than death. However, witches are often viewed as outsiders, or aliens. Some witches respond to this with pride, ignoring whispered slurs and snubs by society. Some witches embrace the role of outsider -- they are eccentric and weird, defying convention.

Witches may adventure in service to their art, collecting strange ingredients and herbs, seeking places of old power. They may wish to avoid the society that condemns them, hoping for acceptance in an adventuring group. The immortal powers to whom they find themselves may call on them for quests or they may adventure for the same reasons others have: curiosity, wealth, fame, and great deeds.

Witches use arcane magic in ways different from wizards and sorcerers and at higher levels they tinker and improvise spells. They also use divine spells and divine curses and blessings that are being powered by the immortal beings with which they have forged pacts. They call spirits and souls to them as servants and informants. They use secret ritual spells and brew powerful potions

---

[24] http://www.woldiangames.com/Woldipedia/index.php/Witch

and are adept alchemists. They are very poor in melee however, because spilt blood interferes with their art.

Witches use both black magic and white magic; there are good witches and bad witches (some people think even the good witches dabble in evil arts). Witches are often dark and quirky, off the wall and unpredictable. Some like to teach lessons that help others, and some just like to meddle -- it may be hard to tell the teaching from the meddling! That suggests a chaotic bent, but on the other hand, witches love to organize into covens, in which they gain greater power and they defer to coven leaders. This tendency is certainly lawful. So in alignment, as in most things, witches are hard to pin down. One special quality of a Witch is that she may use spells of any alignment descriptor without it affecting her alignment although the use her spell is put to might. [25]

GARGUL

Witches draw power from immortal beings and some ally with the gods; some with elemental princes, demon lords, the noble fey, nature, gods now dead, or other places, beings, or forces. This helps makes them outsiders and they may be looked down on by the orthodoxy of traditional religion. Those who worship Gargul, (Gargul God of Death and Life) especially may hate witches; they believe that the Realm of Shadows and the souls of the dead are their special spheres alone -- witches are interlopers and worse. Some few witches avoid this enmity by allying with Gargul himself and avoiding condemnation, but other witches may consider these to be turncoats and traitors. [26]

---

[25] ibid

[26] ibid

Realms of Responsibility

This god collects all the souls and spirits of the dead and makes sure that they arrive at the proper plane of resting and do not roam the World at will. He also ensures that souls born and in some cases even reborn in the proper time and place. He serves both Pantheons in these tasks. He strives against unnatural suffering and death in the World. He tracks down spirits that roam the Realm of Shadow and World itself without proper reasons -- to the consternation of some of the Gods. Gargul is totally dedicated to the elimination of undead from the World.[27]

Appearance

Mortal Form -- Gargul in natural form is a large muscled human with black hair. Some say he looks to be a "Civilized Barbarian of Noble Appearance." Others say he looks similar to Alemi, himself. He appears in dusty well-traveled black robes, with a strange smile that often is mistaken for a grimace. His bearing is once threatening and sad. He is always accompanied by the imp named Gimp.

Avatar For

In pictures, in ritual, or appearing before a group of believers, Gargul appears as a tall figure in a hooded black robe, carrying a book and a crooked staff. The staff glows with a white pure light. Under the robe, one can sometimes make out a crooked smile on his face, or perhaps it's a grimace.

---

[27] http://www.woldiangames.com/cathedral/gargul.htm

Divine Form

In dreams and legend, when his hand forces change upon the World, Gargul seems to be a massive shadowy figure or grey, or a grey lidless eye, or a grey hand that emerges from shadow.

A Gray Lidless Eye

Which is an almost exact replica of its "High Woldian source."[28]

Priests' Appearance

The priests of Gargul often seem cold to the touch. They may wear heavy perfume to mask a slight smell of blood that sometimes surrounds them. They wear grey cloaks, like Gargul, or some black or grey garment. When on missions of importance, a wispy fog may seem to creep from under their cloaks. [29]

WHY SUCH INTEREST IN THE OCCULT?

Knowledgeable Christians point to several reasons for such strong curiosity in the occult. The first is disillusionment with the church and organized religion as it has moved away from Jesus and the Bible as its foundation. The second cause is inquisitiveness concerning paranormal activity; there is a powerful attraction to the occult that appeals to the interest in the unseen. Many begin with "harmless" dabbling, "just for fun," but this can often lead to going deeper into the occult. Third, there is the quest for power; people want control over the future, spirits, or over other individuals. There are three primary categories of the occult world: divination, magic, and demons. Divination is the effort to foretell

---

[28] ibid

[29] ibid, http://www.woldiangames.com/cathedral/gargul.htm

the future and shape their lives accordingly. Folks this puts demons in control of your lives. The divination arts include astrology, zodiac charts, crystal balls, tarot cards, palm reading, psychics, numerology, and horoscopes. The delusory category is magic or paganism. Those in magic make an attempt to control the present by ceremonies, charms, and spells. The magic arts include witchcraft, white magic, black magic, sorcery, Satanism, black mass, wizards and witch doctors.

In our time, there has been a mass exodus from the true Christian faith. The most alarming thing is that millions attend church but they no longer know what they believe because the Word of God is no longer taught. Many churches have become entertainment centers. Many false prophets and teaches have entered in and are preaching another gospel, another Jesus under the anointing of a Kundalini demon and the people thereby lives accordingly. The divination arts include astrology, zodiac charts, crystal balls, tarot cards, palm reading, psychics, numerology, and horoscopes.

Chapter Five
Freedom from the Witchcraft Curses

"But he was wounded for our transgressions, he was bruised for our iniquities; the chastisement of our peace was upon him; and with his stripes we are healed," (Isa. 57:18).

MIRACLE WORKING GOD

Evangelist Fred Carter was holding meetings in our area. Danny Lamb threw Rita across his shoulders to take her to the meeting. Not for one minute did he doubt that God would eventually totally heal his wife. She was terribly sick, dead weight. She hung like a rag doll from his shoulders. Her arms flung loosely as he carried her to the van. They helped her to stagger down the aisle of the building, moving toward the front row. Tonight, tonight might be the night, thought Danny, I know the Lord told me He was going to heal Rita, and I believe Him.

The air was full of hope, faith. That evening Danny grabbed the words of Jesus and held on for the expected miracle. Danny knowing the Devil and his awful works regarded him as his most personal foe. He believed in the Devil firmly, but now sought the power of Christ for victory. Christ was his only hope.

Evangelist Carter knew how to speak the Word of God most powerfully. He had a great anointing to pray for the sick. After preaching, he strolled back and forth with mike in hands worshiping Jesus. The organ music piped softly as the evangelist waited on the Holy Spirit to move with His power. The tent, filled with anticipation, suddenly filled with the power of God. Many miracles began to manifest.

"Don't you love Jesus? ... Praise God. Thank You, Jesus."

"This little sister right here . . . (taking Rita by the hand) . . . You want God to touch you, don't you?"

Rita said, "I do."

Carter began to pray in tongues. He seems lost in a spiritual ecstasy as he strolled back and forth, his Bible high. The organ music got louder in the background. Every eye was glued to the scene, knowing that Christ could do it. All hands extended toward Rita. Suddenly he stopped motioned for the music to bring to a halt. "The powers of God be released in her and begin the work even now," he said forcefully.

"Oh God, help this little crippled lady. Help the little sister to be free in all her limbs: arms, legs, back, spine, bones and muscles . . . Be healed in the Name of Jesus. God give her the victory over it now."

In her direction and every heart dwelt on the power of the Scriptures that could fully deliver even today, as did the Savior when He walked the earth."

The evangelist was walking back and forth and singing softly. Then he stopped and began to talk to the Lord: "Thou hast begun a good work in her. Perform it and perfect it in Jesus." Then he broke into tongues again. Although the words were unintelligible, the man was clearly communicating with the Spirit of God. His face was bright and full of spiritual determination to win the victory in Christ's power. Suddenly his mood changed and in a firm voice he said, "Loosen her . . . We'll be victorious over this . . . Rise and walk, child . . . Step out here and walk with me." He squeezed her hand, a gesture of Christian love.

Rita got up, trembling and stumbling, up for the first time, alone, in a very long time. It was reenacting the third chapter of Acts in which the lame man was healed and walked! "Glory be to

God! Praise the Name of Jesus!" Tears washed the faces of the people as shouts of praise sprang from their lips in great appreciation of what the Spirit of God had done.

"I couldn't walk before!" exclaimed Rita.

"Well, you're doing it now!" Evangelist Carter announced.

Applause and shouts continued to ring forth louder as the organ music crescendo to underscore the miracle. "Hallelujah! Praise God! Praise the Lord! Glory be to God!"

Rita shook her head. She was small in structure; had an innocent face, a little girl's giggle, and made people hope. Giant teardrops of joy flooded her cheeks. "My husband had to carry me everywhere," she testified.

"I believe you." Carter stood with hands extending, to emphasize what was now taking place. She was walking alone!

"Can I walk with her?" Danny asked taking his wife by the hand.

"Sure." Cheers and hand clapping sprang forth again. The air was packed with the reality of the living Christ and His power.

"I can walk! I can walk!" Rita said again and again.

"Well, go ahead and walk then," Reverend Carter exclaimed. "Everybody say, 'Praise your Name, Jesus!" He drifted into tongues again, lost in God, worshiping the King of Glory.

The Lord's presence was precious. Suddenly, it was silent, that beautiful, holy hush that exists when the Holy Spirit is present. Rita had disappeared in the back of the tent with her husband. Hands were high in silent worship of the Lord. Senses had become marvelously acute. Then the mood changed again. The excitement and expectation of God's power charged the crowd with feelings that can only be expressed with shouts and cheers.

"Now that I think about it . . . ." Loud applause overpowered the evangelist's words. "Praise God . . . Glory to God." They shouted. "...Now that I think about it," the evangelist continued, "I remember her stumbling and staggering and being carried in here earlier. Everybody say, "Praise the Lord!" I love to believe God. I try to believe God but when it happens to you, you have to believe God. Say "Amen!""

"Amen!" the crowd replied. You could feel that the evangelist had created a lot of commotion in the camp of evil that day. He got results for God. "Well, here she comes again, folks." Rita and Danny were quickly rounding the far side of the tent, walking at a very quick pace. "I thank you, thank you," Rita repeated fervently running to the evangelist, grabbing his hands. "Thank You, Jesus. Thank You, Jesus," replied Carter, immediately giving the glory back to Jesus where it belonged.

"These people all know that I couldn't walk nor even feed myself. They know me." Rita remarked.

"Well, you can walk and feed yourself now. Hallelujah! Amen . . . Glory to God! I love You, Jesus."

The crowd assembled around the platform. The occupants of the front seats were moved out to make way for seekers, who would be talked with and then asked to sign cards. The cards would be turned over to the local pastors. Personal workers got into the action. The ministers present streamed down to the front. The organist leaned upon the instrument and softly played. The musical invitation continued, while the work for Christ went on up front, except for an occasional appeal from the evangelist.

"Jesus is here waiting for you to come. He loves you. He wants to save you tonight. Praise You, Jesus. Tears of joy washed faces. Hands were raised in praise, as Jesus changed stony hearts and gave gifts of eternal life that night.

Rita's miracle healing was short-lived. Twenty minutes after leaving the meeting, all of the symptoms had returned. We were to

90

discover that Rita's problem wasn't healing alone. She also needed deliverance. The witch's curse needed to be broken, spirits renounced, cast out in the Name of Jesus, (resist the devil and he will flee) before healing would be permanent.

"At this time," related Danny, "Someone in our church told me about a couple by the name of White, (not real name) in another city. He and his wife had been in the deliverance ministry for 14 years. It took us three sessions there but at the end, Rita was pretty clean. First the minister tried to get her to renounce Satan."

"Say, I renounce you Satan . . . I renounce you . . . When she got to Satan's name, she'd give us a devilish look, twisted her mouth in a smirk and say in a playful tone: No, no, and no!"

Rita told us later that it was terrifying, hearing that demon speak through her . . . she said that when she opened her mouth to renounce Satan, this other voice that sounded like her, would say whatever it wanted to say. Also, that she felt "trapped" inside her head, unable to convey her own thoughts and ideas in her own words. But, she said that her spirit was crying out to the Lord and that He knew her heart; and eventually He released her from the curse.

Danny went on to say, "During the first session, Rita asked to go to the bathroom. The Whites had ministered to her for some time. Nothing seemed to be leaving her during the deliverance session. She stayed in the other room for a very long time. So, I went in to check on her. I found her there leaning over the sink coughing and dry heaving. My God, they are trying to kill me here. I want to go home. She kept saying."

"The Whites told me, sometimes demons are very proud and do not want to be seen leaving; so they leave later, after the commands. They Holy Ghost did a complete job on her. She was completely delivered. She's now wearing her wedding band.

There's been no reoccurrences of problems with a heart valve, rheumatic fever, diabetes . . . they're all gone. She eats anything that she wants. Her vision is perfect, the bladder and kidneys - no problem. She's totally healed and delivered. Give God the Glory.

OCCULT FOUNDATIONS

There are two foundations for a person to be able to achieve supernatural power, Jesus or Satan. Seeking power beyond the Word of God and beyond the authority of Jesus Christ finds a person stepping into the world of the witchcraft. The occult is very religious and many are seeking hoping to find for themselves a reason for their life. They want to fill a void in their soul. Instead, they will move into a door that very few people come back. Once ensnared by the Devil, the person's mind, body and spirit is totally bound by the powers of darkness. The only way out is through the grace of God and the Blood of Jesus.

American Christians must learn that the Bible says that God is against anyone that practice witchcraft in any manner. "Manasseh king of Judah hath done these abominations, made his son pass through the fire, and observed times, and used enchantments, and dealt with familiar spirits and wizards: he wrought much wickedness in the sight of the LORD, to provoke him to anger," (2 Kin. 21:6).

The Bible says rebellion is as the sin of witchcraft. When a person turns from God they will walk into rebellion and witchcraft. Witchcraft is the use of every evil spirit in the world to use all Satan's arsenal to destroy any chance of a human being coming into the full power of God.

The word occult means, "powers hidden, unseen," therefore, these bewitching practices are concealed snares to entangle a human being in Satan' world. The spirit of rebellion is working in the world today. It can be identified everywhere. There is a great conspiracy of Satan to control your mind reaches into the entertainment field through television and movies. We also see it working in some churches, medical science, government, business, dying and aging seminars, education, entertainment, lodges, religions, recreation, law enforcement, psychology, mind control, magazines, and rock music, etc.

DECEPTION AND SEDUCTION

The Apostle Paul warns of the spread of heresy from the Christian faith; falling away, a withdrawal, a defection from the Christian Church. The word apostasy conveys the particular idea of the renunciation of a religious or political belief or allegiance. Always remember you can't fall away from something that you've never had. Paul goes on to say in the scriptures that misrepresentation of the truth is a primary avenue for the great end time falling away, or a refusal to accept religious or political beliefs anymore. "Let no man deceive you by any means; for that day shall not come, except there come a falling away first, and that man of sin be revealed, the son of perdition," (I Thess. 2:3). Another avenue is following a strong erroneous belief or illusion. The Bible shows in (2 Thess. 2) the last days that a spirit of "strong delusion" will overtake the whole world. Have you noticed that "another spirit, another Jesus, another Gospel," is being preached everywhere?

God has given them over to the lusts of their own flesh such as "strife and jealousy, greed." The Word of God shows humans descending into unbelief and darkness in Romans 1:21-22, "Because that, when they knew God, they glorified him not as

93

God, neither were thankful; but became vain in their imaginations, and their foolish heart was darkened. 22 Professing themselves to be wise, they became fools,"

These new false Christians are unresolved in their convictions and unstable and unsteady in their purposes are constantly in warfare in their souls as to whom they should serve, God or the world, their own Selves, and Sin. The Apostle Paul loudly and clearly sound out the alarm to the Body of Christ today, (1 Thess. 5:6), ". . . let us not sleep, as do others . . . "

Chapter Six
Witchcraft Possession

I WANT TO KEEP MY DEMON

Rita and Danny give testimony to this by their return to the cross and the Savior who mercifully delivered and healed them from the powers of witchcraft. Because of the tremendous victory Christ had affected in their lives, they took seriously the Scripture, "Heal the sick, cleanse the lepers, raise the dead, cast out devils: freely ye have received, freely give," (Matt. 10:8). They had a crushing burden to see other captives set free, so they brought Louise Carl to me for ministry.

"Lou" was under a witchcraft spell of Della, the same witch who had earlier caused so much torment in the Lambs' lives. I was greeted, "Lou has a demon that she wants to keep! She thinks it is her friend and even knows its name!"

I had seen her before, actually. My mind flashed back. She was sitting in the back row of a meeting with three of her girlfriends. The music was beating joyously. People were dancing, clapping their hands, singing, "God's Not Dead. He's Still Alive." The air was full of the presence of God. Suddenly, Lou pitched forward in her seat, holding her stomach. She gave a piercing scream and appeared to be in great pain. She moaned and groaned. Tears flowed from tortured eyes, her face showing extraordinary stress.

Another woman minister was present. We began to pray for her. The music continued to beat loudly. The people present, caught up in dancing and singing, probably weren't even aware of a demonic manifestation. Her face twisted. She got up and bolted out of the meeting. Later, Reverend Bob Franklyn asked me to go with him to Lou's home to minister to her. Of course, I was always ready to battle for a soul. Several others came with us to pray. When we arrived at her home, she was in bed. She peeped over the covers at us fearfully.

"Jesus can help you Lou, would you like to be born again?"

"No," angrily, her eyes flashing. She was about 18- years old. Yet, her face was already marked with the burden of sin. Her hair hung loosely, framing dark brown eyes. A touch of make-up base did a poor job of hiding deeply entrenched circles under her eyes. Brother Franklyn had a wealth of information. She seemed to like him and was able to carry on a conversation with him in a remote sort of way.

Brother Franklyn took her hand. "Honey, Jesus loves you very much. He died for your sins and wants to help you. He wants to give you eternal life, a spiritual rebirth. (Rom. 3:23), says, All have sinned and have fallen short of the glory of God. Darling do you know that there's not one person on the earth that is just. We all stand guilty before a Holy God. That means a death sentence rests upon everyone that is alive. Unless we receive the sacrifice that Jesus gave us when He died on the cross, we will all go to hell. In (Heb. 9:26), we see He put away sin by the sacrifice of Himself. In other words, He washes us from our sins in His own Blood when we confess our sins and ask Him to take over our life and forgive us."

Lou looked at him with a deadly stare. Her eyes were like cold pools of still water. Her face showed no expression. Brother Franklyn continued to talk to her. "He washed us from our sin in His own blood." Her eyes flickered with mocking contempt. Her mouth dropped into a sneer. He continued, "We've come to set you free. Don't you want Jesus to help you?"

"No, get out of here . . . I don't need you . . . I hate your guts, anyway." Hate, sheer hate and she was such a young person. It was hard to understand that she was capable of having such venomous feelings. One could see that she hurt deeply, though.

"We are not going to harm you, darling."

"Get out,' she growled. "I don't want to talk to you," she looked panicky now, and her voice was shaky.

"Jesus can help you."

"I hate Him; too . . . don't talk to me about Him. Leave me alone." She had the most horrible look in her eyes. You see. The evil spirit was saying all this, manifesting through her. She became increasingly violent and extremely strong.

Loosening a person from the powers of darkness can sometimes be fairly easy but other times exceedingly difficult. It is a factor, to the degree of being possessed by demons, as well as the person's willing the demon's presence to leave, to be able to be free.

Brother Franklyn attacked the demon. She wrestled and kicked. She shouted, convulsed, screamed and tried biting anyone she could grab. Glazed eyes flashed with hatred and fire. There were eleven people there. Each one was restraining a part of her; but, with a strong thrust she broke loose, grabbing a big man and throwing him across the room like he was a rag doll! It was unbelievable, but demon-possessed people may have great, supernatural strength. I never attempt to deliver a person unless they want to be free to serve Jesus.

"I bind you in the Name of Jesus," Brother Franklyn loudly commanded. Suddenly she became calm and her head slumped to her side and she seemed to be in a trance. But just as quickly as the calm came, the demon rose up again began to thrash about. I'd never seen anything like it before . . . I'd never had to hold anyone down like this. I've always believed and still do, if you have the power to command demons out, you have the power to make them leave peacefully, harming no one. However, I was not in charge here. I did a lot of praying. Brother Franklyn pressed the demon to leave for many hours but it did not budge! It was there to stay and had every right to be there because Lou had not confessed Jesus Christ as her Savior.

Lou had two roommates who were frightened, unbelieving, with horror. The sight was enough to drive the hardest heart into the arms of Jesus, in terror. Everyone's eyes were wet with compassion as real demons continued to hold and torment the helpless, wounded girl as a prisoner.

Mary, a roommate, laid her head in her hands weeping uncontrollably. I took her into my arms, holding her as her body trembled with fear. It was then that she came to realize the terrible strength of the "Enemy of our Souls." I've never believed in the devil before tonight; but, after seeing what he's doing to my friend, I know beyond a shadow of doubt the devil is real. What can I do?" I gave her the plan of salvation!

"Honey, accept God's Word that He loves you and wants to give you an abundant life. (Jn. 3:16), tells us, 'For God so loved the world, that He gave His only begotten son, that whosoever believeth in Him should not perish, but have everlasting life." I then showed her (Jn. 10:10), "I am come that they might have life and that they might have it more abundantly."

"You must truly repent and turn away from sin because it separates you from God."For all have sinned and come short of the glory of God'. (Rom. 3:23), says Christ is God's provision for us. 'But God commendeth His love toward us, in that while we were yet sinners, Christ died for us,' (Rom. 5:8). Jesus Christ is our only mediator to God. Therefore, you must receive Jesus as Savor and

98

Lord by your personal invitation." I quoted (Rev. 3:20), " Behold, I stand at the door, and knock: if any man hear my voice, and open the door, I will come in to him, and will sup with him, and he with me. 21 To him that overcometh will I grant to sit with me in my throne, even as I also overcame, and am set down with my Father in his throne. 22 He that hath an ear, let him hear what the Spirit saith unto the churches."

She repeated the sinner's prayer, "Lord, I repent of my sins. I ask you to forgive me. I open the door of my heart and receive you as my Savior and my Lord. Take control of my life and make me the kind of person you want me to be!" Janice, the other roommate had received Christ earlier at the meeting.

Many were still dealing with the demonic force totally in control of Lou. Finally, Brother Franklyn called Lou's own personality back and told the demon to recede, saying, "Lou, come back . . . Lou, come back. The real Lou must surface." She returned to normal just as suddenly as she had previously disappeared under the power of the demon. Rubbing her eyes as though coming out of a deep sleep, she flashed a smile. Her face had relaxed. She was totally unaware of her previous violent behavior. She was now perfectly normal.

Brother Franklyn again tried to lead Lou to Christ. Her roommates pleaded with her to accept the protection of Christ. They both pledged to stick with her and help her. But she continued to stand firmly against Christ.

CONQUERING POWERS OF DARKNESS

Meanwhile, months later, Lou stood on my front door step saying that she still had a demon that she wanted to keep. One thing I knew, total submission to God and resisting Satan is absolutely necessary for deliverance. I knew it would be a difficult week. I didn't know just how terrifying it would turn out.

Occultists' works are cloaked in secrecy. Satan hates exposure. Many church people seem to hate his exposure also. Therefore, people possessed or oppressed by Satan are told to go to a psychiatrist. Many find themselves languishing in mental institutions. While the casualty list grows, we find many church people only interested in what Christianity can do to prosper themselves! Only Judgment Day will tell the tales of horror of the damned because of the slumbering saints of our day.

The Bible shows us that Christ has already conquered Satan's powers of darkness. "Having spoiled principalities and powers, he made a shew of them openly, triumphing over them in it," (Col. 2:15). Christ has already made a spectacle of the powers of darkness with the work He performed on the cross. The idea of spoiling is manifestly a victory that Christ won on the cross. Evil spirits are stripped of their legal right authority to exercise dominion over us. They are His defeated foes, Satan and all his power, all possible enemies. We must exalt the victory of Jesus on the cross He has led all in triumph.

BOUND BY THE POWERS OF DARKNESS

Christians must never seek help, guidance or healing from an occultist. Yes, if any Christian seeks these powers, they will be lured and then bound by the powers of darkness. Many have discovered from their shock and terror that it is Satan that is behind these sources of powers. Sadly, they find out that the real contact of their guidance and supernatural sway is demonic. These victims become confused and unable to pray. They drop away from church and many fall away from the faith and never return. Deliverance ministries are hard to find in America.[30]

What does the First Commandment say? (Exo. 20:2-5), God says, "He is the Lord our God and we are not to have any other gods before Him." The first commandment also warns us that God is jealous and won't tolerate our seeking power or guidance from any other god." Thou shalt have no other gods before Me," (Deut. 5:7). Involvement in the occult is breaking the first commandment (2Cor. 4:4), "In whom the god of this world hath blinded the minds of them which believe not, lest the light of the glorious gospel of Christ, who is the image of God, should shine unto them."

God loves us and has forbidden it to us for it so very dangerously, (1Tim. 4:1), "Now the Spirit speaketh expressly that in the latter times some shall depart from the faith, giving heed to seducing spirits, and doctrines of devils . . . " (1Tim. 4:2), "Speaking lies in hypocrisy; having their conscience seared with a hot iron." Whatever we have seen, or heard, or touched, or experienced through any of our senses has an effect on us, no matter how long ago.

Isaiah 47:9-15 shows God's attitude toward the occult and the dangers which face human beings who traffic in any of these evil arts and sciences. When entrapped by them and judgment comes there is none to help except God.

Christians today must totally commit their lives to Jesus Christ. They cannot swim in both pools. The Word says, (1 Cor. 10:21), "Ye cannot drink the cup of the Lord, and the cup of devils: ye cannot be partakers of the Lord's Table, and of the table of devils." Once a person turns away from God, Satan is there ready to give them a counterfeit faith, false prophet, psychic, or

---

[30] H. A. Maxwell Whyte, Dominion Over Demons (Banner Publishing), p. 175.

false religious experience. Unfortunately, help is rare once the victim is engaged. The Scripture prophesied that occult activity would be increased in the latter days.

Author, Merrill F. Unger has written: Although demonic activity in human history has always been undeniably great since the sin of our first parents exposed mankind to its grave attacks. Yet, the full fulfillment of its destructive powers upon the world is restrained for the end of the age. Demonism bears a striking relation to the doctrine of the last things. All classes of human beings Jews, Gentiles and the Churches of God, (I Cor. 10:32), will be soundly affected by the last-day upsurge of evil supernaturalism. [31]

Concerning the question, can Christians have a demon, and did Dr. Unger change his mind? He certainly did; and not only his mind, but his method. Despite all he so scripturally established in his first book, in this one he reversed all in this second book, *Demons in the World Today*

They [missionaries] claim to have witnessed cases of repossession among converts of ancient idolatrous cultures, such as in China and India, and also among aboriginal peoples and primitive civilizations that live in servile fear and abject bondage to Satan and demons. The claims of these missionaries appear valid. [32]

In this book Dr. Unger quoted accounts given by missionaries and others, mainly Armenian and charismatic, concerning the experiences of "demon possessed" believers. He submitted none of these accounts to the Word and he did not

---

[31] Merrill F. Unger, *Demons in the World Today* (Tyndale House Publishers). Why a second work on the subject of demonism, while the first, *Biblical Demonology*, is still in print?

[32] (p. 117).

contest any of them. Rather, he made such remarks concerning them as "thoroughly authenticated," "this seems very reasonable," "quite probably," "would seem to confirm," "it is only reasonable to conclude," and "supported by experience and observation."

He also favorably and without question quoted such authors as Hobart Freeman, Kurt Koch, C.S. Lovett, J.A. McMillen, T.J. McCrossan, J. L. Nevius, J. Penn-Lewis, A.B. Simpson, Charles Ussher, and V.R. Edman--all of whom teach that believers can be demon-possessed.

For some time Dr. Kurt Koch has been purported by most to be authority on demonism. This man was incredibly naive being completely taken in by any and all stories and claims concerning the "revival" of Mel Tari, *Like a Mighty Wind*.[33] Certainly Dr. Edman's subjective claims went far in toppling Dr. Unger from objective truth into the pit of subjectivity:

For many years the late chancellor of Wheaton College, Dr. V. Raymond Edman, taught that a Christian under certain circumstances could be invaded by demon powers. His first-hand experience with crude demonism, as a result of missionary labors in Ecuador in his earlier years, gave Dr. Edman an understanding of the subject of demonism not possessed by purely theoretical Bible interpreters.

In 1955, three years after the appearance of *Biblical Demonology*, *Dr. Edman wrote me a letter in which he stated his convictions on the subject*. At the time, I espoused the purely theoretical position which did not square with the authenticated facts of experience.[34]

How about experience squaring with the authenticated truth of Scripture? So, three years after Dr. Unger presented his *Biblical*

---

[33] http://www.amazon.com/Like-Mighty-Wind-Mel-Tari/dp/0884190803
[34] *(What Demons Can Do to Saints, p. 61)*.

Demonology stand that believers could not be indwelt by demons, he referred to that stand as a *"purely theoretical position."* And just what did he mean by *"authenticated facts of experience"?*

For that answer we must go back 20 years, to the early 1930s. Dr. Unger had several Christian women in his early pastorate that he believed to be demon-possessed. And he still held that belief when he wrote his anti-possession *Biblical Demonology!*

Some 40 years after his pastoral experiences, and 20 years after his anti-possession stand in *Biblical Demonology*, he wrote:

Believers can be hindered, bound, and oppressed by Satan and even indwelt by one or more demons, which may derange the mind and afflict the body.

One woman, who excelled in the gift of intercessory prayer, was nevertheless constantly the center of a disturbance because of lack of tact and wisdom, due apparently to some alien spirit indwelling her.[35]

The writer remembers well the occasion of a prayer meeting when this woman was delivered from this evil spirit, as she and a group of us were on our knees in intercession. All of a sudden, as she quietly prayed, the demon [!] in her gave an unearthly yell that could be heard for a block and came out of her, frightening the group almost out of their wits. After falling into an unconscious state for a minute or two, the woman regained consciousness and rose to her feet, joyfully confident that she had been set free from an evil power.[36]

Here we have a Pentecostal woman's typical "relief" in a too-quiet prayer meeting. That will get the attention of the uninitiated! In this and similar cases, Dr. Unger's diagnosis was

---

[35] http://withchrist.org/MJS/ungerm.htm
[36] *(Demons in the World Today, pp. 185,186).*

demon possession without question. Coupled with this false conviction, and the pressure of the missionary letters and other claims, our brother's subjectivity was complete. Six years after writing his second book on demonology, a third was produced.[37]

Certainly Dr. Edman's subjective claims went far in toppling Dr. Unger from objective truth into the pit of subjectivity:

For many years the late chancellor of Wheaton College, Dr. V. Raymond Edman, taught that a Christian under certain circumstances could be invaded by demon powers. His first-hand experience with crude demonism, as a result of missionary labors in Ecuador in his earlier years, gave Dr. Edman an understanding of the subject of demonism not possessed by purely theoretical Bible interpreters.

In 1955, three years after the appearance of *Biblical Demonology,* Dr. Edman wrote me a letter in which he stated his convictions on the subject. At the time, I espoused the purely theoretical position which did not square with the authenticated facts of experience,[38]

WITCHCRAFT REVOLUTION

In view of the extent to which America and the Christian Church has, in many instances, are infected by the occult, Christian workers are faced with a double task. One is to enlighten and warn; the other to counsel and help those in need. Since occult experience is a religious (spiritual) issue, the treatment is not to be found in psychiatry or psychotherapy.

Persons who have subjected themselves to demonic forces become a direct target or torment from them. Deliverance comes

---

[37] http://withchrist.org/MJS/ungerm.htm
[38] *(What Demons Can Do to Saints, p. 61).*

through Christ alone. A person can, through faith and submission to Calvary, overcome all powers of darkness. It was for this purpose that the Son of God appeared that He might destroy the works of the Devil. "And wheresoever he taketh him, he teareth him: and gnasheth with his teeth, and pineth away and I spake to thy disciples that they should cast him out and they could not," (Mk. 9:18).

We can forget medieval times and folklore. These demons are for real and active! Americans tend to think that these kinds of devils are just fantasy or imagination. I'm telling you that they are for real! They are supernatural evil spirits that are being invited into our homes because many open a sexual perversion door through television, movies and evil magazine. When they are invited in, they are very hard to deliver because they are "pleasure devils" that give joy to the flesh of their victims. Having sex with many people will bring their sexual refuse into their bodies. All the spirits that are in these sexual partners these spiritual chains go back for thousands of years.

You must remember, these are "feel good" devils and just as some get hooked on drugs and cigarettes and you can't get free, so it will be with these devils. In the beginning they may give you pleasure but in the end, they will kill you! Try to find help before it is too late! These demons have sex with both men and women as the person sleeps, AND SOME OF YOU KNOW IT. It's not a dream, and it is not your imagination, its evil supernatural experience!

106

SPIRITUAL INFECTION

Many souls are being deceived by powerful seducing spirits and are falling away from the truth that Jesus Christ as Lord and Savior. Christians who are spiritually asleep generally have certain features about them. Some of them are as follows: They believe that they are safe and sound, secure, senseless, happy-go-lucky, religiously careless, and unconcerned about their souls, their families', country; negligent of their duties like prayer, Bible Study, fellowship with other believers, and witnessing, not considering their spiritual enemies or the warfare in which they should be engaged.

These slumbering Christians are given to a carnal self-confidences and sinful indulgences. They are stupefied and blinded by besetting sins; living as though there is no tomorrow or an eternity and judgment awaiting them when they leave this world. (Rom. 11:8), "(According as it is written, God hath given them the spirit of slumber, eyes that they should not see, and ears that they should not hear;) unto this day.

Christians are willfully ignorant of God's Word and His Will for their lives; and rebellious and avoid of any serious means of instruction; generally unbalanced, extreme, and excessively corrupt in their morals.

We had a woman to come through our ministry that was the Sunday school teacher to the youth in her church. She was a Satanist! She told us, many witches and Satanists go right to the children in "children church" where they can pollute them. These times, it is hard to convince Christians to work in church because many just want to receive the Word, dance and sing to be blessed. It seems that Satan's agents are more zealous than Christians, so they infiltrate and fill the gap." Imagine that church, Satan sends his agents right into children' church to steal the Christian children! Some molest these young people and draw them into perverted life styles.

Another example, I'll call this women Terri who told me that she had joined a Satanist group and had practiced Satan worship for many years. One day, she went to a church to see a "drama." The next thing that happened to her is that she began to manifest. Christian began to pray for her. She was writhing and fighting against them. She fell into another dimension and black out. When she came back, everyone was praising the Lord. She asked them what had happened to her. They told her that she had become "born again." How ridiculous! How can a person become born again while unconscious? She eventually married the piano player of the church and tried to make him fall away from Jesus and being unsuccessful, she took the Sunday school class to teach the children.

Terry's foot was twisted in the reverse direction and when she walked, she had to drag the foot. She told us that she had a familiar spirit called "Albert." She said that Albert had twisted her foot after a car accident. While she was in the hospital, Albert told her that if she would give him her foot, he would heal it. She gave him her foot, and he twisted her foot! Terry went on to tell me that every night, Albert got in the bed and placed himself between her and the husband. She had a spirit called, "a water spirit," in Africa and also known as a spiritual husband.

When we ministered deliverance to her, we led her to command Albert to give her back her foot and release it in the name of Jesus. After that, we delivered her from the spirit of Albert and prayed for Jesus to heal her foot. It immediately began to be loosed and the foot turned around and became normal. Regrettably, after much deliverance, Terry fell away from Jesus and invited

Albert to come back into her life. Her foot returned to the crippled condition and twisted to the opposite direction but worse than before. Regrettably, after much deliverance, Terry in her rebellion invited Albert to come back into her life. Astonishingly, her daughter's foot became changed exactly like her mother's foot and Albert made the daughter crippled!

Jesus warned in (Jn. 10:10-15), "The thief cometh not, but for to steal, and to kill, and to destroy: I am come that they might have life, and that they might have it more abundantly. I am the good shepherd: the good shepherd giveth his life for the sheep. But he that is a hireling, and not the shepherd, whose own the sheep are not, seeth the wolf coming, and leaveth the sheep, and fleeth: and the wolf catcheth them, and scattereth the sheep. The hireling fleeth, because he is an hireling, and careth not for the sheep. I am the good shepherd, and know my sheep, and am known of mine. As the Father knoweth me, even so know I the Father: and I lay down my life for the sheep."

(1 Thess. 5:6-7), "Therefore let us not sleep, as do others; but let us watch and be sober. For they that sleep in the night; and they that be drunken are drunken in the night."

(Rom. 13:11), "And that, knowing the time, that now it is high time to awake out of sleep: for now is our salvation nearer than when we believed." (1 Cor. 15:34), "Awake to righteousness, and sin not . . . "

(Eph. 5:14), "Wherefore He saith, Awake thou that sleepest, and arise from the dead . . . "

(Rom. 12:11), "Not slothful in business . . . "

Chapter Seven
Walking in Agreement With Witchcraft

"For we wrestle not against flesh and blood, but against principalities, against powers, against the rulers of the darkness of this world, against spiritual wickedness," (Eph. 6:12).

WAGING WAR

Every ounce of Satan's territory that you take for Christ is a battle. It's a struggle. It's warfare. We are end time saints living in a demonized world which is the same demonized world that the first saints lived in. They were not fearful of devils and witchcraft powers. They acknowledged their reality and by taking spiritual authority over them, they vanquished them! Thomas Carlyle wrote twenty-one words that if the Church would take to heart could change its spiritual life:

"Our business is not to see what lies dimly at a distance, but to do what lies clearly at hand." We must stand in Christ's power and battle for souls. Jesus said: "And I say also unto thee that thou art Peter, and upon this rock I will build my church; and the gates of hell shall not prevail against it," (Matt. 16:18).

WITCHCRAFT CRISES

Lou was a pretty girl. When she was in her own personality, her eyes were soft as a deer's. She appeared to be the All-American girl next door. She had just recently graduated from high school. Lou had asked Jesus one night to save her.

She had recollected her early days: brutality, degradation of her alcoholic father and grandfather. They had both raped her and then had placed her into a mental institution. She was bitter, hating them.

After she finally got out of the institution, in desperation, she turned to witchcraft and séances. As she searched for freedom, memories of her demented father and her grandfather, and their abuses, continued to plague her. Her back bore livid scars from the belt that had slashed her stubborn, unwilling body into humiliating submission. She'd never forget nor forgive this anguish. She was bound by guilt, fear, rejection, hate, and now witchcraft.

Several months before I met Lou, one of her best friends had died in an auto crash. She had grieved constantly about her and become very withdrawn. Rita said that she came to the meeting one night and did actually forgive her father and grandfather for raping her. She cried and asked Jesus to save her. But, two other friends were killed that very same night in an auto crash! This seemed to push her further into herself. After all, they had all attended school together, worked at the same place after graduation . . . even participated in witchcraft together.

"When she went to the meeting, she asked for salvation and did forgive them for raping her," Rita reported. "A measure of deliverance occurred, but she admitted to us that she still has a spirit that is her 'friend'. She does not want it to leave! She even knows its name!"

I told Rita, "A number of conditions must be met by a person if prayer is to bring deliverance: willingness to turn from all sin and contact with evil spirits, forgiveness of all persons, complete surrender to the Lordship of Christ in every area of life. We can only free her by breaking Satan's legal right to her life and we can do that only by her renouncing each sin. (2Cor. 4:2). Then we can command the demons to go."

I started a fast. I knew that we could not free her because she had not met the conditions for deliverance just listed. When a person believes a demon is a friend, they have to be brought to the point by the Spirit of God to want to be free. Freedom comes only when one takes a firm stand against spirits. We simply could do nothing at this point but pray, fast, and talk Scriptures to her.

We took her to our meeting the next day. Under heavy oppression, she sat with head bowed, hands in her lap. Under tremendous conviction, she did not, however, respond to an altar call but, instead, left the room abruptly.

Later, in my home, the demon surfaced and again took her personality over completely. Remember: the first time that I saw it exposed, eleven people were holding her down. This time, there were just the four of us. I put my hand on her stomach, commanding the evil thing to leave in the Name of Jesus. She acted as though my hand was like fire, burning her . . . she began to groan, shrieked that it hurt her. I was only lightly touching her. She wrapped her hand around my wrist trying to force it off but I kept it there. Later, I noticed my wrist was black and blue from her strong grip. Those marks remained for the rest of the week!

Oh, how that demon hated the touch of Jesus! Her body was rigid, now drenched in perspiration. Her eyes were not focusing. Veins stood out on her neck, pulsating rapidly. Foam would show in her mouth but she kept her mouth tightly shut to keep the evil spirits inside as they were being pressed to leave. We ministered to her for more than an hour, but the demons did not leave. They knew their rights. Without her total commitment to Christ, they had power to stay. Lou seemed out of touch with reality. We tried not to upset her any further. She seemed to be hanging on a thread. We were all very gentle with her.

One thing I've learned over the years: I am not the personality involved in the deliverance conflict. It is Christ IN ME! Also, it is not the person who caused the battle, but the Devil(s) within them. The battle is always a supernatural one, fought in the Spirit by the power of Christ working through me. His power is only limited by our faith AND the will of the person involved. Deliverance always comes when Biblical conditions are met. But, God will never step over a person's will to set them free, just as He will not make people get saved. It really is their decision.

Transference of Spirits shows how Satan transfers his demonic spirits to humans. The Bible shows that the mind can be manipulated by supernatural forces. "But their minds were blinded: for until this day remained, the same veil taken away in the reading of the old testament; which veil is done away in Christ" (2 Jn. 6:14). These devils use deception to transfer spirits through the mind "Satan disguises himself as an angel of light (2 Jn. 11:14), appearing to men as a messenger of that which is good and wholesome to indicate that, truly, he comes from God.

GREAT AUTHORITY

The late, H. A. Maxwell Whyte once had a dramatic experience in terms of deliverance authority: "The Apostle James tells us that the devils believe and tremble at the Name of Jesus. This should help us to understand that we have great authority over these demons. We can afford to deal with them as defeated foes.[39]

---

[39] H. A. Maxwell Whyte http://www.amazon.ca/Casting-Out-Demons-Maxwell-Whyte/dp/0883684683

"I once had a spectacular experience which helped me to realize this fact. I was talking to a brother minister in our sanctuary. Suddenly, a drunk lurched into the church and started to insult us. Realizing that I was face to face with a demon, I rebuked it in Jesus' Name and commanded it to be subject to me. The results were extraordinary.

"The man started to jump up and down and curse the Name of Jesus. Then he pulled of his jacket and threw it into the air. All the time, I was binding and rebuking Satan. Then he tore off his shirt and threw it away, and put his hands into his pockets and pulled out all his money and threw the coins all over the church.

"He then came forward to where we were sitting and began arguing that he knew more about 'religion' than we did. I continued to rebuke and bind the demons. Finally, he fell to the floor and started to spin round and round as a top. The demons were completely under control, and it was a very interesting experience to be taking dominion over the Devil this way.

"Suddenly, the man stopped spinning, got to his feet, started back to where his shirt was lying, put it on, and began to pick up his scattered coins. I helped him retrieve as many as I could: Then, after I had helped him on with his jacket, he sauntered out of the church very peacefully.

"It was a dramatic demonstration of the power we have over demons." [40]

HOW DOES AN INITIATE BECOME A WITCH?

When a person becomes a witch, he or she has to enter into a pact with Satan to worship him. In making this covenant with the

---

[40] ibid

devil, the initiates promise to serve him. Moreover witches have their own liturgy which is a parody of the liturgy said by Roman Catholics.

A MODERN SATANIC GROUP

Local satanic groups are called "grottoes" and their rituals and ceremonies are little more than a mockery of Christ. Following is a sample of what a typical ritual might include, as suggested the Moody article.[41]

Every first day evening just before midnight, a group of men and women gather at a home in San Francisco. There, under the guidance of their high priest, a sorcerer or magus sometimes called the "Black Pope of Satanism," they study and practice and ancient art of black magic. Precisely at midnight they perform satanic rituals that apparently differ little from those allegedly performed by European Satanists and witches at least as early as the seventh century. By the dim and flickering light of black candles, hooded figures perform their rites upon the traditional satanic altar-the naked body of a beautiful young witch . . . calling forth the mysterious powers of darkness to do their bidding. Beneath the emblem of Baphomet, the horned god, they engage in the indulgences of flesh and sense for whose performance their forbearers suffered death and torture at the hands of earlier Christian zealots.

All Satanists are not witches or wizards, but most dabble in black magic. Their altar often has a naked woman on it, is symbolic of a primal goal: to satisfy any physical desire.

Moody began as an observer but was drawn in as a willing participant. He was impressed by their sincerity. "They firmly

---

[41] Be Free, Pat Holliday, Moody Magazine, San Francisco, 1966, the Church of Satan Anton LeVey

believed in what they were doing!" At the same time, they wanted their activities to remain secret in order to prevent ridicule, censure, and even prosecution. They felt isolated by their bizarre behavior, but they continued anyway, since Satanism provided a sense of identity and seemed to provide answers to their problems.[42]

In San Francisco, 1966, the Church of Satan was founded by Anton LeVey and Satan Worship is activity being practiced throughout the world. Churches are being broken into and its equipment stolen while cemeteries invaded for black masses held in mockery of the Lord's Supper.[43]

The Italian scholar Guazzo listed some of the ancient requirements for becoming a witch:

Denial of the Christian Faith: "I deny the Creator of heaven and earth. I deny my baptism. I deny the worship I formerly paid to God. I adhere to the devil and believe only in thee." Trampling on the cross, which accompanied this oath, had been from very early times as an important part of the ritual.[44]

Rebaptism by the devil of a piece of clothing.

Symbolic removal of the baptismal chrism (the consecrated oil mingled with balm).

Denial of godparents and assigning of new sponsors.

Token surrender to the devil of a piece of clothing.

Swearing allegiance to the devil while standing within a magic circle on the ground.

Requests to the devil for their name to be written in the Book of Death.

---

[42] ibid
[43] ibid
[44] http://www.questia.com/library/book/stefano-guazzo-and-the-english-renaissance-1575-1675-by-john-leon-lievsay.jsp

Promise to sacrifice children to the devil, a step which led to the stories of witches murdering children.

Promise to pay annual tribute to the assigned demon. Only black-colored gifts were valid.

Marking with the devil's mark in various parts of the body . . . So that the area marked became insensitive. The mark might vary in shape, a rabbit's foot, a toad, or a spider.

Vows of service to the devil: never to adore the sacrament, to smash holy relics; never to use holy water or candles; and to keep silence on their traffic with Satan.

THE WITCHES' CIRCLE

At the Sabbat a circle nine feet in diameter is drawn on the ground or floor using a ritual knife call the "athame." Within the circle is a five-pointed star known as a "pentagram." Tools denoting the elements-earth, air, fire and water are placed on the altar. A high priestess conducts special rituals and while standing in the circle, invokes demons to materialize. At a major annual Sabbat, she will ask Satan to appear. An animal, often a goat, is sacrificed. The witches then proceed to a feast that includes drinking wine and strong liquor.

When the feasting is over, the witches begin to dance sing and chant. Some dance with broomsticks in commemoration of an ancient fertility rite. As the dancing becomes more uninhibited with a high state of excitement bordering on hysteria or a trance state is achieved, a sexual orgy follows. A major annual Sabbats, according to claims, Satan himself comes materializes and engages in intercourse with the witches. (Some witches claim to have a ceremonial marriage with Satan himself), women who reportedly have had intercourse with Satan have testified that this sexual activity is a very harsh experience. They submitted to it because it represented an affirmation of the evil bond between them.[45]

FESTIVALS

European folklore tells of two major festivals for witches, April 30, the grand Sabbat, known as Walpurgis Night and October 31, known as All Hollow's Eve. This is known today as Halloween, the latter is the night when according to witchcraft, the barriers between the worlds of life and death and thin as veils, allowing the dead to walk among the linking. During these two major festivals, witches gather in great numbers to form a congregation or as they call it, a coven.

Witches normally meet monthly during the full moon meetings may vary, however from as few as five witches to as many as several thousand. These meetings are called "Sabbats." [46]

Every ounce of Satan's territory that you take for Christ is a battle. It's a struggle. It's warfare. We are end time saints living in a demonized world which is the same demonized world that the first saints lived in. They were not fearful of devils and witchcraft powers. They acknowledged their reality and by taking spiritual authority over them, they vanquished them! Thomas Carlyle wrote twenty-one words that if the Church would take to heart could change its spiritual life:

"Our business is not to see what lies dimly at a distance, but to do what lies clearly at hand." We must stand in Christ's power and battle for souls. Jesus said: "And I say also unto thee that thou art Peter, and upon this rock I will build my church; and the gates of hell shall not prevail against it," (Matt. 16:18).

---

[45] ibid
[46] Halloween, Pat Holliday, http://www.miracleinternetchurch.com/ebooks

Chapter Eight
Discerning Witchcraft Powers

I see confused, bewitched people come through prayer lines seeking relief from demonic occult bondage. As I minister to these poor souls, many times, church people stand in unbelief that such powers even exist! May God help us in these hours of darkness?

THE STUBBORN WITCH

It was now a Wednesday night, and we were still praying and attempting to break through the demonic forces controlling Lou. She continued to stand against meeting the biblical conditions for deliverance that she so desperately needed. Demons have every right to stay in a person that walks in agreement with Satan and his demons. Lou's demons were manifesting and trembling.

God gives His disciples the same power that Jesus had when He ministered on the earth. The Word of God says that Christ destroyed the devil's power. "And having spoiled principalities and powers, he made a shew of them openly, triumphing over them in it," (Col. 1:15). God reveals wisdom to the church, "To the intent that now unto the principalities and powers in heavenly places might be known by the church the manifold wisdom of God," (Eph. 3:10). God reveals the believers' position in power, "Nay, in all these things we are more than conquerors through. Him that loved us," (Rom. 8:37). "For I am persuaded, that neither death, nor life, nor angels, nor principalities, nor powers, nor things present, nor things to come." Verse 38; "Nor height, nor depth nor any other creature, shall be able to separate us from the love of God, which is in Christ Jesus or our Lord," Verse 39.

However, as we continued to put pressure on the demons controlling Lou, she became more adamant and would not repent from her involvements of practicing witchcraft. We continue to battle for her soul and working with her to bring her to repentance and acceptance of Jesus as her personal Savior.

Also we knew that witches meet on Wednesday across the country and that they would be working in her town against what we were trying to do for her. We prayed spiritual warfare prayers, binding and caging their demons. We had relentlessly dealt with Lou since Monday, quoting the Word of God, telling her she had to make a choice. The Word of God says: "But I say, that the things which the Gentiles sacrifice, they sacrifice to devils, and not to God: and I would not that ye should have fellowship with devils. Ye cannot drink the cup to the Lord, and the cup of devils: ye cannot be partakers of the Lord's Table, and of the table of devils," (1Cor. 10:20, 21).

In order to help her, Lou simply had to make a choice, Satan's demons living within her or Christ's divine protection over her life, by renunciation of the Devil's power but she continued to walk in agreement with the evil demons inside her.

She was resting on the couch. Her eyes began twitching and moving around and around like a pinball machine in action. They began to move sideways like snake's eyes. Her pupils were now dilated to the point that no color was noticeable: two black coals. Her eyes continued to dart back and forth for a very long time.

Danny remarked: "That's exactly what Rita did when she was sick. She's seeing demons. We used to have to make my wife stay in bed because she couldn't walk. But this is the same thing." Lou slowly moved to get up. Danny got up to stop her. Suddenly, her eyes sank into the back of her head. It was as though the balls beneath had shrunk away and only the whites were showing.

120

"Leave her alone . . . I want to see what's going on here," I suggested. Her eyes returned a glassy stare. Slowly, getting up to a sitting position, she swung her feet to the floor. She was in a total trance-like state. Her eyes were still weaving. She stood up, shakily, and began to try to walk, staggering and stumbling. I said, "She looks like a zombie or a puppet. That's it, a puppet on the end of a string." Staggering across the room, legs like rubber. "Of course! It's voodoo. She's a Zombie under the power of a voodooist." I had never seen anything like it, this is Incredible! These powers of darkness were in complete control of her body and mind! I continued to watch her as she stumbled back to the couch. It had taken her nearly 15 minutes to walk across the room in that condition. She reached the couch and slumped and collapsed like a rag doll.

Rita started talking. "That's a spirit of Voodoo," she repeated. "Pat, the sad thing is, I can take you too many people in our town that are in the same condition, just like her. They walk around and stumble, like drunks, in a trance," Rita related.

"Many," I asked?

"Yes. I can take you to at least thirty," Rita answered.

"My Lord, what are the Christians doing?"

"Nothing" she replied.

"Nothing, that's incredible?"

"That's right," Rita replied, "people must travel to other parts of the state to find help."

"Extend mercy, Father. Help me to see spiritually in these last days," I prayed. "The Church is so asleep. The Word of God says Christ is the head of all power and "God elevated Christ above all principalities and power," (Col. 1:16). We also believe your Word, Father, that You will send the Holy Spirit to war against these demons in Lou. We believe that the power of Jesus more powerful than Satan and his demons because You said, "And ye are complete in him, which is the head of all principality and power." (Col. 2:10). Also we are reminded according to the scriptures that Jesus is above every power. "Far above all principality, and power, and might, and dominion, and every name that is named, not only in this world, but also in that which is to come." (Eph. 1:21).

We take authority over every deceiving demon that has ensnared Lou and command you to loose her. We believe that "God so loved the world that He gave His only begotten Son, that whosoever believeth in Him might not perish," and ask the Holy Ghost to open her understanding so that she can receive Jesus in Jesus' name.

Older Christians are leaving the battlefront almost totally to neophytes. (A vast majority of Christians today are ignorant of the nature and operation of evil spirits). Many are fearful of supernatural things. Much of Christ's ministry was devoted to casting devils out of tormented people. Christ stated that if we are true believers, these signs shall follow us that believe. "In my name they shall cast out devils," (Mk. 16:17). The essence of the Christian ministry is personal service. The earliest ministry of the Church was that of the Apostles. As the meaning of the word, "apostle" indicates, they were men "sent out on a mission to continue the work of Christ." The Word of God has never told us to cease their beginnings. Christ was a devil driving minister. Jesus set the people free and we must do the same. Casting out demons is a very specialized ministry which, when properly understood, involves unusual qualities of faith, prayer and fasting (Matt. 17:19-20). If we do our part, God will perform His Word.

The Bible teaches that God has given us a spiritual armor but that it is our responsibility to put it on. (Eph. 6:10-18). That's where Satan has been getting the victory. We, many times, haven't put our armor on. We haven't been using our weapons . . . fasting, prayer, the Name and Blood of Jesus, the Word of God, the power of the Holy Ghost and fighting the battle of faith. We are simply not doing what the Word of God says . . . The Word works every time - God doesn't fail.

We must begin or continue to war in the heavens and break the strongholds that are capturing millions in our country and throughout the world. These people are facing the deaths of infidels. We must get and increase the burden for the lost!

WHITE WITCHCRAFT

In the world of witchcraft, white witchcraft is ruled by the same evil forces as rules black witchcraft. Both movements are commissioned by Satan.

Modern white witches, claim to be heirs to an unbroken religious tradition stretching back into primeval history. They worship the Great Mother, the earth mother, the symbol of fertility and the oldest and most elemental of the ancient gods. White witchcraft insists that it is religion and not an evil cult. [47]

White witches believe there is a distinction between white magic and black magic. But the source of power between white and black magic is the same source, Satan! It is that simple, both are demonic! Remember, any supernatural power that is not association with Jesus Christ and His Word is coming from Satan!

Wicca is the cult of neo paganism, or white witchcraft that has been flourishing in the west since the 1960s. The groups maintain that their "Old religion" is not connected to Satan

---

[47] Pat Holliday, Witchcraft and deliverance, http://www.miracleinternetchurch.com/ebooks

worship. The gods of Wicca are Mother Goddess who ruled the Harvest god who ruled fishing and hunting.

William Schoelbelen, a former high priest in Wicca, explains that there are many differences between Wicca groups. In his book *Wicca: Satan's little White Lie,* he describes some of the variation he found. Some groups perform their ceremonies nude, while others wear robes. In some group's members are scourged with a whip during group practice ritual sex and sexual orgies; others abstain from sexual ceremonies.[48]

He goes on to explain: that there are, however, a few common elements in all Wicca and neo-pagan practices. [49]

Bewitching demons will draw its followers into the pit of hell. The history of witchcraft is sketchy, since ceremonies and beliefs are only orally communicated. Witchcraft rituals have been traced to worship of the Greek goddess Artemis, Diana of the Romans, the Egyptian moon goddess and the fertility goddess of the Canaanite. Modern witches believe in two primary deities: Hecate, the Greek Goddess of ghost, and Pan (Lucifer), the god of the woods and shepherds. Witches insist their Pan, even though horned and cloven-hoofed, is not the same Lucifer condemned in Scriptures.

Just think about this. Vice President Gore wrote a book in the eighties, called, *Earth in Balance,* which challenges' Christian to worship mother earth. He says that they are ignorant if they keep their minds closed to other forms of religions. He claims to be a Southern Baptist.[50] What a shame, what a deception! Wicca is a cult of neo paganism, or white witchcraft that has been flourishing in the west since the 1960s. The group maintains that their "old

---

[48] Chick Publications. *Wicca: Satan's Little White Lie* William Schnoebelen
[49] ibid
[50] http://en.wikipedia.org/wiki/Earth_in_the_Balance

religion" is not connected to Satan worship the gods of Wicca are Mother Goddess, who ruled the Harvest god who ruled fishing and hunting.

MYSTERIOUS SECRET THINGS

There are conditions for successful deliverance from demons. You must be absolutely honest with yourself. You must have a willingness to turn from and confess all known sin. You have to renounce of all contact with evil spirits; forgiving all persons; and complete surrender in every area of life to the Lordship of Jesus Christ. "Whosoever shall call on the Name of the Lord Shall be delivered . . ." (Joel 2:32).

The word "Occult" is defined as knowledge beyond human understanding, mysterious, "secret things." "Hidden knowledge belongs to the Lord, our God: but those things which are revealed belong unto us," (Deut. 29:27). God and Satan are the only two sources for supernatural power. God's grace and power is available to you but first you must believe that He is, and renounce all contact with the satanic occult realm. Many are drifting into the occult because they are spiritually curious. A person cannot exist in a spiritual vacuum. He will either have Christ or Satan, but he will not have an empty soul.

If a person chooses to go into the darkness looking for God, they will end up demon possessed. Once demon possession happens, only Jesus Christ can deliver that person. The Bible shows demonic activity and shows Jesus casting these demons out. "And in the synagogue there was a man, which had a spirit of an unclean devil, and cried out with a loud voice," (Lk. 4:33).

A WITCH CHOOSES JESUS

In October 1982, Irene A. Park, author of *The Witch that Switched* [51] spoke in the churches in our area. She said, "Halloween is nothing for a Christian to play around with." In her book, *The Witch That Switched*, she tells the moving and forceful story of Jesus' victory in her life. She grew up in the world of witchcraft, familiar spirits, voodoo, drugs and pornography. In the realm of Satanic power, rising to the position of High Priestess for the State of Florida, only to see herself being destroyed by the very demons that she had faithfully served.

She had been given up to die by doctors, police and her own satanic clan. Irene's salvation, deliverance and healing, a mighty testimony to the power of prayer; the Lord told two bold Christian women to fast and pray for a woman called Irene Park. They obeyed Jesus and believed for her conversion by praying and fasting 40 days for her soul! Imagine that, most Christians are too busy to come to a prayer meeting to pray for their families.

At the end of their fast, Jesus told them to go to her home. "Just tell her that I love her." Irene was being guarded by two adopted Apache sons and two vicious pit bull dogs. When the two Christian women walked past Irene's guards, they just blinked their eyes and stood with their arms folded. The dogs rolled over and fell asleep.

"Irene," Faith said, "We know what you are doing here and Jesus also knows. He sent us here to tell you that Jesus loves you!" The two women turned and left.

Irene was furious. She went to her satanic altar and conjured her devils to kill the two women. She could not believe that they

---

[51] Irene Park, *The Witch that Switched* cdmin.com/IrenePark.htm

had the nerve to come into her place and tell her His message. Suddenly her demons turned on her and began to attack her. She called her sons to bring her heroin. She took several hits but nothing could stop her pain. The demons continued to attack. She collapsed. Her sons came to rush her to the hospital. The doctors said there is no hope for recovery. Every organ in her body was dying. Irene insisted that her sons take her back home. She said that she did not want to die in the hospital. Driving home, she saw a Christian tent ministry and told her son, "Take me to the tent." They were husky, strong Indians and carried her into the tent. She cried out for Jesus to save her and He saved her that night and she's been preaching His gospel for years.

Irene is one lady delivered by the hand of God. I am telling you there are millions now dabbling with these destructive powers of the darkness. The Church is silent and totally unaware that a Satanist revival is going on and Christian people are being ensnared. Many will never walk out of the witchcraft powers because the workers are few.[52]

Saints, we can no longer ignore what is happening. We must meet the occult revival by pulling the strongholds down through prayer and fasting! We must meet this spiritual crisis with Biblical principles to set the captives of Satan's kingdom free.

---

[52] ibid

127

Chapter Nine
Defeating Witchcraft Powers of Darkness

"The night is far spent, the day is at hand, let us therefore put off the works of darkness," (Rom. 13:12).

CONTROLLING POWERS

Three weeks after Lou left my home, she was still walking in agreement with the evil witchcraft force that could control her on demand, and I came to her hometown to hold an evangelistic meeting. It was there that I again witnessed six people rebuking the evil spirits present in Lou. They were tightly holding her to the ground while she wiggled, kicked viciously and screamed, her eyes bulging and teeth bare. The Devil was really putting on a show and many present were fearful.

Someone took a handkerchief that the evangelist had held in his hand while preaching under the anointing of God. It floated down on her stomach like a feather. Although her eyes were closed, she seemed to "know" the moment it touched her stomach! She groaned like a wounded animal and quickly snatched it away from her, throwing it across the room. Another person picked it off the floor and dropped it on her stomach again. She flinched and shrieked, snatching it off. The interesting thing about this manifestation was that there was no way she could even see the handkerchief being put on her stomach, her eyes were closed and certainly, under normal circumstances, she wouldn't have been able to feel it. But, she did feel it because the power of the anointing of God was on it.

The demon knew each time that the handkerchief was put on her stomach and the demon fought, cringing and screaming as if scalding water had been poured on her.

Finally, the evangelist told the people to let her alone. She jumped to her feet and rushed out of the tent in terror under the control of the demon. She went, we learned, directly to Della, the witch. She wasn't there. Lou was found later walking incoherently along the side of the road babbling unintelligently to an unseen force. Later, she was seen on several occasions visiting the witch's place. "One cannot sit at Christ's table and at the table of Satan, simultaneously," I said, "To be delivered from occult demons, the infected person must sever all relationships with friends or associates who continue to practice occult. The Lord can send someone stronger, more mature, not in need of deliverance, to witness to them!"

The next night, I was ministering in the church and Lou showed up with a big smile and a giant bear hug, acting like any normal teenager greeting a friend. I noticed during the meeting, she left for long periods of time but she'd always return. Nothing unusual happened that night concerning her. The Holy Spirit seemed to be drawing her, but God did move in the church mightily and many were healed and baptized in the Holy Spirit.

After that, Lou returned the next day to Danny and Rita's home. She was holding hands with John, Rita's son, for lunch. Although John had witnessed much of our struggle in dealing with evil forces controlling Lou; he told us that loved her. He shared that they had attended Senior Prom together. She was his first date and his first love. He said that he had committed himself to her while she was visiting my house during our attempts to deliver her. They announced to us their plans of marriage and Danny and Rita were very concerned. When Lou was not under the powers of

129

darkness, she appeared to be like a normal 18-year-old. However, we all understood that if deliverance failed to come and she was not saved by Jesus. She would never be normal or stable mentally and John would also be tormented. So, we all joined hands and I prayed for God's perfect will in John and Lou's lives because once ensnared by the Devil, the person's mind, body and spirit is totally bound by the powers of darkness. The only way out is through the grace of God and the Blood of Jesus and deliverance.

I explained to them that if they will not submit their lives to Christ as Savior, then, Satan will take advantage and bind and possess them with his demons. "Lou, If you have never been to the foot of the 'old rugged cross' . . . you are lost! Jesus said, **"He who comes unto me I will in no way cast out.** The Bible says, 'If thou shalt confess with thy mouth, the Lord Jesus, and believe in thy heart that God raised him from the dead, thou shalt be saved," Rom. 10:9. Lou gave no response to the pleas for her salvation and John was saved.

The following night, after most people had left the meeting, Lou lingered behind. "Can I talk to you alone?"

"Sure." I walked over to the edge of the platform and sat down. She whispered into my ear: "I saw the demon, "Blackman," (not referring to people of color) today, Pat. It was really gross. I mean really ugly. I'm scared to death. I don't want it anymore. Why doesn't it go?"

"Honey, if you truly want it to go, the demon must leave in Jesus' Name. But you need to be one hundred percent for Christ and filled with the Holy Spirit." She nodded seriously.

"But, I've already got the Holy Spirit."

"Oh, where did you get the Holy Spirit?"

"I got it your house, Lou replied."

"No, you didn't."

"I thought I did, she said."

"No, Lou. I never told you that the Holy Spirit baptized you. Remember you did not want Jesus to save you. You did not get deliverance from those demons either."

She brushed hair from her face, listening. There was a long pause. "I'll do anything.... I really want to be free," she firmly replied. Her eyes were desperate and fearful.

"Will you stay away from that witch and renounce all your occult activity?" Sin had become her companion and although she was 18-years-old, she looked haggard and old. I continued to minister to her. "Jesus gave us power and authority over unclean spirits to cast them out . . . heal diseases . . . and preach the Kingdom of God," (Matt. 10:1, Lk. 9:12, Mk. 2:14-19).

"Yes."

"Okay, let's see what God will do." She rubbed her trembling hand as she stood up. I placed my hand on her forehead and she immediately surrendered to the power of the Holy Spirit. She floated to the floor like a feather, slain under the power of the Spirit. I led her in a basic prayer of salvation and then renunciation of Satan's power. The prayer of renunciation is important in cases of occult oppression because these activities are of contact with the power of darkness and explained that these demonic contact binds through successive generations: (Deut. 28:45, 46), transferring occult/familiar spirits down the family line, until the sins are renounced, repented of and curses broken, spirits cast out."

Lou said, "I want to be free, Jesus."

I had someone read Deuteronomy 28 breaking the curses and released the blessings over her in Jesus' name.

I explained those who were praying for her that satanic powers will enforce their claims upon descendants who are completely unaware of the fact of hereditary complicity and who

131

often have had no contact with sorcery themselves. When that person is saved by Christ, Satan will continue to try to enforce his claims to them. A prayer of renunciation officially cancels all of Satan's rights.

We see in the Bible, "But have renounced the hidden things of dishonesty, not walking in craftiness, nor handling the Word of God deceitfully; but by manifestation of the truth commending ourselves to every man's conscience in the sight of God," (1 Cor. 5:2). "Will you renounce witchcraft?"

"Yes." She repeated the simple prayer: "Father, I've sinned. Please forgive me, be my personal Savior and take over my life . . . I renounce all witchcraft sins in Jesus' Name! I give my heart to You."

"Now seek the Holy Ghost, Honey; He will empower you so that you can live for Jesus. The Word of God says "you shall receive power after that the Holy Ghost has come upon you," (Acts 1:8). This gift of God will give you power in witnessing, not only in words but in claiming healing, deliverance; in prayer; in understanding the Word; and power to overcome sin and live a victorious life for Christ. It's for only born-again Christians. (Lk. 11:13), tells us when you have truly become one of God's children, then Your heavenly Father will give the Holy Spirit to them that ask Him."

"We are going to lay hands on you just as Paul did in (Acts 19:6), to the twelve believers at Ephesus, worship Jesus. Raise your hands to the Lord, close your eyes and let your mind dwell on Jesus. Ask your Father in heaven for what He has promised you. Start praising Him. Remember, He will not make you speak in tongues; you have to allow Holy Spirit to use your vocal cords, as the Lord places a strange word in your mouth, speak them out boldly. The Holy Spirit brings out of your spirit." Some Christians had stayed to back me with prayer. She said a couple of hallelujahs when suddenly a demonic power took over her body again. Her facial expression changed and darkness flooded over her face. From the utterances, I knew I was again in the presence of the denizens of Hell!

Suddenly the demon spoke, "She is mine,"... "You cannot have her," the demon growled. The air hung heavy as ungodly embedded creature gazed at me. Her eyes had a fearful disturbed look, face a wild distraught expression. I remembered the Word of God (Lk. 10:19), "Behold, I give unto you power to tread on serpents and scorpions, and over all the power of the enemy: and nothing shall by any means hurt you. Notwithstanding in this rejoice not, that the spirits are subject unto you; but rather rejoice, because your names are written in heaven." It is comforting to know that the Word of God backs one up at times like this.

"I will never leave," the demon snarled. "She belongs to me and made an oath with her blood to serve me forever. You cannot have her. This is my house" The demon sulked and raged. Her lips snapped tightly shut but her body was trembling and jerking. She fell on the floor and began crawling like a snake.

The atmosphere became nerve-racking as I spoke to the evil snake spirit firmly: "You have no power here. I bind all your power over Lou's life in Jesus Christ's Name. She has made a choice to serve Jesus and has renounced your stupid powers. I rebuke you and command you to leave!"

The snake spirit looked at me through double lidded eyes and hissed, "Never! And you can't make me go, this is my home. She's gone too far and belongs to me."

When Satan is invited in, he does not always leave easily. He must be driven out, forcefully. Jesus promised that "the gates of hell shall not prevail against us." (Matt. 16:18). I ignored the chatter of the demons. They moaned and groaned as I continued to press them to leave. "I bind the demons of rebellion, witchcraft, covetousness, greed, materialism, worldliness, gossip, slander, deception, spiritual blindness, spiritual and sexual perversions, adultery, lust, incest, fornication, oral sex, anal sex, whoredom, hate and all the bondages under the sun."

"No," the demon defiantly snarled, "I won't leave and you can't make me go, she wants me to stay. I help her and protect her from her dad. She will die without me." The demon twisted and tried to get up but an invisible angel had it bound to the ground.

"You foul evil demons, loose her. Today I am standing in my position of authority in Jesus and accept the responsibility of walking in Jesus Christ delegated power as is shown in Mark 16:17-20, "And these signs shall follow them that believe; In my name shall they cast out devils; they shall speak with new tongues; 18 They shall take up serpents; and if they drink any deadly thing, it shall not hurt them; they shall lay hands on the sick, and they shall recover. 19 So then after the Lord had spoken unto them, he was received up into heaven, and sat on the right hand of God. 20 And they went forth, and preached everywhere, the Lord working with them, and confirming the word with signs following. Amen."

"Lou belongs to Jesus, you foul demons must leave. I command you to be bound in according to Matthew 12: 25-29, "Jesus saith unto him, I am the way, the truth and the life: no man cometh unto the Father, but by me." (Jn. 14:6). "For there is one God, and one mediator between God and man, the man Christ Jesus," (1 Tim. 2:5), you bow your knee to the name of Jesus."

"No, she's mine; I've been here a long time, since she was born. I will never leave." The demon distorted her face and she took on the feature of a witch.

Once you are in a battle, you must stay focused on the power of Jesus. "I take domination over you, Satan, in the name of Jesus Christ that you are bound according Matthew 18:18 and you will depart from me with all your demons. I bring the blood of Jesus Christ between us and resist every effort of Satan and His wicked spirits to confuse and block me from the will of God. I choose to be changed by the renewing of my mind. I pull down all strongholds of Satan and his fortresses of evil in the name of the Lord Jesus Christ according to 2 Corinthians 10:3-5.

All those present could see the manifested demons and began to pray and claim protection of Christ's Blood. The terrible gaze of the evil thing working through the young girl fell on each of them and they could clearly see witchcraft's effect. A peculiar, heavy feeling hung in the air but there was not one who doubted that Christ would set her free. Jesus told His disciples to heal the sick and cast out devils (Matt. 10:7, 8) and that's what we were doing. God was on our side and we knew it.

Suddenly she struggled strongly to get up. The Lambs and the rest present, familiar with her possession, immediately moved to hold her down. I remembered that not only had Jesus Christ cast out evil spirits but He had commissioned His disciples to do the same works (Mk. 6:13). Eventually they returned with joy saying, "Lord, even the demons are subject to us in your Name," (Lk. 10:17).

"Don't touch her, Jesus and His angels are more powerful than those devils. They are in subjection to His name." The people took away their hands and formed a prayer band . . . sometimes singing about the Blood of Jesus . . . "There is power, power, and wonder-working power, in the Blood . . . of the Lamb." The demon tired to get up again. The men pinned her to the ground. "Leave her alone! Take your hands off her. Those demons don't have the

135

power to stand against the Word of God, the Name of Jesus and His power. They must remain subject to the Name of Jesus Christ. That Name above all names by which every knee shall bow and every tongue confess that Jesus Christ is Lord."

The struggle for Lou's soul continued. In the past, they had the demon put up a tremendous struggle (displaying great paranormal strength). It had acted violently and made itself look stronger and more powerful than the Word, the Name of Jesus and the ministers involved, because many people there were ignorant of the true power of Christ. Jesus is truly more powerful than all the demons in the universe. The Word of God says: "Having spoiled principalities and powers, He made a show of them openly, triumphing over them in it," (Col. 2:15).

Suddenly she began to thrash about. The people rushed to hold her down. Their fingers were digging into her skin. "Take your hands off of her. I've been casting demons out for many years and I've never had to hold people seeking deliverance down in the past and I'm not going to start now. If we can tell them to go, then, I believe, we have the power to tell them to go peacefully! There is not one scene in the Bible of anyone holding down a demon possessed person while the Word of God went forth to cast them out. Satan is a powerful foe, but he was decisively defeated at Calvary. The Word says we are "more than conquerors in Christ."

When they reluctantly took their hands away from her arms and legs, the evil thing reacted quickly with a lunge tried to get control of the situation. I pointed to the demon with my finger and commanded the demon to be still. "Don't you move? You have no power except to leave. You are weak and caged and must obey the name of Jesus." I glanced around the room at the faces of the people watching. Unbelievable horror stamped on their faces, clutching their Bibles tightly.

"Why will you ask proof of the veracity of One who cannot lie; the devils themselves declared Him to be the Son of God; will you mistrust Him?" I took my Bible and laid it on her stomach. Oh, how the demon hated that! The demon began to recoil and began to moan and groan like it was in great pain. It tried to push the Bible of her stomach, but it was now so weak it could not even budge it. No one had to hold her this time because that demon was under the control of the power of God and the commanding Word of God. I knew that shortly we would overcome now.

Thousands of thoughts must have been racing through Rita's mind, particularly because she wept softly, watching the power of demons wane. Everyone in the room was aware of a powerful demonic presence in Lou, at the same time; the authority of Jesus was covering everyone as they prayed. Opening the Bible, I began to read and remind the demon who he was. I beat him up with the Word of God, telling him just who he was, according to God. Nothing but the Word of God and the Name of Christ are needed at a time like this. I hammered him constantly with the Word while everyone prayed and sang songs about the Blood of Jesus. I quoted Scriptures concerning Christ's supremacy, power and Satan's inferiority. The Son of God came out of that tomb, the keys of hell and death dangling at His belt Revelation 1:18, "This was total victory!" 'For this purpose the Son of God was manifested that He might destroy the works of the devil,' (1 Jn. 3:8). You are defeated tonight by His name."

The Word says, "For by Him were all things created, that are in heaven, and that are in earth, visible and invisible, whether they be thrones, or dominions, or principalities, or power; all things were created by him and for him," (Col. 1:16). "This scripture says you were created by Christ. Therefore, we know that you must be subject to Him in all things. You have no power," I reminded the evil spirit. It reacted by making a low growling sound and baring the girl's teeth. Her face made many strange contortions. The evil thing kept hold of her and leered at me in the most threatening, terrible way. I was touching an unclean, totally malefic being from Hell.

The demons were very weak and Lou went limp like a noodle. Her eyes went to the back of head and only the whites were showing and she fell into a deep trance. She looked dead. I quoted the word, Mark 3:11, "And unclean spirits, when they saw him, fell down before him, and cried, saying, Thou art the Son of God." The people were wearing faces full of total fear. "You cannot kill her, I command you to leave in Jesus' name."

I continued to press the demons with the power of the name of Jesus and the Word of the God. The Bible says: "And having spoiled principalities and powers he made a show of them openly, triumphing over them in it," (Col. 2:15). "You remember you killed Him and it's by His Holy Blood that we are saved. It's by His Blood that we have authority and power over you. Don't forget, you tried to kill Him but He's alive and powerful. He's defeated you by His sacrificial love for Lou. She belongs to Him now and you must go by the power of the Name of Jesus."

The demon was now trembling and whimpering like a whipped puppy. It was now so weak that it could not even lift Lou's arms. He howled, "I don't want to hear the name of Jesus. Don't say His Name; leave me alone, you're driving me crazy!" Every eye was on Lou. Faith was now very high and you could tell they all had a greater respect for the use of the Word of God after seeing its effect on these evil demons. "Please, let me stay. You don't know how mean the Devil is, he'll. . . he'll . . . Oh, help me . . ." the demon screamed in terror.

Rita stood with a Bible in her hands. She was bold and fearless. She read the scripture aloud: "And there was war in heaven: Michael and his angels fought against the dragon and the dragon fought and his angels, and prevailed not; neither was their place found any more in heaven. And the great dragon was cast out, that old serpent called the Devil and Satan, which deceiveth the whole world, he was cast out with him," (Rev. 12:7).

"Shut up, shut up!" The evil thing growled and stared hard at Rita hatefully. "I'll come back in you!"

"I'm not afraid of you. You're defeated," Rita said.

"You are the dumbest demon I've ever dealt with. You've exalted yourself all over this community," I said. "You've even revealed the reality of demons to many people who never believed in them before. Why, people have been saved because of you showing off yourself and "power," over Lou's life! You are the first demon I've ever seen that has actually helped spread the Word of God. Now the only power you've got left is enough to leave Lou!" Everyone started praising God and clapping their hands.

I changed tactics. "Lou, tell it to go. You don't need the thing anymore. You've got Jesus." Appealing directly to the person, urging them to use their own will and authority to tell the demons to go, this speeds deliverance, because getting their will involved in the battle helps to drive the demon out. At first, her chin balled up and quivered, tears rolled freely, teeth pressed tightly against her bottom lip.

Then Lou started to co-operate and began challenging the demon to leave! "GO! I don't want you anymore." Everyone present had to agree that the mighty evil spirit was totally overcome by Jesus' power. It tried to thrash about and wipe the floor with the little strength that was left. Still nervously whimpering when I told the demon, "You are powerless. See. You can't even move her arms now." The drooling, salivating devil was trying to move her arms to move the bible off of her stomach. The only power I give you is the power to leave, in the Name of Jesus." I spoke according to the pattern of the Apostle Paul. "You evil spirit, I command you in the Name of Jesus Christ to come out of this woman and leave her alone," (Acts 16:18). The demon suddenly left! Hallelujah!

Suddenly, there was a commotion in the rear of the church. I looked up to see a young man about twenty-two-years-old pushing his way down the aisle. His hair was oily, matted and thin, dirty shirt, jeans and his boots made loud clicking sounds as he moved toward us. He looked drunk or drugged.

"Where is Lou," he said in a very loud coarse voice. "She's my niece and I want to see her. What are you Christians doing to her?" A few of the men were trying to stop him from coming to the front of the church and he brushed them away and continued to march forward.

I stood up and spoke to him. "Hello. My name is Pat. What do you want here?"

"I came to talk to my niece, Lou. What are you doing to her?"

"I'm just praying for her. She's fine. Jesus is helping her. No one is hurting her here. We love her very much."

Lou was still on the floor but her eyes were open. When she saw her uncle, she quickly got to her feet without help. Her uncle told her that her father was waiting outside to take her home with him. I wondered how they knew she was here. It was now about twelve midnight and not many people are to be found in the churches at that time. Did an evil spirit tell them?

"No!" Lou's eyes were wide with fear. "I don't want to see him. Make him go away. I'm afraid of him." She was now holding

140

on to me very tightly. Her fingers were digging into my arms and her whole body was trembling in fear.

Her uncle came closer to me. "Can I talk to her a few minutes alone?" he asked.

"Only if she wants to talk to you," I replied.

She shook her head. "I guess I'll talk to him. He loves me and won't hurt me." They walked into a small room just to the right of the altar and then he closed the door. We waited for about five minutes and they did not return. We became concerned that he might try to force her out against her will, so I opened the door and told them that I had to leave.

"Just one more minute . . . ." The uncle pleaded, eyebrows raised.

"All right, one minute, I must leave, it's very late you know." I was exhausted. The church had been packed that night. I had been ministering many hours. Lou's deliverance had taken a long time. I wondered again about her relatives' appearance at the church. Odd that they knew where to find her, finally, they walked out of the room; her uncle had his arm around her shoulder and then he left the church.

Lou warned me to stay in the church. Her eyes were wide with panic and shock. "Pat, don't go outside. You don't know my father. He's mean . . . really mean. He's capable of doing anything. He's been drinking all day."

"It's very late. I've ministered since 7:30 pm and I want to go home to rest. First, I'll go out and talk to your father." Lou grabbed my arm, holding me firmly, now pleading with me to stay saying, "Please don't go . . . don't go out there. He'll kill you. He'll kill us all. He carries a shotgun." Her fingernails dug sharply into my skin, tiny sweat beads stood out on her forehead and bitter tears streamed down her cheeks.

Lou told me that her father, Ed, had spent the previous night threatening Rita and Danny. He had stayed in an orange grove across the street from their home, with a gun shooting it in the air. The police had been called but they did not arrest Ed. They told him to go home and sleep. I put my hand on Lou's shoulder and looked her in the eyes and said, "I'm not afraid of your father. I've got Jesus inside of me Who is stronger than your father, Ed can't hurt me. Now, please let go of my arm and let me go."

Max, my traveling companion and I walked away leaving her standing with outstretched arms and a pathetic fearful expression on her face. She started weeping softly as I opened the door to the street. Max followed as we walked across the street to Ed's truck. We could see three figures standing next to an old beat up truck. The night was clear with a big moon in the sky but the air was muggy, hot and sticky. When we came close, the smell of alcohol and tobacco that hung oppressively in the night air. Heavy drinking, obviously looking for trouble, we caught them be surprise when we boldly walked over."I'm looking for Ed," I boldly said.

"I'm Ed," He sneered. He stepped to the front of the other men. He was about 5'10, with cold piercing, blood-shot eyes. He was clearly an out-of-control red neck in dirty, torn overalls; holding a cigarette tightly between his teeth. Perspiration beads sat on his forehead. He appeared mean-spirited, very spaced out. He spit on the ground and sneered at us. The other two men backed him up with eyes bulging and jaws jutted out, ready for a fight.

Fear was trying to attack us, but we stayed high in faith. "What are you doing here? Do you need prayer? Are you looking for Jesus? I'm Pat Holliday, a minister of the Gospel."

He peered at me in disbelief. He was shocked because I was supposed to be frightened by his gun. He pressed the double-barrow shot gun into my stomach. "Nope, I've come to take my daughter home. His laconic answer was underscored by a defiant, hateful tone. He searched my face for reaction of fear.

I smiled at him softly saying, "I bind you and forbid you to shoot me or Max in Jesus' name."

Max said, "Mister, your daughter told me that she did not want to go home with you. She wants you to leave. She's fine now. We've been praying for her. She will not come out of the church as long as you stay here."

"Well, I ain't leaving . . . You can't tell me she's O.K. She called me and told me that Lamb guy is trying to kill her. I'm taking her home with me right now. That blankety blankety no-good bum . . . "he threatened to kill him. Ed was now pacing back and forth like a caged animal, very stirred up. A high flush appeared on his cheeks and an unnatural glaze in the eyes indicated drugs and demonic activity.

Max stepped forward, her voice firm: "Your daughter is going to be all right. We love her and are trying to help her. I know you don't like that, but it's true. Now, why don't you get into your truck and go home and leave your daughter alone? Let Jesus help her."

Eyes popping, he looked at Max threateningly. "No, I ain't leaving without her, you shut up." His voice was cruel and harsh, lips a thin line, legs apart, gun in his hand and he forced spit between his teeth to the ground. He again shoved the shotgun into my stomach. I looked into his eyes and softly, I said, "Jesus . . . the blood of Jesus, I bind you in Jesus' name. I forbid you to shoot me."

Suddenly we heard a scuffle as Danny ran across the street to get into his van. Fire began to flash in Ed's eyes as they caught a glimpse of him, his face reddened progressively with sheer hate and anger, Ed suddenly ran toward Danny with his fist ready to clobber him. He took a quick swipe but missed. His eyes glassy from drink and demon power, "You blankety blank, I want my daughter back." Foul language and sheer hatred dripped from his mouth and his abusive language cut through the night, rubbing nerves bare. I could see something looking through Ed's eyes at Danny.

Danny, a new Christian, reacted quickly by springing to defend himself with his fists. He was ready to return the punch when Max stepped between the two, threw her hand right in front of Ed's face and said: "Satan, I bind your power in Jesus' Name." She rendered him powerless. Ed stood stunned by the power of her words. She certainly was brave in the face of his bullying spirit. I quickly took Danny by the hand and led him toward his van. I told Danny, "Let's not act in the flesh; we are Christians." Meantime, Rita ran from the church and got into the van. They were scrunched down on the floor board. He got into the van and drove it close to the church door and Lou quickly got in and they tried to speed away.

Now Ed ran and stood in front of the van with his gun waving. "Go ahead and run over me, you no good blankety blank crude pot," his foul-mouthed language filled the air but no one was afraid of him. His arms were extended, jaw stuck out stubbornly then suddenly he rushed to the driver's side and took another quick swing with his fist at Danny through the van's window, screaming offensive obscenities.

Again, Danny's face flushed with anger, he was already half out of the van to counteract the blow when Max suddenly pushed the door closed, catching Danny's neck between the body and the door. He got released and sat back in the driver's seat and pressed hard on the gas. The van's wheels squealing, surged forward, gathering clouds of dust. In one instant, it was at the next corner.

The men with Ed stood with their mouths gaping open with absolute unbelief at the crazy scene that was playing out in front of them. Ed ranting and raving jumped into the pickup truck and scratched off after them. The air was full of powdery dirt, trailing behind like a whirlwind. It had been a strange evening.

"What should we do? Follow them, Pat?" Max asked.

"No, God is in control. I'm tired and going home to get some sleep." We joined hands and prayed for Rita, Danny and Lou's safety and bound Satan's power. Then we prayed for Ed and the men with him, binding the powers of the demons.

Dropping into bed, exhausted, I thought: Anyone who thinks working for Christ is boring and easy; they should come with me sometime!

The next day I learned that the Lambs and Lou had spent the night at the sheriff's office. Finally, they left at six in the morning with two deputies escorting them home, only to find Ed hiding in the orange grove which he had again staked out the Lamb's home all night. The deputies made him leave the grove and sent him home.

That next evening Lou came back to my meeting. "I'm leaving for New Jersey tonight, Pat. I can't marry John. I like him, but I just can't forget how awful I felt when my father raped me. I just can't think of having sex with anyone. Thanks for all that you have done for me. I'll never forget you as long as I live."

"Be sure to stay close to Christ. Get into a good Bible believing church. Stay away from sin and Christ will continue the work He has started in you." The Scripture warning is plain: a person must sever all relationships with friends and/or relatives who continue to practice occultism. I felt it was best for her to go at this time.

Recently, I received an encouraging letter from Lou, she said, "Max gave me Wednesday night's tape of your sermon against witchcraft. I really enjoyed it. I've tried to get several people to listen to it but they won't. I've tried telling my aunt and uncle about demons, satanic powers and what happened to me. Most of the time they don't even bother listening, my Uncle always says: "You can make the Bible say anything you want it to." And my aunt always says "Aw pooh. There ain't no such thing as demons". Last night all of us went to the drive-in movies and saw a horror movie called *Beyond the Dead*. This lady in it was possessed. I told Aunt Bell that's the way I was except I didn't throw up green stuff. She just laughed at me and said, "You talk about the weirdest stuff, Lou. You know that I don't believe in that crap."

"Pat, I'm attending church . . . I'm trying awful hard to stay straight. Believe me; it is hard. Everyone here smokes cigarettes and, Pat, my uncle's always trying to make me drink. It hurts his feelings when I won't! He drinks every day, sometimes a lot during the day. I plead the Blood of Jesus over everybody and bind Satan and all evil away from the house and I loose angels around everyone just like you taught me!"

All hope for deliverance is through His Holy Name!

Jesus prayed: "I pray, Father . . . that thou shouldest keep them from the evil," (Jn. 17:15). The answer to the problem of the rise of witchcraft is revival and the discovery that it is possible to have a personal relationship with Jesus Christ and to experience the power of God. Healing, physically, mentally and spiritually brings new life through His grace and recreation of the spirit.

I thank and praise Him for that. Coming to know the Lord Jesus Christ personally as the resurrected, living Savior is the greatest thing that can happen in a person's life.

Again, we need to ask ourselves if we are fulfilling the great commission which the Lord has given to us. He instructed His disciples not only to preach that the kingdom of heaven is at hand, but also to heal the sick and cast out devils. He is as ready to honor His Word as ever, and our faith, likewise, if we are obedient to His commands. Signs and wonders would indeed follow because He is just the same today!

HIS CHURCH WILL GROW IN DISCERNMENT

"And this I pray, that your love may abound yet more and more in knowledge and in all judgment (perception, discernment); That ye may approve (test, discern) things that are excellent; that ye may be sincere and without offence till the day of Christ; Being filled with the fruits of righteousness, which are by Jesus Christ, unto the glory and praise of God." (Phil. 1:9-10).

"The night is far spent, the day is at hand, let us therefore put off the works of darkness," (Rom. 13:12). Deliverance Power of Jesus is through His name. "So will they fear the name of the Lord from the west and East. His glory from the rising of the sun; when the enemy comes in like a flood, the Spirit of the Lord will lift a standard against Him," (Isa. 59:1).

FREEDOM

Christians can live free from mental torture, panic, envy, hatred, pride, self pity, addiction, gluttony and all other forms of bondage, oppression and defilement!

There are two main causes for a person's inner problems.

The first point is what the Word calls "the flesh, or the 'old man." The old man that part of the person that is the carnal nature of the person's flesh and it is the rebellious person's will that is being influenced and tempted by Satan. "Knowing this, that our old man is crucified with him, that the body of sin might be destroyed, that henceforth we should not serve sin," (Rom. 6:6).

That ye put off concerning the former conversation the old man, which is corrupt according to the deceitful lusts; 23 And be renewed in the spirit of your mind; 24 And that ye put on the new man, which after God is created in righteousness and true holiness."

"Lie not one to another, seeing that ye have put off the old man with his deeds; 10 And have put on the new man, which is renewed in knowledge after the image of him that created him," (Col. 3:9-10).

The second cause for inner problems is the working of evil spirits. Demons will tie themselves to the person's mind or flesh. They will not relinquish their evil hold unless compelled to do so by a Christian that is empowered by Jesus.

"Submit yourselves therefore to God. Resist the devil, and he will flee from you," (Jam. 4:7).

DEMONS ARE REAL

Many Christians are totally unaware of the reality of indiscernible world of demons. They are real!

The Bible says that my people perish for a lack of knowledge.

"My people are destroyed for lack of knowledge because thou hast rejected knowledge, I will also reject thee, that thou shalt be no priest to me: seeing thou hast forgotten the law of thy God, I will also forget thy children," (Hos. 4:6).

Multitudes are tormented because people choose to ignore the power to cast out devils. The word of God declares, folks can be bound by Satan,

"And others, tempting him, sought of him a sign from heaven. 17 But he, knowing their thoughts, said unto them, Every kingdom divided against itself is brought to desolation; and a house divided against a house falleth.18 If Satan also be divided against himself, how shall his kingdom stand? Because ye say that I cast out devils through Beelzebub. 19 And if I by Beelzebub cast out devils, by whom do your sons cast them out? Therefore shall they be your judges. 20 But if I with the finger of God cast out devils, no doubt the kingdom of God is come upon you. 21 When a strong man armed keepeth his palace, his goods are in peace: 22 But when a stronger than he shall come upon him, and overcome him, he taketh from him all his armour wherein he trusted, and divideth his spoils," (Lk. 13:11, 16).

TESTIMONY OF A WITCH

Another witch, called Doreen Irving, testified after salvation the following experience: "When I went into churches and the Blood of Jesus was mentioned, strange satanic things began to happen. I fell on the floor . . . I was unaware that I was doing it . . . hissing like a snake, screaming and shouting. I threw Bibles over the heads of the congregation nearly missing the preacher. All sorts of evil manifestations occurred. NO ONE KNEW WHAT WAS WRONG WITH ME! NO ONE! Some said I needed to see a psychiatrist . . . No, I didn't need a doctor, and I needed deliverance from demons. To think, some Christians don't even believe in demons at all. Yet no one realized that I had demons and was on the brink of suicide, for Satan stood by my bed with his great hairy hands and tried to choke me many nights." [53]

"I was no stranger to demons. I had called on them and they came to my aid. I thought I controlled them, but actually, they had control of me! I knew of the reality of demons, but the Christians seemed to be totally ignorant of my need. I needed to be delivered. They needed to be cast out. One day I met a Baptist pastor and he knew what to do! It didn't take seven minutes or seven days, but seven long months before I was delivered from witchcraft, unclean spirits, tormenting, and lying spirits . . . During the deliverance, I would be unconscious of what went on, but when the last one came out with a loud piercing scream . . . I knew that I was free! I'm a new creature in Christ. I have a new garment. A new song . . . I don't wear witches' robes anymore. I have a new robe of righteousness!" (Isa. 61:10). [54]

Bible says, "And these signs shall follow them that believe; in my name, they shall cast out devils; they shall speak with new tongues," (Mark 16:10). This is the "Great Commission" of our Lord and Savior, Jesus Christ. He commanded those who believe upon Him to take power over demon spirits and cast them out in His Name. In these last days, there will be multitudes of people needing to be set free. The ministry of the church of Jesus Christ is to set them free.

A Satan worshiper describes going to a Satanist temple: "When I got to the temple, I was led in blindfolded to the back of a large hall. The blindfold was removed. I saw about 600 people standing. There were no seats because when everyone worshiped

---

[53] Paperback: 179 pages Publisher: Thomas Nelson (May 1981) ISBN-10: 0840757719 ISBN-13: 978-0840757715
[54] ibid

Lucifer, they prostrated themselves on the ground. On the wall hung effigies of Lucifer: half man, half beasts, cloven hooves and all; up front was a large platform draped in black; by the side of the platform was a high altar; on it were knives, cups and vessels made of real silver.

The lights dimmed and they lit the flaming torches while everyone prostrated themselves on the ground as the chief Satanist sat on a throne, robed and hooded. The robe was embroidered with snakes and dragons, and flames of fire rose from his seat. Around him in a semicircle were thirteen priests and priestesses of Satanism. They removed his hood. Wails and prayers to Lucifer the great god of darkness, death, and mystery arose. The air was pregnant with evil . . . I stood glued to the spot in the back, unable to move, hypnotized. I was captured by the mystery and power and started going regularly to the temple where I witnessed filthy diabolical things going on.

We were taught, incorrectly, that Lucifer was wrongfully ejected from heaven but one day he would regain his rightful position and rule the heavens, the earth, the sky, and the seas. Then the Christian Church would be vanquished and overthrown. But, before all this could come about, evil must increase. Wickedness must grow. Nothing is sacred in the Satanists' temple . . . Nothing and they will stop at nothing.

Lucifer used to appear to us. We saw him sometimes as an angelic being and sometimes as an ugly grotesque figure, true to his nature. There was no doubt in the minds of the Satanists that Lucifer existed. We heard his voice and saw him often enough. I became a Satanist when I agreed to obey all of the 48 rules. Here are a few of them: 1) You must never tell anyone what goes on in the Satanist temples, or where the temples are. 2) No one is late for a meeting. If one arrived late, he or she was stripped naked and strapped to a wooden post and flogged by the chief Satanist himself in front of everyone. (It was considered a gross insult if anyone came in late. In the Satanist temple, they were most devout, and time was nothing). 3) The Bible was never to be read. It was mocked and I myself have held a Bible on the altar in white hot flames and the bible disintegrated to dust in my hands without leaving one scar.

I witnessed many animal sacrifices. At my initiation, a rooster was sacrificed and then I dipped my finger into the blood signing an oath that I would love, honor, and obey Lucifer the rest of my life. I called Lucifer my master, and by demon power I could levitate. I was able to kill a bird in flight with a wave of the arm. I was into soul travel and much more . . . The first Christian meeting I attended I was very uncomfortable. Suddenly Satan said, 'Get out of this meeting, you're mine!' "I said, 'Wait a minute.' It was then that a great struggle began for my soul, and I realized that these powers were truly controlling me. I was not, as I had thought, controlling them! But, Christ's power is stronger. It prevailed. Today I am a born-again Christian, washed in His Holy Blood set free!"

Chapter Ten
Occult Stepping Stones to Witchcraft

"For rebellion is as the sin of witchcraft, and stubbornness is as iniquity and idolatry. Because thou hast rejected the word of the Lord, he hath also rejected thee from being king," (1 Sam. 15:23).

CHASING NIGHTMARES

American media have found a new horror story to promote that will draw people to accept the powers of darkness as being just fun and game and nothing to worry about. Full page advertisements and articles show these powers as helpful . . . not harmful. A typical advertisement may read: "Whatever it is you need or want, Witchcraft can get it for you quickly, easily, and automatically, say these experts. You'll discover how it can bring abundant and overflowing wealth, find or bring back a lover, ward off evil influences, and much more . . . Step-by-step in plain English, with complete easy-to-follow instructions!"

We had ministered to Tillie and she received Jesus Christ as her personal Savior, the Baptism of the Holy Spirit and deliverance from witchcraft. She boldly called the leaders of the coven and told them that she would not be coming back.

"They called me last night, Pat, about midnight and said, we'll pick you up at 1:30 tomorrow for the meeting. I told them that I wasn't going to the meeting. They just said, okay." But early this morning, my doorbell rang. I thought it was one of the ladies in the apartment building. These kinds of people (occultists) have got ways of knowing things. Anyway, I answered the door. I thought it was a neighbor wanting some sugar or something. But there was a man and woman from that occult group standing there. They claimed that they wanted to come in, just to talk. After I closed the door, I offered them a cup, but they refused. "You'll be down to the meeting this afternoon, won't you?' I told them, 'no." Then I turned to go back to the kitchen, as I remember. Suddenly, from behind, I felt something around my neck! It was powerful that it about broke my neck. There are still the rope marks on my neck, Pat. They were strong. Something snapped in my mind. I staggered, opened my mouth and out came a loud croaking sound. That must have frightened them. They let me go, and moved toward the door, but paused before they left! "There'll be more!" they shouted.

I was stunned! My head was in bad shape. I ran over, slammed the door and locked it, looked out of the peephole, but they were gone. Really, I thought they were going to kill me. I think they would have, too, if I had not made that strange noise. They got scared someone would hear them and come catching them. Probably, it was the blood of Jesus Christ that protected me, or I would be dead today. My girlfriend, Jamie warned me that I could be standing on the street corner and they'd try to run over me or jump out and capture me by shoving me into the van. I guess I'll have to watch out. But Pat, I've had to bear some marks on my body for the sin, but I'll never go back! They can kill my body, but they can't touch my soul. Christ is worth it all. Before I knew Jesus, this traumatic experience would have thrown me into epileptic seizures . . . but, I didn't have one then. "People are going to have to pay a price for the gospel. What I went through yesterday makes me know Him in His suffering and His resurrection power. I did what you told me to do and I'm going to come out on top. Something came over me that Tuesday at your meeting and it hasn't left me. I promise you, Pat - the occult life for me is over."

Tillie, everyday, I want you cover yourself with the blood of Jesus. Paul says we are living in physical bodies in a material world. At the same time we are in a war, but the war is not being fought out in the physical or material realm. It is in a different realm. He explains in the Bible 'For the weapons of our warfare are not carnal but mighty in God for pulling down strongholds...' and the demons use humans to do his dirty work. However, Jesus will protect you. It is true; a person has no resistance at all to demons without Christ. The Word says in (Phil. 4:13) "I can do all things through Christ who strengthened me." The natural person without Christ is spiritually weak and highly susceptible to infestation by demons. There is little one can do about fighting off evil spirits if Christ is not dwelling inside. You are free; Tillie and Jesus will protect you."

OCCULT PROBLEM

I have written *The Walking Dead* because of the rise and social acceptance of witchcraft in America. We have entered the supernatural age of progressive interest and involvement in the occult. Satan's ambassadors are very successful and extremely evangelistic, capturing spiritual slaves. I also believe satanic worship, coupled with human sacrifices is widespread and happening now! New York's Queens County District Attorney, John Santucci claims he has evidence supporting "Son of Sam" killer, David Berkowitz' bizarre assertion that a devil-worshiping cult helped him murder six people. Since his conviction, Berkowitz has claimed that he was a member of a New York-based satanic cult whose secret members were responsible for shootings that killed six and wounded seven people!

Fiendish devil-worshiping cultists' arson the verge of spawning an insane bloodbath of murder and terror in cities and towns across the country; recently, while I was evangelizing in Miami, a young girl who had escaped from a group of Satan worshipers told a frightening tale of human sacrifice and kidnapping: "They find old people who have no relatives and put them in cages. They torture them with hot irons and within three days their hair will actually turn snow white from terror! They tie them to a pentagram table (a table with a five-pointed star, a witchcraft symbol, on the top). Then they sacrifice them to Satan! The Satanist temple is located in a very elite section, she reported. On September 5, 1982, a noted University of Florida nutritionist, Dr. Howard Appledorf, was found tortured and slain. He had been bound and gagged. His killers had put an ice-cube-filled canvas bag over his head and knotted it at his neck, police said. There were all kinds of words written on the walls; predominately the word "murder" spelled backwards, as in some killings that took place out West." Backward spelling of murder was a theme of the horror movie, "The Shining."[55]

The police said they also had found cryptic "apologies" to the corpse. Appledorf's nose had been smashed, and at least one cigarette had been extinguished on his stomach. Appledorf also was tortured in other ways, but Ward would not reveal them. Signs were all around that a strange cultic murder had taken place.
[56]

Reader's Digest, July 1982, reports 100,000 missing children a year! The figures are estimates. But the few known facts are

---

[55] Editorial, Florida Times Union, 7/28/82, p. 10.
[56] ibid

appalling: Thousands are murdered annually; then number of missing children is rising; and **no one** is keeping an accurate count.

"Kids who just disappear present a big problem that people had better start opening their eyes to," said Detective Sergeant Dick Ruffino of the Bergen County, New Jersey Sheriff's Office. [57]

When Adam Walsh was abducted from a Fort Lauderdale-area department store in 1981, it caused fear and revulsion throughout Florida, with the shock waves reaching Washington, D.C. During the fruitless 15-day search for the 6 year-old, his frantic parents, John and Reve Walsh, learned many things about the American people and about the nation itself. The grieving Walshs were buoyed by a great outpouring of generosity. They were appalled to find, however, that there was no central agency that kept a nationwide file on missing children. Fishermen found the remains of Adam in a canal in back of a neighborhood in Vero Beach, 90 miles from the site of his disappearance. Despite their heavy burden of sorrow, the Walshs embarked on a crusade to remedy the relative lack of national attention given missing children (as contrasted with vehicles and even large appliances!).[58]

The state of Florida, in response, passed a Missing Children's Act and Senator Paula Hawkins, R-Fla., introduced a Missing Children's Act in Congress. The bill remained bottled up in committee a year after Adam's death, despite enough Congressional sponsorship to assure its passage. It languished in committee because of opposition from the U.S. Justice Department. [59]

---

[57] Geoff Clark, Florida Times Union, 9/6/82, pp. 1A-2A
[58] Gary Turback, "100,000 Missing Children A Year," Readers Digest, July 1982, p. 60.
[59] Editorial, Florida Times Union, 7/28/82, p. 10.

Several reasons were given by the Justice Department for opposing the bill. The reasons included the fear that the measure "may interfere with the FBI's management prerogatives to modify or expand the criteria" that govern what information is put in the FBI computers. "What we're asking for is a pure bill... to link up agencies nationally..."

Each missing child case has its own poignant drama and irony. In July, 1976, 12 year-old Dee Scofield disappeared while running an errand at a Florida shopping center. Two days later, a classmate reportedly saw Dee looking out of a van window, desperately forming the word "help" over and over with her lips. Dee was never found.

Parents always ask the inevitable question: *Why? Why would someone steal a child? Why my child?* Could some of these deaths be attributed to satanic cults?

Arne Johnson, a 19 year-old charged with the bizarre murder of Alan Bono, age 40, was using demonic possession as his defense: The soft-spoken teenager claims he was possessed by the devil when he suddenly flew into an uncontrollable rage and fatally stabbed his best friend in Brookerfield, Connecticut.

In Belle Glade, Florida, Wayne Callender, and a 23 year-old murderer of an elderly, sleeping couple explained: "The Devil promised to make me rich if I killed them." Such statistics continue to swell daily, while millions dabble in psychic phenomena, witchcraft, black magic, voodoo and satanic cults. [60]

The most publicized psychic activity in America and the one which people in great numbers are embracing today is divination. This goes under the names of: telepathy, ESP, clairvoyance, hypnotically trance, spiritualism, psychic research, etc. Although

---

[60] ibid

the term "psychic research" has a respectable sound, it involves the same old witchcraft referred to many times in the Bible. Sorcery or traffic in familiar spirits is strictly forbidden in the Scriptures. (See Lev. 20:6; Lev. 20:27; Is. 8:19).

OCCULT RESPECTABILITY ADVANCED

The American media have found a new horror to promote. Full page advertisements and articles show these powers as being helpful... not harmful. A typical advertisement may read: "Whatever it is you need or want, Witchcraft can get it for you quickly, easily, and automatically, say these experts. You'll discover how it can bring abundant and overflowing wealth, find or bring back a lover, ward off evil influences, and much more... Step-by-step in plain English, with complete easy-to-follow instructions!"

Magazines and newspapers do not seem to realize the terrible forces they are unleashing on the deceived individuals who will respond to the power of witchcraft. Hundreds of thousands have become spiritual slaves. They are captives because of the media's spiritual blindness. They don't see the psychics, for example, as dangerous influences on society.

Research at major universities has given a measure of respect to precognition, telepathy, clairvoyance and clairaudience. For years, Rice University has been studying positive and negative thought vibrations, but the first notable acceptance of parapsychology in the scientific community came at Duke University in 1930

. Receiving a grant in 1927, the institution began a program of ESP study under the direction of Dr. William McDougall. Later, biologist, J.B. Rhine and his wife, Louisa, received even greater notoriety for their part in the Duke studies. Satisfied that the scientifically exacting tests of London psychologist S.G. Sole had demonstrated the reality of telepathic communications, early experiments relied heavily upon mediums and psychics in search of proof that life exists after death. Later efforts graduated to the use of symbol-inscribed cards and sophisticated electronic measurements for discovering the psychic sensitivity levels of different types of volunteers.[61]

The discovery and verification of ESP, psychokinetic, clairvoyance, telepathy, precognition, psychometrics, and other forms of psychic power have produced evidence that the human mind exists separate from the brain in a non-physical dimension beyond space, time, and matter. The late Dr. J.B. Rhine, father of American parapsychology, declared:[62]

The evidence of PK along with that of ESP establishes the case for the reality of mind in spite of the fact that a couple of generations of psychologists had been trying to discourage the idea and supplant it with a model of mechanistic behaviorisms. "The man in the pulpit... was right in preaching that the human spirit is something more than the material of his body and brain." [63]

Dr. Milan Ryzl (formerly of the Czechoslovakian Academy of Science) has summed up the implications of recent laboratory discoveries: "Apparently, we are heading toward the finding that our 'physical' universe is only a part of a more extensive reality... (Where) the former contradictions between 'matter' and 'spirit' disappear... We can further assume... parts of the human personality that exist outside the material universe... This could

---

[61] Dr. William McDougall. Later, biologist, J.B. Rhine and his wife, Louisa, Duke University, Louisa E. Rhine, Mind over Matter: Psychokinesis, New York, 1970, pp. 190-191.
[62] ibid
[63] ibid

survive even after the material part has been destroyed by death. There are indications that what we know as the 'material world of physics' is only a part of a far wider reality..."[64]

More recently, Stanford Research Institute (SRI) had opened shop on the subject—with aid from the United States Government.[65]

Science has moved into the spirit dimension where it is ill-equipped to venture. Despite the sophisticated scientific instruments and computers, scientists are no less vulnerable to spiritual deception than anyone else.

THE HOLISTIC HEALTH CULTS

As early as 1973, the World Health Organization had recommended that the medical profession accept the validity of native cures such as those used by witch doctors. Recognizing the fact that about 80% of its 4 million whites consult witch doctors, in 1979, Witwatersrand University in Johannesburg staffed a special medical clinic with witch doctors. Witwatersrand psychology professor, Dr. T. Leonard Holdstock had expressed the belief that the "mind power" used by witch doctors can diagnose and treat the mentally ill. Dr. Herbert Benson of the Harvard Medical School has also recently expressed the belief that modern medicine may have much to learn from the "mind power' of witchcraft. Voodoo and witchcraft are among the folk remedies now studied by candidates for a bachelor's degree in nursing at the University of

---

[64] Dr. Milan Ryzl (formerly of the Czechoslovakian Academy of Science). Lecture by Dr. Walter Martin, "ESP and Parapsychology."

[65] Stanford Research Institute (SRI) Milan Ryzl, Parapsychology: A Scientific Approach, (New York, 1970) pp. 389-390.

Alabama. These are only a few of the indications that medical science has been turning back to its occulted origins.[66]

In Roman mythology, Aesculapius was the god of medicine. His symbol was a staff with a snake coiled about it. According to the legend, he had received a healing herb (drug) from a serpent's mouth. The connection between the serpent and sorcery (*pharmakia* in the Greek New Testament) has continued to the present day. Aesculapius' staff now has not one but two serpents coiled around it in the familiar and honored emblem of modern medicine. The tradition behind this symbol is kept alive by the medical profession. Though the name of Jesus Christ and prayers to God the Father have been excluded from our schools, at the time they receive their M.D. degrees, graduates of medical colleges still repeat in unison the ancient Hippocratic oath which begins: "I swear by Apollo the Physician, by Aesculapius, by Hygeia, Panacea, AND ALL THE GODS AND GODDESSES." [67]

PSYCHIC EXPLOSION

When the Society of Psychical Research was founded in London in 1882, its original intent was to separate the psychical from the supernatural. Instead, the two realms gradually blended into what is now known as parapsychology. Psychics today embrace every form of occult practice, including fortune-telling, Eastern religion and astral projections.

A recent issue of *Psychic Life* carried articles on astral travel, reincarnation, psychic healing, meditation, spirit guides and prayer to "Your God" - whatever that might be. Psychics are being used by police to help solve murders and give "valuable information" in

---

[66] Ralph Wilkerson, ESP or HSP, (Anaheim, California: Melodyland Pub., 1978) p. 115.

[67] Dave Hunt, The Cult Explosion, (Irvine, California: Harvest House) pp. 117-118.

other crimes. The use of mediums or psychics by institutions and conservative law enforcement agencies is not new and, lately, it has become commonplace. With society generally accepting the validity of ESP, the increase of psychic activity can be seen everywhere. A book recently published in the San Francisco Bay Area, *The Psychic Yellow Pages,* has a 177-page directory listing 130 "genuine" Bay Area psychics, astrologers, holistic centers, palmists, numerologists, graphologists, tarot card readers and research organizations.[68]

CASSADAGA

Typical of the many spiritualist groups around the world is the community of Cassadaga, Florida, located in the misty lake country a few miles southwest of Daytona Beach. More than 100 spiritualists live in Cassadaga, and 24 of them are "certified mediums" who make their living communicating with the dead to obtain information for paying clients.[69]

The usual trivia that pours through mediums is only incidental. In Casssadaga , as everywhere else, the real purpose of the spirits is to preach the same Cosmic Gospel that UFO cults receive by psychic transmission from "Space Brothers"... that there is no death, that Jesus did not die for our sins... that God is not personal but a Force... that all men are divine and only need to realize it. And that godhood can be achieved through occult enlightenment, mystical power, and generating good karma (how can one have 'good' karma or 'good' anything when *Satan* is the controller of all these mediums?) The central theme is always, "You won't really die, for there is no death."

---

[68] San Francisco Bay Area, *The Psychic Yellow Pages,*
[69] Lecture by Dr. Walter Martin, "ESP and Parapsychology."

A 1979 study by The Times Magazine showed that of 250 forecasts made by the "leading psychics" for the previous year, only six could be listed as "reasonably fulfilled!" Nonetheless, "prediction issues" outsell every other tabloid year after year.[70]

MYSTICAL REVOLUTION

Psychic prophets, astrologers, spiritualists, ESP, hypnotists, flying saucers, space saviors, mind mixers, mind manipulators, mind movers, false prophets of the East, witchcraft, devil worshipers, séances, occult games and occult movies are presented as having the answers to all of life's problems. People have been sold the bill of goods that occultism is exciting and wonderful.

Occultism is big business, representing a billion dollars each year! Supermarket and drugstore racks are full of books and magazines promising to tell you the hidden secrets of the "other world" (or you own psyche). More than a thousand daily newspapers carry astrological forecasts, and few would dare drop this popular feature. Computers pop out "instant horoscopes" for about twenty dollars. Two well-known country clubs in Florida have "Psychic Nights," when they invite fortune tellers and psychics. These nights are packed to capacity with seekers. Shopping malls hold a "Psychic Fun Day" as a money-making, promotional gimmick. People pick the methods to predict their future and are given material to help them to join the groups. People today have an insatiable thirst for knowledge of the "other world."[71] Many are convinced that life holds mysteries beyond what our five senses reveal. They are right!

---

[70] 1979 study by The Times Magazine
[71] ibid

Everyone from presidents to common people, the educated to the unlearned, the spiritualist to the entertainer, is affected by this intense yearning to know how to cross the bridge between two worlds. That the "beyond" exists is commonly accepted today.

GODDESS CONSCIOUSNESS

There is a reawakening today of "goddess consciousness", which the L.A. Times reported upon in 1978 as the spiritual power behind the women's movement and that the Force is really female is one of the foundational beliefs in witchcraft. This is expressed in the terms "Mother Nature" and Mother Earth". The head of a witches' coven must be a woman. Witchcraft is known as the "Old Religion (Wicca); it claims to be as old as the human race. It began with Eve's deception by the serpent. Witches worship 'the Force', which they believe permeates all of nature; and they use it in their spells. The connection between the environmental (back-to-nature) movement, the women's movement (the matriarchal cult), and witchcraft is undeniable. Of the many persons involved, most are believed to be unaware of this.[72]

WITCHCRAFT AND THE WOMEN'S MOVEMENT

An accredited course held at the University of California at Santa Cruz in April, 1978, illustrates what is happening in our universities and the real spiritual power behind the women's liberation movement Billed as a course to raise the consciousness level of participants in the women's movement the study program was called "The Great Goddess Re-emerges". Women had to be

---

[72] L.A. Times reported upon in 1978

turned away from the course, which could only accommodate 450 students. Participants danced bare-breasted on the campus to the beat of bongo drums in scenes reminiscent of "frolicking wood nymphs." [73]

The following excerpts from a L.A. Times Article covering the course speak for themselves. Remember, this was a University of California course for which credits were granted... "...Eerie monotones... reverberated on the U.C. Santa Cruz campus. Cheers and whoops went up for the goddesses of your choice - Isis, Astarte, Demeter, Artemis, etc... The event was indicative of burgeoning spiritual dimensions of the women's liberation movement in America..."

Christine Downing, head of San Diego University's religious studies department, estimates that many, if not most spiritually sensitive women in the women's movement are willing to replace the biblical God with a frankly pagan and polytheistic approach. Witchcraft is aiding the women in their search for roots and rituals, without the connotations of evil usually associated with witchcraft. A Santa Cruz woman said, "Some of the women think of themselves as witches, but not all."[74]

A brief, unscheduled appearance met with enthusiastic applause, was made by Z. Pudapest. A self-described witch - the Goddess movement knows her more as a leader of the Susan B. Anthony Coven No. 1 in Los Angeles and a charismatic spokeswoman for a mean brand of Wicca, an ancient women's religion (witchcraft) The goddess movement, also called the women-spirit movement, apparently considers its first major

---

[73] University of California at Santa Cruz in April, 1978,
[74] Dave Hunt, The Cult Explosion, (Irvine, California: Harvest House) pp. 117-118.

gathering to have been a conference attended by about 1200 women at the University of Massachusetts in late 1975.[75]

The ancient Mediterranean world, pagan Europe, native American and Hindu traditions are all sources for goddess imagery, Dr. Christ (rhymes with 'grist') said. (Dr. Christ is head of San Jose State University's women's studies program). A religious phenomenon virtually unknown outside feminist circles, "goddess consciousnesses will be widely known in three to five years, predicted Dr. Christ.[76]

THE WITCHES' CRADLE

That the relationship between mystical experiences and psychic phenomena is well-established indicates that the same spirit beings create both for the same purpose. Parapsychologists have developed a free-swinging platform called a "witches' cradle," patterned after devices used by witches centuries ago. When deprived of all light and sound, the subject occupying the platform experiences altered states of consciousness due to the subtle movements of the "witches' cradle." Psychic powers are manifest while in the cradle. At the same time, the subject has mystical experiences very much like those of TM practitioners. Typical is the following report during a laboratory experiment:[77]

"I am expanding, expanding... I can... read the secrets of the universe... beautiful forms are alive... unity unified; it is the experience of the Unity... as if all were unified in me!"[78]

---

[75] Wilkerson, op. cit., p. 113.
[76] ibid
[77] ibid
[78] Stanley Krippner, Song of the Siren, (New York, 1975), p. 75.

YOUTH SEDUCTION

Even teenagers are being seduced. Satanic demons operating through occulted oriented rock performers have flourished throughout the land. The Beatles had a record called, *"Revolver"*. The song was teaching meditation. It said: "Turn off your mind, relax and float downstream, listen to the voices - are they not speaking...?" It was about spirit beings guiding you into cosmic-consciousness.[79]

"Sgt. Pepper", had all kinds of enticements to get kids into LSD. *"Magical Mystery Tour"* had a lot of Eastern mysticism in it. They encouraged the use of LSD, and then later advocated Maharishi Mahesh Yogi after they'd quit taking drugs and gotten into TM. The Beatles, I think, were largely responsible for initiating hundreds of thousands of kids in the U.S. and England and Europe into the Eastern way of thinking. [80].

AC/DC's *"Dirty Deeds Done Dirt Cheap,"* released in 1978 said it all. Their "deeds" included lyrics too explicit to quote in this book. *"Highway to Hell"*, was delivered with a lascivious growl by lead singer, Bon Scott, with a direct lyrical invitation for Satan to claim his soul. Scott declared hell to be the "promised land," and warned that nothing would stop him from cashing in his "season ticket" for a one-way ride. One night at 33 years of age, Scott's arrogant affront to God was literally fulfilled... He died of an overdose.[81]

In the K (ings) I(n) S(atan's) S(ervice) album *God of Thunder*, children can be heard crying: *"I don't want to go to that place."* Other lyrics include: *I gather darkness to please me"*, *"I*

---

[79] Circus, August 26, 1980, p. 22. Beatles, Revolver
[80] St. Pepper Circus, August 26, 1980, p. 22.
[81] C/DC's *"Dirty Deeds Done Dirt Cheap,"* released in 1978

168

command you to kneel before the god of thunder and rock and roll", "The spell you're under will slowly rob you of your soul."

Gene Simon extends his tongue (a sign of demon worship; and they refer to themselves as demons while on stage).

ELO/Electric Light Orchestra sings: "We'll see if eternal life is meant to be." The real message hidden in backward masking is: "For He is the nasty one - Christ, you're infernal." (Infernal means inferior, abominable, and inhuman).

In Led Zeppelin's *Stairway to Heaven.* The eerie words sound like a message from the dead..."*Satan is Lord". "I'll give you 6-6-6." "Jesus betrayed us". "I sing because I live with Satan".*[82]

These messages are heard when the recording is played backward! This is the very latest thing in rock music; subliminal messages hidden in the music. You don't hear them when the record is played forward but if you reverse the music, the hidden message can be heard. Psychologists maintain that the hidden messages can be heard and our mind can decipher them subconsciously. The sales pitch is implanted into the mind then as truth because our conscious mind filters out 'untruth' allowing only 'truth' to settle in to our subconscious. Backward masking and other subliminal advertising/messages are used by Satan to implant lies as truth into peoples' minds!

If someone told you to worship Satan as god, you'd probably reject that. Your mind would reject that thought. But when these thoughts enter the brain backward or subliminally they pass consciences thought of the brain without being filtered by the conscious mind and without being rejected. The thoughts are then stored in our subconscious mind for future us as truth! If you

---

[82] ibid, Circus

169

receive this backward information, you'll not only receive it, but you will begin to believe it, also!

Raunch and Roll's Oat Arkansas' *the Day Electricity Came to Arkansas* begins with demonic sounding laughter... then they say: *Dog se e; Dog se e; Natas. Natas.* Translated: *Satan he is god. Satan he is god.* This is how they are programming our youth to receive Satan as god![83]

JoAnn said, "I owned a dance school in Washington State for 23 years and spent a lot of time with teenagers in classes. After teaching there for 11 years, I met the Lord Jesus, and then burned the old worldly music . One jazz dance student objected to the new Christian pop music and wanted the world's rock hits to be played, sulking and interrupting the class to express her opinions. I took the opportunity to share the latest newspaper article concerning the 3 recent teenage suicides in our area's towns... all mid-teens, all shot themselves with shotguns (very difficult to do), after police searches of their rooms, all reportedly had the same heavy metal 'music' cassettes with song lyrics depicting hell as a great party place and telling listeners to kill themselves if their parents and teachers didn't understand them; is this a coincidence? I doubt it. The demon music god in that girl raged and screamed out, "I don't have to listen to this!" Then she stormed out of the studio, (or rather, her demon took her out) - never to return. Her idolatrous worship of 'her music' was greater than her love of dance, apparently.

The rest of the class was as shocked by her behavior as they were my sharing about backward-masking in 'their music'. They stayed... they were Christians. The worst record I'd had (before Jesus) and the hardest to burn, melted with an eerie whistle coming

---

[83] 15. Billboard, No. 1, 1980, p. 34.

170

out of it and bright turquoise flame... a "Queen" record containing the piece, *"Another One Bites the Dust"* - a few of the teenage students that had attended a summer dance workshop at Whitman College had learned a dance to that song there, so I bought the record. They taught the dance to a young man who had a poor relationship with his Dad - abusive. He went away to Pacific Lutheran College after graduation and within a few months, had killed himself there.

Later on, I heard that the Queen record had backward masking that said, "Smoke marijuana" on that song. (It had a depressing, funeral dirge rhythm, too). Some of the other records, Beatles' LPs, melted with chartreuse-colored flames and shrieks coming out of them. (Records, tapes, C.D.'s, videos, books and art figures that contain demons are very hard to make burn. They will usually make unusual sounds or have weirdly colored flames); note: one should bind the demons to the object, telling them to remain there 'til judgment day, or if burning the object, bind the demons, forbidding them to enter anyone or anything else, and to go to the feet of Jesus, immediately]."

Aleister Crowley, a 20th century Satanist wrote a book, *Manual on Magic.* On pages 481-482, he advises: "Think backward, write backward, speak backward, walk backward are the ways to get into the other world." Thus, "I am he" would be said, "eh ma I".[84]

Pink Floyd in *Goodby Blue Sky* through backward masking says: "Congratulations, you've just discovered the secret message. Address your correspondence to..." and the beat goes on while the most popular groups are those who identify themselves with

---

[84] Aleister Crowley, a 20th century Satanist wrote a book, *Manual on Magic.* On pages 481-482,

witchcraft, drugs, sex and Satanism. They brazenly place satanic symbols on the album covers.

WARNINGS FROM EXPERIENCE

Harold Sherman, author of *Thoughts Through Space,* an expert in the field of telepathy, gives some serious warnings to those who week to meddle in psychic phenomena. He points out that the sovereignty of the human mind is definitely endangered by the practice. He found at times when he became attuned to the subconscious that a panoramic series of mental images and impressions rushed through his mind which he could not control. These unbidden experiences were frightening. They took a terrific emotional toll and he had serious physical after-effects. He said that it required a great exercise of will power to overcome these forces that were seeking control of his mind.[85]

Mr. Sherman declared that in his explorations into telepathy, he suffered a loss of health from emotional and physical strain which resulted in stomach ulcers, causing hemorrhages which nearly took his life.

The physical menace of the occult affects dissenters also. In *Be Free,* I cited the experience of Tillie Damon, who had been strongly connected with the occult:[86]

"They called me last night, Pat, about midnight. They said, 'We'll pick you up at 1:30 tomorrow for the meeting.' I said I wasn't going. They just said, 'okay'. But early this morning, my doorbell rang. I thought it was one of the ladies in the apartment building. These kinds of people (occultists) have got ways of knowing things. Anyway, I answered the door. I thought it was a

---

[85] Harold Sherman, author of *Thoughts Through Space,*
[86] Pat Holliday, Be Free, http://www.miracleinternetchurch.com

neighbor wanting some sugar or something. But there was a man and woman from that occult group standing there. They wanted to come in, just to talk. I went in the kitchen to get a cup of coffee. I offered them a cup, but they refused. 'You'll be down to the meeting this afternoon, won't you?' I told them, 'no'. Then I turned to go back to the kitchen, as I remember. Suddenly, from behind, I felt something around my neck! It was powerful. They about broke my neck. There're still the rope marks on my neck, Pat. They were strong. Something snapped in my mind. I staggered, opened my mouth and out came a loud croak. That must have frightened them. They let me go, and moved toward the door, but paused before they left! 'There'll be more!' they shouted.

"I was stunned! My head was in bad shape. I ran over, slammed the door and locked it, looked out of the peephole, but they were gone. Really, I thought they were going to kill me. I think they would have, too, if I had not made all that noise." They got scared someone would hear them and come, probably. "It was the blood of Jesus Christ that protected me, or I would be dead today. My girlfriend, Jamie said I could be standing on the street corner and they'd try to run over me. I guess I'll have to watch out. But Pat, I've had to bear some marks on my body for the sin, but I'll never go back! They can kill my body, but they can't touch my soul. Christ is worth it all. Before I knew Jesus, this traumatic experience would have thrown me into seizures... but, I didn't have one then.

"People are going to have to pay a price for the gospel. What I went through yesterday makes me know Him in His suffering and His resurrection power. I did what you told me to do and I'm going to come out on top. Something came over me that Tuesday at your meeting and it hasn't left me. I promise you, Pat - the occult life for me is over."

A person has no resistance at all to demons without Christ. The Word Philippians 4:13 says, "I can do all things through Christ who strengtheneth me." The natural man without Christ is spiritually weak and highly susceptible to infestation by demons. There is little he can do about fighting off evil spirits if Christ is not dwelling inside.

Dabbling with the occult and developing one's potential paranormal powers can be dangerous. No safeguards exist for those who invade strange territory. Dr. Allen Y. Cohen, a California clinical psychologist, asserts, "There are at least 2,000 documented cases of individuals needing psychological help, (as a result of) trying to develop psychic powers."[87]

Even the psychological sophisticated are vulnerable when experimenting in this realm. Harmon H. Bro's observations in this regard are enlightening:[88]

"The proportion of casualties (among the sophisticates) in the modern West who seek to cultivate psychic ability is probably quite large. A quick review of twenty-two cases of individuals training in psychic capacity for four months to twenty years shows that about half of the cases achieved positive results with favorable consequences for their careers and health. The other half show mental and physical illness, divorce, vocational calamity, drug addiction and sexual deviation."

---

[87] Dr. Allen Y. Cohen, a California clinical psychologist,
[88] Laile E. Bartlett, "What Do We Really Know About Psychic Phenomena?" Readers' Digest August, 1977, p. 86.

LACK OF KNOWLEDGE

Witchcraft or occultism is only a vague doctrine in most seminary training although the Bible has much to say about such manifestations. Most ministers have never been called upon to deal with someone who is under the influence of an evil spirit. However, due to the widespread phenomenon of the occult, we will begin to witness more and more people who must be freed from evil spirits, not in Africa or some remote regions of the world... but here in America. Nineteen centuries ago the Apostle Paul warned Christians: "Beware, lest any man spoil you through philosophy and vain deceit, after the tradition of men - after the rudiments of this world, and not after Christ." (Col.2:8).

Many have suffered greatly because they started investigating these things and have eventually been brought to destruction when they have attempted to free themselves from it. Homes have been broken up. Suicide and lunacy have afflicted those who, once in it, dared to seek deliverance from its power. I have ministered to many people in mental institutions who were bound by occult devils. Those who have found deliverance can only give thanks to God for His grace and mercy.

There are, however, many thousands who have been unable to get free from the Arch-fiend because they have never been told of the saving power of the Lord Jesus Christ. They are just as unaware as if they lived in the depths of heathen lands that if they call upon the Name of the Lord, they shall be saved. This seems incredible in this so-called Christian country, but it is nevertheless a sorrowful fact.

Hal Lindsay wrote of the occult: "I believe that people are given superhuman powers from Satan in order that they may promote his work on earth. We are only at the beginning of this

175

explosion.   There will be inventions which will come from the spirit world and fantastic displays of miracles and wonders that the ancient Scriptures predict would occur in the days just before this present civilization would end." [89]

Mr. Lindsay stated further: "I do not believe this trend of history has happened by chance.   Satan does not want a world that rejects the supernatural;   he wants a world that is 'religious' and accepts super-naturalism, because it sets the stage for him to be worshiped in the person of the coming world leader known as Antichrist." [90]

[89] Hal Lindsay, Satan Is Alive and Well on Planet Earth, (Grand Rapids, Mich. Zondervan Publishing House, 1972), p. 40.
[90] Hal Lindsay with C.C. Carlson, The Late Great Planet Earth, Grand Rapids, Michigan, Zondervan Publishing House, 1970.

Chapter Eleven
Witchcraft

Charles Williams wrote in Witchcraft: 'It is cold, it is hungry, it is violent, and it is illusory. The warm blood and intercourse at the Sabot do not satisfy it. It wants something more. It wants souls.

SATAN'S POWER

Witchcraft is the use of a person employing satanic power. It is Satan's way of imposing his will upon your will and enforcing emotions, behaviors, or circumstances on people they would not otherwise want. Witchcraft cause to be endured, its power primarily though curses and spells.

Satan is the instrument of this power. He uses human vessels to work his powers. His agents obey his will. Satan must have a willing vessel in order to accomplish his foul deeds.

"How art thou fallen from heaven, O Lucifer, son of the morning? How art thou cut down, which didst WEAKEN THE NATIONS? They that look upon thee, saying, is this the man that made the earth to tremble, that did shake kingdoms?" (Is.14: 11-16).

Sorcery operates by Satan's supernatural power and is released through drugs, fetishes, potions, (conjured by wizards' and witches') drink or food that has been ritualistically fashioned to bind the person. It can be released in music, charms, and fetishes.

The Bible says that witchcraft is the root of all rebellion. "For rebellion is as the sin of witchcraft, and stubbornness is as iniquity and idolatry. Because thou hast rejected the word of the

177

LORD, he hath also rejected thee from being king," (1 Sam. 15:23).

Satan's power is real! The Bible says that he has power. "...and power was given him over, ALL KINDREDS, AND TONGUES, AND NATIONS," (Rev.13: 7).

SATANIC AGE

Divination is fortune-telling, or forecasting the future under the power of a demon. People want to know about the time to come. Sometimes soothsaying can be found in the church masquerading as prophecy. Many Christians get caught up in some prophetess or prophet to tell them "what God is saying about them. Really, if you want to know what God is saying about you, study His Word." "But strong meat belongeth to them that are of full age, even those who by reason of use have their senses exercised to discern both good and evil," (Heb. 5:14).

This is the Satanic Age and the world is looking to receive the Antichrist. "...The fourth beast shall be the fourth KINGDOM upon earth which shall be diverse from all kingdoms and shall devour THE WHOLE EARTH, and shall tread it down, and break it in pieces," (Dan.7: 23).

WHO BELIEVES IN WITCHCRAFT?

After all, witchcraft was a problem of the Dark Ages and we are living in the greatest age of knowledge advancement the world has ever known. You may think that only a few off-balance kooks are interested in witchcraft, but you would be wrong! Multitudes believe and practice witchcraft and their numbers are growing every day. In Germany, thousands are engaged in witchcraft. England has thirty thousand practicing witches! The British Parliament revoked the ancient Witchcraft Act in the Fifties. They reasoned: why have antiquated laws on the books when something doesn't exist?

The New Testament agrees with the Old Testament. "Now the works of the flesh are manifest, which are these; Adultery, fornication, uncleanness, lasciviousness, 20 Idolatry, witchcraft, hatred, variance, emulations, wrath, strife, seditions, heresies, 21 Envying, murders, drunkenness, revellings, and such like: of which I tell you before, as I have also told you in time past, that they which do such things shall not inherit the kingdom of God," (Gal. 5:19-21).

CAN WIZARDS AND WITCH'S REALLY FLY?

The Bible also reveals that witches and wizards can really fly. Let's look at what the Scripture says about this.

The Bible, in (Ezekiel 13:20), bears witness to certain women who are practicing witchcraft to "hunt for the souls of men, to make them "fly." These "soul catchers make them "fly." "Wherefore thus saith the Lord GOD; Behold, I am against your pillows, (wherewith ye there hunt the souls to make them fly), and I will tear them from your arms, and will let the souls go, even the souls that ye hunt to make them fly." In verse 18, these women are shown sewing "pillows" (objects used in association with magical practices) and "kerchiefs" or (magical veils) which they put over the heads of those consulting them, as if to fit them for receiving a response, that they might be rapt in a spiritual trance above the world. Some believe that the words, "your kerchiefs" are nets, or amulets to catch the souls of men."

Note the comment of God, "Hunt the souls of My people." The word hunting means hunt down, track down, prey upon, go in search of, quest after, hound, and search for . . . Souls, minds, individuals, and humans. In other words, witches and wizards, "hunt for the souls of my people."

Most people mistakenly assume that witchery cannot act physically or spiritually on a Christian. They unwisely think that being born again automatically protects against any sort of course, spell or hex, etc., that is sent by people practicing witchcraft. The Scripture points out those Believers are a sought-after target of witchcraft which is hunting (catching or snaring) Christian individuals (mind, will, emotion). Face-to-face with witchcraft some people can be brought into a certain state into bondage, thus becoming captives, having their souls restrained.

Then the words appear, notice the phrase, "to make them fly," this means turn to witchcraft and they will learn astral projection or soul travel. The word fly is a most interesting word when you take into account witches and wizards all testify that they are able to "fly." They call it "soul travel" or "astral projection." They claim their spirit can leave their body to spiritually travel to other places. They maintain that their fleshly bodies stay in place with demon spirits guarding them and keeping them alive while they are on these excursions.

THE RISE OF WITCHCRAFT

There are twenty-five million into cults! One witch believes there are nearly ten million practicing witches in America! The same source said there are four million that are official registered with Witchcraft Centers. Arthur Lyons wrote in *The Second Coming: Satanism in America*: "The Satanic Age started in 1966. That's when God was proclaimed dead, the Sexual Freedom League came into prominence, and the hippies developed as a free sex culture."

(February 22 1917 - October 26 1982) was an English witch, astrologer, psychic, and occult author. She wrote more than 60 books on occult and esoteric subjects. She was dubbed "Britain's most famous witch" by the BBC. A famous British witch and medium claimed that the witch population has exploded 40 percent in America during the past five years, with more than four-hundred covens scattered across the country. In news releases, Miss Leek claimed to be 560-years-old, if one counts "previous reincarnations." She died October 26, 1982. An antique dealer and part-time newspaper columnist, she practiced astrology and numerology. A prolific writer, she did more than anyone else to popularize witchcraft in America. Her books are taught in many universities. Someone said of her: "She has made so much money that she forgot how to cast a spell." The Bible says, "Thou shalt not suffer a witch to live," (Ex. 22:18).[91]

WITCHCRAFT'S POLITICAL ACCEPTANCE

Louise Heubner, mother of three children, has been proclaimed 'Official Witch of Southern California'. Eugene Debs, a public official, once gave her a ceremonial scroll when Heubner cast a spell to increase the sexual vitality over Los Angeles. A vast amount of publicity resulted. Debs then realized the respectability he had given to witchcraft and disavowed the scroll). Promptly, the witch revoked her spell! She has a weekly column in twenty weekly newspapers; a book, *Power through Witchcraft,* and two

---

[91] http://www.reference.com/browse/wiki/Sybil_Leek

record albums: Seduction through Witchcraft, and Coven Witchcraft. Selections on the latter album include titles such as: *"Black Sabbath"*; *"For Unlawful Carnal Knowledge"*; *"Pact with Lucifer"*; *"Wicked Woman"*; *"Dignitaries of Hell"*; and *"Satanic Mass!"*

We have been carefully lulled to sleep concerning the dangers of the forces of witchcraft. Occultists are "In!" Many believe it's a harmless joke to see men and women in long black robes, claiming to be witches and warlocks. Hard questions must be investigated: Are witches and demons just superstitious fairy tales handed down from the Middle Ages? Are these figments of one's imagination? Are they endangering the public's peaceful right to exist; should they be given media coverage, with the "other side" being given equal time; should the Church be concerned about them and should Pastors warn their congregations about the spiritual dangers of witchcraft?[92]

Satanism is one of the most obscure manifestations of witchcraft. Several years ago, Anton Szander LaVey, founded the First Satanic Church in San Francisco, dedicated to sensual indulgence, vengeance, and all sin. Mr. LaVey decries "good" witches; he preaches evil and wields black magic. (His 'church' isn't open to visitors). Telephone inquirers are told that they should first read the Satanic Bible. If they're in agreement with its teachings, they may then make written application for membership.[93]

---

[92] Louise Heubner, 'Official Witch of Southern California'. Eugene Debs,
[93] Anton Szander LaVey, founded the First Satanic Church in San Francisco,

182

Chapter Twelve
Witchcraft Religious

"And he caused his children to pass through the fire in the valley of the son of Hinnom: also he observed times, and used enchantments, and used witchcraft, and dealt with a familiar spirit, and with wizards: he wrought much evil in the sight of the Lord, to provoke him to anger. 7 And he set a carved image, the idol which he had made, in the house of God, of which God had said to David and to Solomon his son, In this house, and in Jerusalem, which I have chosen before all the tribes of Israel, will I put my name forever," (2 Chron. 33:6-7).

Witchcraft is being promoted in newspapers, magazines, books, and on radio and television. Everywhere you turn, you will find it being advanced in the world once, and the only witches we heard about in America were the ones in fairy tales and Disney movies. Now, witchcraft is a very real force, festering openly in our society."

WHITE AND BLACK WITCHCRAFT

Many modern witches claim to be heirs to an unbroken religious tradition stretching back into primeval history. They worship the Great Mother, Gaia, the earth mother, the symbol of fertility and the oldest and most elemental of the ancient gods. White witchcraft insists that it is a religion and not an evil cult.

White witches believe there is a distinction between white magic and black magic. But the source of power for white witchcraft, white magic is the same as that of black witchcraft and black magic. It is all from the same Devil. Remember any supernatural power that is not association with Jesus Christ and His Word is of Satan. Black and white is both demonic. There is no such thing as good and bad, witchcraft. The Bible warns, "While they promise them liberty, they themselves are the servants of corruption; for of whom a man is overcome, of the same is he brought bondage." (2 Pet. 2:19). A dictionary might say: "A witch is a person who practices witchcraft."

What is witchcraft? It is an art practiced by witches." Another dictionary might say: "A witch is a person who practices magic." An encyclopedia relates: "The use of supposed supernatural powers for antisocial needs." Notice "supposed." You see. Many of the intellectuals in our lifetime have denied supernatural power - any supernatural power God or Satan. Of course, we, as born-again Christians, should realize that there are two supernatural powers in the world. One is the supernatural force of Satan and his demons. The other, the supernatural force of Christ and His angels and there is no such thing as a neutral power in the universe. A more scholarly definition might be: "Witchcraft takes many forms - but, in every case, it is antisocial."

If you were to ask a witch if there were different types of witchcraft, the answer would be, "yes," a "black" witch practices magic that will aid selfish needs no matter how it affects others. A "white" witch claims to have power to heal the sick and give them protection from evil spirits, and to be concerned with helping others. The Bible makes no distinction between white or black witchcraft. It all comes from the same source: Satan.

Evangelist, former queen of Black Witches in Europe, Doreen Irving, in her book, Freed from Witchcraft, writes: "When I returned from England, my time was spent visiting covens. Many new ones were springing up and were important to

184

encourage new members. White witches were swelling their ranks; therefore, we also had to attract new members. We didn't mention blood sacrifice that would've caused fright.

Irving wrote, "White witches joined the ranks of the black witches and we learned from them. I will mention here that although white witches claim never to harm anyone, I can say that I've known white witches who did harm people. Practices called voodoo by black witches were followed by white witches, who use "fith fath" - a doll made of clay in the image of the person they wish to harm. They use a pin on this image to seal the lips of the person represented. They tie a cord to the legs of the image to inflict pain in the person's legs. When someone is rendered speechless or when he is made to suffer pain in his legs and is unable to walk, he is certainly being harmed.

We read. "And I will cut off witchcrafts out of thine land; and thou shalt have no more soothsayers" (Mic. 5:12). The Devil is not good. Even though he may pretend to be good, he's evil. Therefore, both witchcrafts are evil and destructive. There are many that accept the premise of something called "white magic." To suggest that white magic is beneficial in nature is to say that there is a pious side to the devil. The idea of a personal devil is very rare in our world but very real in the pages of Scripture and in "second and third world countries!" (Ezek. 28:12-19), shows Satan in his original, angelic state without sin . . . then describes his sin and fall. (Isa. 14:12-17), reveals him as the deceiver of nations who wishes to sit on the throne of God.

He uses witchcraft to accomplish his diabolical ends. He leads uninformed people into a life of occult spiritual bondage. This is the dark side of Satan and there is no light side. Trudge into his territory of supernatural practices and you run the risk of achieving his ends whether you want them or not. The price is subjection to him. Jesus said: "He that is not with me is against Me." When you say "no" to Christ, you are actually-truly saying "yes" to Satan!

WITCHCRAFT - THE OLD TIME RELIGION

Witchcraft is sometimes referred to as the Old Religion terminology, meaning that it is older than Christianity. It is a Nature religion. The forces of the world around me are considered manifestations of divine power. It is pantheistic. The image of the Mother Goddess representing the forces in Nature was eventually given a companion; the horned god . . . representing the male principality. The "horned god" is not really Satan, although he looks the part, explain the witches. They say that he is "Pan," the Roman god of Nature who was half-goat and half-man.

It doesn't help the witches' cause when they speak of Pan as Lucifer, a name that the Bible confers upon Satan. The ancestry of the Old Religion can be traced back to Artemus of the Greeks, and Diana of the Romans, and perhaps to even the moon goddess of the Egyptians and the fertility goddess of the Canaanites.

Interestingly, John Todd traveled across the country trying to warn the Christian Church of the rise of Witchcraft. Controversial in Christian circles, claims to have been a high priest in the International Witchcraft coven of thirteen. He once passed out a diagram in a meeting supposedly outlining the "structure" of Satan's kingdom as shown in (Eph. 6:10-12). At the top is Lucifer, Cherubim Beelzebub. You must continuously pray to God for protection of these people and for one another.

186

Here are the seven high-ranking, major principalities of Hell that are taught to witches. This will give you a clear understanding of possessions and who causes them and why. They are listed so that YOU will be able to properly deliver or refer someone to be properly delivered from demonic forces.

PRINCIPALITIES

REGE - controls the occult, blue aura, hallucinogenic drugs, LSD, "speed," marijuana and Christian gossip. Rege causes you to become depressed, so you go to Rage, the demon of the occult and drugs, and he sends you to **Bacchus**, the demon of addiction. It's all one big circle in which they'll try to keep you trapped forever.

LAZERS - Controls Demon of Sexual lust, homosexuality, bisexuality, adultery, masturbation, pornography and other such sexual pleasures.

BACCHUS - Demon of addictions, such as drugs, and alcohol. And, tobacco, and foods.

PAN - Controls mind, mental illness, rejection, nerves, and depression.

MEDITI - Demon of hate, murder, killing, war, jealousy, envy and gossip and non-Christian gossip.

SET - Demon of death. There really is such a thing. He causes of death by doctors. He is listed with 39 major causes of death by doctors.

CHRISTIAN DEMON DISCONTENTMENT - A principality only used against Christians! - This particular demon has no set name. He is so powerful that most won't even bother him. They just let him go on his merry way to do his dirty work. Getting Christians to talk about each other through gossiping and causing strife within the church and among the brethren (Lev. 19:19; Ps. 15:1-3). He will also try to weaken a Christian's walk with the Lord *by* making him content, fail to live up to church commitments, such as tithing, soul-winning, church participation and much more.

Under these names are countless unclean spirits and each one of them is under the strict control of a commander.

Todd claims that these powers make up the categories within each principality. Now, I'm not promoting John Todd. He professes to be a former witch once on the Council of Druid of Thirteen in America. He says this council is connected to an organization called the Illuminati, which has been in existence since 1776.[94]

He alleges these people are running everything in the world, including American Presidents and they are the force behind the strong witchcraft and satanic movements in the world. The Illuminati, he states, furnishes all the money for these movements. He claims further that people like Sybil Leek, Lady Sheba, Lorka (and Todd, himself) are, or he claims, have been on this council.[95]

He lays out a plan of world domination by the Illuminati. Many have written that Todd is just a strange man, with an immense imagination, seeking attention. However, witchcraft is on the rise in our country. There are thirteen members in a coven: six men and six women, and a high priest.[96] They meet once a month on a night with a full moon. This monthly meeting is called an esbat (beast). In addition there are eight Sabbaths. Typical dates include the two

---

[94] http://en.wikipedia.org/wiki/John_Todd_(occultist)
[95] ibid
[96] ibid

traditional Druid festivals - the eve of May Day (April 30 and All Hallows Eve October 31, and seasonal festivals of winter (February 2), spring (June 23), summer (August 1, and fall (December 21). The bible of the Old Religion, The book of the Shadows, describes their rites, cures, charms, and spells, and is read at every meeting.[97]

WITCHCRAFT'S EVIL POWERS

These days, you can enroll in a course in Witchcraft in many schools and colleges. Some are: Holly Stoke Free University, San Diego State College, New York University, the University of South Carolina and the University of Georgia. There are sixty-eight institutions of higher learning in America that now have courses in witchcraft. Make no mistake about it. Witchcraft is gaining wider respectability and following. It was once assumed to be a religion for the superstitious, uneducated folk; but, no more! Doctors, teachers, businessmen, as well as housewives and college students may form the thirteen members of a coven. A hardware clerk, a sign painter, an airline employee and an Air Force officer could be members of another typical coven.

So far, you might think witchcraft innocent. You might wonder why witches were persecuted in ancient times. But look a little closer . . . "It's a nature religion," says one of their priests. "Sex always has been an integral part of our rituals. Witches have always used drugs (hence the proclivity for doctors and nurses to be involved!). Animal and human sacrifices are practices (very easy to do under 'medical auspices' and in abortion clinics!) It is a religion of freedom, joy in the sensual

---

[97] ibid

189

appetites and in Nature. The witches take off all of their clothes. They call this 'becoming sky-clad' and immerse themselves in salt water to 'become purified.' Then, stark naked they form a nine-foot circle and sing "Blessed Be." They chant and dance to taped music until they work up a good sweat, while incense is burning in brass censers. Broomsticks, yes, are sometimes used, following an ancient fertility ceremony. They drink wine and tea and listen to readings from *The Book of Shadows*.

They are naked because they believe the human body has tremendous forces which clothing can cut off. New members are initiated into the coven. They are blindfolded, and with hands tied behind their backs, they are led naked (or sometimes clad in light robes) into a ring of witches and wizards. The high priest refers to their belief in reincarnation and worships the powers of Nature. The ceremony is conducted by the high priestess. Second and third "degrees" in witchcraft often involve sexual intercourse; but, there is a surprising lack of uniformity among the covens on the proper procedure. In some covens sexual intercourse is a part of the third degree. Degrees are developmental stages of witchcraft.

Remember the Charles Manson case that "Family" was a group of people operating under the powers of witchcraft?

Ed Warren, self-proclaimed demonologist, told The Weekly World News: "Fiendish, devil-worshiping cultists are on the verge of spawning an insane bloodbath of murder, mutilation and terror in cities and towns across America. Satanic worship and human sacrifices are going on right now. It's not fantasy. It's a very real and dangerous situation. We can't run away from it."[98]

---

[98] Ed Warren, self-proclaimed demonologist, told The Weekly World News:

Incredibly, at almost the very hour that Warren was making his chilling warning, four people were being brutally murdered in Columbia, S.C., in a house police said was temple of Satanic worship!

The victims of the ritualistic massacre were shot in the back of their heads at point blank range. Their blood-spattered bodies were sprawled at the foot of a small altar. "We know from talking to neighbors that the people in the house practiced black magic, witchcraft and the occult," Sheriff Frank Powell said. The house was filled with boxes of seeds, leaves and incense," the deputy added. "I've seen places like this before and I knew what that house is. It's a place where devil worshipers meet. It's a temple of the damned."[99]

CHRIST'S SUPERIOR POWER

"For by Him were all things created, that are in heaven, and that are in earth, visible and invisible, whether they be thrones, or dominions, or principalities, or powers; all things were created by Him, (Jesus) and for Him" (Jesus) (Col. 1:16).

The devil can only dominate humans through their rejection of Jesus. (Life would be intolerable if all the demons had their way. But, like Satan, they are under strict limitations. They are not able to create anything and can only produce after their own kind). Most people are kept from becoming demonized by the natural protection of their wills. The "will" (the mind that says "yes" or "no") is the wall that keeps demonic influence out. When that wall is broken down by sin, demons may then come in. When a person no longer is able to control his will, the

---

[99] ibid

demons take control and that new, strange personality will manifest. A person may also inherit curses and accompanying spirits that are generational, as well as just be "hit" by satanic attacks or witchcraft. This type of demonization is not caused by their sin. It can be "assignment" of persecution or oppression. Spirits can oppress people from inside or outside of them!

Familiar spirits can cause psychotic traits such as paranoia and Schizophrenia (split personality) because there are innumerable classes of evil spirits, each having a personality of its own. They seek to gain possession of living bodies and souls so that they may express their own habits, personality traits, appetites, lustful desires, etc. Thus, we have what is called split personalities, the paranoid - the possessed. When the living, human spirit is completely overthrown, subdued, conquered, suppressed, and locked up in a cell inside the body and taken over, possessed completely by familiar spirits . . . then, we have the "insane."

Witches say that if they send out an evil spirit and the mission of that evil demon is not successful, it will come back tenfold on them. This is why, said former witch, Mike Warnke in *The Satan Seller*, says they did not like to send demons out to Christians. If unsuccessful, those demons would return to them in great anger. The demons would serve witches but hated to serve man and only did at the bid of Satan. If witches gave them any occasion, they would come back on them.

Christ's mercy is extended to all who will confess, forsake, and ask for forgiveness for their wicked ways. Hell was not prepared for humans but for the devil and all his angels . . . and all who fail to accept Christ as Savior, (Matt. 25:41). A person can "will" to go to hell! (Deut. 28) shows the blessings and the curses. The curses fall on those who serve other gods

Disobedience to God's law in/by visiting Satan's occult camp will result in suffering, sickness, sorrow and despair and often early death, unto grandchildren and great-grandchildren. While I was ministering in Miami, a lady who had been a gypsy was helped into the Church. She could hardly walk. She confessed and renounced her occult involvement and was instantly set free. She was then able to walk without help and all the pain vanished. The next day I heard that she'd walked for four hours shopping in the Sun Mall.

There are forgiveness and deliverance in Jesus Christ. Open renunciation and repudiation of all occult sins must be made. Then cleansing may be received by resisting the evil forces by faith in Jesus and His shed Blood. The occult line that has run through a whole family can be broken!

It is true, according to the old adage that the devil "trembles when he sees the weakest saint upon his knees." But just as true that he and his cohorts tremble when they see the weakest saint, in any activity of the Christian life, put his faith in his all victorious Lord, for then, the saint becomes their strongest foe. The powers of darkness stand in awful fear and dread of Him who "spoiled principalities and powers," and dread Him who "made a shew of them openly, triumphing over them in it," (Col. 2:15).

They experience that same fear and dread of any believer who will dare by faith to count on his union with his all victorious Lord. Such a believer becomes Satan's prime target. All hell's artillery is hurled against him, because he constitutes the deadliest enemy which the powers of darkness possess. But, be courageous! God will come to our aid, deliver us, and even send in legions of angels on assignments on our behalf!

193

THE DEVIL IS A POWERFUL FORCE

John heard words that describe our time: "Woe to the inhabitants of the earth and of the sea. For the devil is come down unto you, having great wrath, because he knoweth that he hath but a short time," (Rev. 12:12). We can now see his workers very busy in the world filling it with rebellion, terror and fear. Irene A. Park, a former witch and Satan worshiper, tells us: "Make no mistake to think that witchcraft and its current expressions in our society are not the result of some innocent fad."

Nearly all the spreading of occult practice in America is being done by people firmly in the hands of the Devil, who in exchange for power and wealth, have fully yielded their souls to his work.

There is a definite power structure in satanic order. To be able to work up the ladder of Satan's domain, a person must consecrate his entire being to doing and becoming evil. To perform the supernatural power of darkness, one must devote time to study and meditation.

Everything that Satan offers is a counterfeit of the real thing but if one will devote himself to the Devil, he promises to give that person power, wealth and authority - not the real thing, but power based on fear instead of love; wealth in money, but not wealth of the soul; and authority based on deceit rather than truth.

In many ways, witches; covens and Satanic cults are not much different from most mystical orders and brotherhoods, secretive sisterhoods, fraternities and sororities, all of whom are based on secret covenants. With Satanists, however, there is no such thing as a "good" or "white witch" (this is another demonic deception).

A witch must submit not only his soul, body and spirit to the Devil, but also his family (if married) to also be used as tools and vessels of Satan at his discretion. based on the creeds and vows made during the secret initiation ceremonies in most Satanic orders, the Devil has every legal right to use (or dispose of) the person or any member of his family for his purposes. It is much like playing Russian roulette with your soul (and your family's lives).

This really gives insight into the power and control that Satan has over his followers. Most people are not afraid of witchcraft because they don't know the reality of its powers and the spiritual implications of it. It has been on the rise in our country since the 60's and now it's more than fortune telling or mind reading. People are now becoming spiritual and psychic captives . . . hurt by crippling forces - with very little chance of escape.

SPIRITUAL EYES MUST OPEN

The Church must address itself to the rise of witchcraft and voodoo. So many people are being injured and, unfortunately, most ministries simply are ignorant and do not know what to do. Mrs. Penn-Lewis wrote: When the existence of evil spirits is recognized by the heathen, it is generally looked upon by the missionary as 'superstition' and ignorance; whereas the ignorance is often on the part of the missionary, who is blinded by "the prince of the power of the air," to the revelation given in the Scriptures, concerning the satanic powers. Many in the service or our Lord have been spiritually blinded. [100]

We simply must discern the enemy and his power in order to overcome him. There are many demons in our churches. What do the clergy do with the possessed? They send them to doctors who drug them and give them shock treatments. Many are in worse shape than before they sought treatment. Satan's works must be treated spiritually by the power of God. The Bible tells us about Satan and his demons but it also shows us the armor and the weapons that we need for this battle so that through Jesus Christ; we may be more than conquerors.

The Catholic author, C. S. Lewis wrote in *The Screwtape Letters*: "There are two equal and opposite errors into which our race can fall into about the devils. One is to disbelieve in their existence. The other is to believe and to feel an unhealthy interest in them! They themselves are equally pleased by both errors, and they hail a materialist or a magician with the same delight."

Many Christians have chosen to ignore the Devil, thinking they will not have to do battle with him. However, the Scripture says: "Submit yourselves to God, RESIST THE DEVIL, and he will flee from you," (Jam. 4:6-7). The fear of demons comes from the demons themselves, whispering fearful thoughts into the minds of people. The entire church must begin to battle against the powers of darkness to see real victory. People must be liberated through God's saints speaking the Name of Jesus to set the captives free. We have nothing to fear because Christ is greater. If Christians don't cast out devils, who is going to do it?

---

[100] Jesse Penn-Lewis, War on the Saints
http://www.apostasynow.com/wots/Contents.html

Many might disagree that there is an unseen world of spiritual beings in the universe. But, the Scriptures tell us there is a personal Devil. "Ye are of your father the devil," (Jn. 8:44). He is aggressive according to (1 Pet. 5:8), "Be sober, be vigilant; because your adversary the devil, as a roaring lion, walketh about, seeking whom he may devour, whom resist steadfast in the faith . . ." Therefore, we must fight both a defensive and offensive warfare. (Eph. 6:10-18 and 10:12).

Satan stands behind every aggressive move of anti-Christian endeavor. Witchcraft is anti-Christian and one of the greatest sins in the history of Israel and Judah! It brought great punishment. It is prevalent today and is the scarlet sin of the social realm. The treachery of witchcraft weakens minds, damns souls, wreck homes and lives.

Witchcraft is both sensual and sexual, making one lose a sense of sin. It seeks to deceive both the secular and religious people. Witchcraft is rebellion. SIN. Man has been blinded by Satan, the god of this world (2Cor. 4:34). Man needs salvation to rescue him from darkness and open his eyes to the new life, and that in Christ (Acts 26:18).

Somehow the world has failed to see the real meaning of the powers of darkness that keep it bound and the redemption of Christ that delivers from the authority of sin. Salvation through the Blood of Christ brings man home from exile to walk with God (Eph. 2:13). Man without Christ is bound by the chain of sin (Mk. 5:1-5). However, being born-again makes it possible for man to be free to live for the Savior, free to serve the Savior, free to enjoy the Savior (Jn. 8:32; Mk. 5:15).

Witchcraft is not allowed for Christians. Yet, some "Christians" claim that it is. It is the root of rebellion against God, man aligning himself with Satan and his power. To see witchcraft as a gift from God is sheer ignorance of the basic teaching of the Bible. A Christian must bend to God's will. He cannot seek to bend God's will to his. "Thou shalt not learn to do after the abominations of those nations. There shall not be found among you anyone . . . that useth divination, or an observer of times, or an enchanter, or a witch, or a charmer, or a consulter with familiar spirits, or wizard, or necromancer. For all that do these things are an abomination unto the Lord," (Deut. 18:9-12).

Exposure and intercession through prayer are desperately needed. Christian warriors are also needed to set the captives free. Divination and sorcery were designed to obtain from supernatural or superhuman beings, information concerning the destiny of individuals, nations and causes. Satanism is openly, profanely anti-Christian. Naturally, those who profess to these powers like to be reckoned to be in special accord with God, however, so serious did God consider this demonic practiced that the law in the Old Testament was that a witch was to be put to death. "Thou shalt not suffer (permit, allow) a witch to live," (Ex. 22:18).

There is no sin under the sun that cannot be seen or forgiven and washed in the Blood of Jesus Christ. I have seen many occultists or witches and warlocks come to Christ. Praise Him for His sacrifice. As Brooks Alexander has said,"...the spiritual anemia of the West has left this generation ravenous for reality, and therefore vulnerable to any spiritual counterfeit offered in the name of Truth . . . this development opens up new vistas of Christian apologetics that have barely been touched before."[101]

---

[101] http://www.scp-inc.org/staff/BrooksAlexander.php

Christians need to be diligent in seeking an informed understanding of what its direction is and what it means within the context of the spiritual warfare to which we are called."

Cults of all kinds are gaining new stature and acceptance through the popularity of entertainers and public leaders, who openly admit their involvement and often their favorite cults. Lon Tinney, Production Manager for special Effects in Star Wars has made a lengthy endorsement of L. Ron Hubbard's *"Dianetics"* for a national Scientology advertisement. In an obvious attempt to promote TM, Talk show host, Merv Griffin had Maharishi Mahesh Yogi on his show several times, while refusing to have as guest Rabindranath Maharaj, a former Hindu guru, saved, to present the other side. The wide influence affected for Mormonism by the Osmond family is well-known. California's governor Brown has been described as "one who has been touched by the spirit of Zen (Buddhism).[102]

CHURCH REACTION

Satan, though defeated, is still the most subtle of enemies. He is able to cleverly conceal himself from human sight. A master of camouflage, he has been able to deceive people to the point of having them think he doesn't even exist! Even many theologians and church men are persuaded that he is simply a figment of the imagination or a mythological character of bygone days. The devil must be exposed before he can effectively be opposed! Revealing him and his evil purposes is the task of God's people in this age.

---

[102] ibid

POWER OF GOD

Mel Tari, a man who witnessed the outpouring of a great revival in Indonesia, describes his observation of the state of American churches in the early Seventies. His words read like a prophecy for today. Mr. Tari writes in *A Mighty Wind* (17) "Before I came to the United States, I said, "Lord, I'm from a heathen country, and when I go to America, which is a Christian country, what will I tell them? I have no message to them. We still have need of missionaries from America to come to our country and preach the Gospel. But when I got off the plane in Los Angeles, I began to understand why God had sent me to America. At first I was excited; the airport building was so big and new. After I had walked and walked, I reached a large room where many things were for sale. Everywhere I looked, I saw dirty books, bars with liquor, and people smoking. What's wrong, I thought? God, help me!"

"I got into the taxi, and by that time I was sad and sick. But it got worse. On every street corner there were signs with liquor, and people cursing the Name of God."

"What's wrong?" I asked my friends. "Is this really America where the coin says In God We Trust I remembered what the Lord had spoken to me: "You have one message for the people of America: That is their need to get back to the simplicity of the Word of God and not only back to the Bible, but back to the simplicity of the Word."

"Now that I have been in America, I realize that America's greatest problem is that the Church doesn't recognize that demonic power is real . . . Satan has blinded your eyes until you do not even see the problem."

There are two kinds of magic power; black magic and white magic. Black magic is where the power may be used to kill someone. I don't think America has very much of this. However, when I read your newspapers, I think this, too, is coming to America.

"White magic is what is affecting America today. By white magic, I mean the demonic power you use for something good, like healing people or having fortune tellers tell good things. Most Americans are so blind to demonic powers that they think they are hearing God, when it is really demons. We can't blame most of the people, for if sheep do not have green grass, they will eat dry leaves.

"The pastors in America must make sure they feed their sheep the green grass. Why do people go to fortune tellers and look at the horoscope? It is because the church has lost the gift of prophecy. So the church member finds out about the future from the demons. All this demon power is a counterfeit of spiritual gifts."[103]

"The only way to save ourselves from this is to see God's power in action in our lives. That's the only way."

Two things happen when people read the horoscopes. First, they have committed sin because God said don't do it. Second, a demon binds them. For this bondage they don't need forgiveness - they need deliverance. These two things are totally different.

Today, we often pray about the sin, but rarely do we pray for deliverance. We need to put into practice (Matt. 18:18). "Verily, I say unto you, whatsoever ye shall bind on earth shall

---

[103] ibid

201

be bound in heaven; and, whatsoever ye shall loose on earth shall be loosed in heaven."

It is said of Martin Luther that whenever he was assailed by Satan, he shouted at him, "I've been baptized!" When Satan appeared at the foot of Smith Wigglesworth's bed, he simply said: "oh, it's only you," and he turned over and fell asleep. A seminar professor reacted with great alarm when I mentioned Satan's name to him. The professor had planned to teach a course on hypnosis. "That's of Satan," I said. His eyes widened with great fear . . . "Don't mention Satan to me," he said.

"Why not," I asked?

"He appeared at the foot of my bed when I attended college," he replied. "What did you do?" I asked. He said, "I ran from him!"

Thank God. We Christians have the authority to chase him out!

The Church must stir to action with passion and compassion for souls walking in great darkness in these latter times. As I evangelize, Satanists and witches are frequent visitors at meetings. Some come to work their spells against me. Others come as human chalices to receive demons expelled from the repentant ones into their bodies. (They believe that the more evil spirits they have to control and control others with, the more power they will move in. Warlocks many times use gullible, weak vessels as chalices to bring back demons that they will assign their evil works).

Some are convicted of their evil, repent, receive Christ as their deliverer; others leave in the same darkness because they WILL TO WALK with evil. These "walking dead" continue on the highway to hell. The Christians have been sleeping concerning the rise in witchcraft and its new respectability. Like the Devil, many Christians feel if they ignore it, it will go away. NOT SO, the Bible says: "Submit yourselves to God, resist the devil and he will flee from you" (Jam. 4-7).

Consequently, the witches are seeing many powerless churches, unaware concerning their endeavors. Therefore, some are not afraid to attack the churches' members with their powers of darkness! Many witches and warlocks have infiltrated churches, prayer groups, and other Christian areas, pretending to be Christian, even running forward during altar calls, faking repentance and salvation. The covens send them out on assignment into churches to destroy the pastor, break up the church and do everything to shut down the prayer groups. This is why the Church needs to operate in discernment, parking a donkey in a garage do not make it a car! We must awake and go forth under the power of the Holy Spirit to warn, discern and deliver people from this ungodly power.

CHURCH GIVEN GREAT POWER

The ultimate aim in Christian service can only be salvation of the lost and the glorifying of His Name. We need willing workers who would stop at nothing in order to bring to Christ needy men and women all around us. God is seeking people today prepared to sacrifice their all for His work . . . men and women willing to lay their lives on the altar and leave there without taking them back again.

"In Roman mythology, Aesculapius was the god of medicine. His symbol was a staff with a snake coiled about it. According to the legend, he had received a healing herb (drug) from a serpent's mouth. The connection between the (serpent and sorcery *pharmakia* in the Greek New Testament) has continued to the present day. Aesculapius' staff now has not one but two serpents coiled around it in the familiar and honored emblem of modern medicine. The tradition behind this symbol is kept alive by the medical profession. Though the name of Jesus Christ and prayers to God the Father has been excluded from our schools, at the time they receive their M. D. Degrees of medical colleges, graduates still repeat in unison the ancient Hippocratic Oath which begins: "I swear by Apollo the Physician, by Aesculapius, by Hygeia, Panacea, and ALL THE GODS AND GODDESSES."[104]

GOD OF HEALING

"The blessing of the Lord be upon you . . ." (Psa. 129:8). Sickness - A blessing or a curse?"

God says, "I am the Lord that health thee," (Ex. 15:26). That word of promise will endure forever!

"Blessed be the God and Father of our Lord Jesus Christ, who hath blessed us with all spiritual blessings in heavenly places in Christ: "

Benefits concerning people that have obeyed God by choosing Jesus Christ's Blood Sacrifice.

THE CENTRAL MESSAGE OF THE CHURCH

The Church was purchased with the precious blood of the Eternal Son of God, therefore, like Him is eternal. Jesus said, "Upon this rock" (Petra) "I will build my church." The Church is not built upon Peter, but it is built upon Christ. Every born again member of the church shares mutual citizenship and each belongs

---

[104] http://en.wikipedia.org/wiki/Asclepius

to the household of God, "Now, therefore, ye are no more strangers and foreigners, but fellow citizens with the saints, and of the household of God," (Eph. 2:19).

There is a divine person living in the true Church. Each member of the church is indwelt by the Spirit of God, "Know ye not that ye are the temple of God, and that the Spirit of God dwelleth in you?" (Cor. 3:16).

The members indwelt by the Holy Spirit form a glorious temple where God dwells in a special way by His Holy Spirit, "In whom ye also are builded together for an habitation of God through the Spirit," (Eph. 2:22). The Holy Spirit indwells permanently each Christian and the corporate body of Christians in the church. The church is the dwelling place of God.

The Christian has a unique relationship with Jesus. Jesus is shown as the Head of the church and the members are called His Body. He has given his believers a power of attorney to act against the power of Satan. It is essential to believe the gospel and everything it teaches for believers, (2 Tim. 3:16-17). Repentance and renunciation of all sin and wrong doing is another requirement (Acts 26:18; 2 Cor. 6:17.) A Christian's obedience to the gospel and seeking to be endued with power (Lk. 11:13; 24:49; 5:32). Surrender to God, walk and live in the Spirit, (Rom. 8:1-2, 8:10, 13-16; Gal. 6:26; Col. 3:17.) Learn to pray in faith, (Jam.1:5-8.)

In these last days, when God is pouring out His spirit so abundantly on His people, Satan is coming against us in great power, trying to defeat the Church and rob us of victory. But that does not mean we have to be cowering victims, powerless against this Deceiver. The Scriptures tell us in 1 John 4:4, "Ye are of God, little children, and have overcome them: because greater is he that is in you, than he that is in the world." In

Romans 5:20, "And where sin (Satan), does abound, there does grace (God's love), more abundantly abound." We need never be fearful - only aware of the enemy. With that awareness should be awareness of who we are in Christ.

A line is being drawn in our day and there is no middle road. We must choose to walk with God by His Word. (Deut. 18:9-12), shows us that God hates sorcery and witchcraft and warns His people not to perform these sinful abominations. We must walk perfect with our God. We must not fear these people. God hates witchcraft but loves and wants to save those who are into it! We've been anointed with greater power (Lk. 10:19-20) power to set the captives free!

This shows Jesus transferring His power to His followers. "And when he had called unto him his twelve disciples, he gave them power against unclean spirits, to cast them out, and to heal all manner of sickness and all manner of disease," (Matt. 10:1). Jesus gave the Church His power from the very beginning and that omission continues until this day. "And these signs shall follow them that believe in my Name shall they cast out devils; they shall speak with new tongues," (Mk. 16:17).

Satan wants us to ignore the rise of these evil powers. They seek to control our government, churches, schools, and the entire social structure and when Christians ignore, they sleep: they don't pray, rebuke the devil, wrestle for victory in the heavenlies. Satan is defeated only when he is face to face with the mighty name of Jesus and Christians exercising their faith by using Jesus' superior supernatural power. Satan is already defeated, legally because Christ's power prevailed - we must just appropriate that victory in each situation and every area, individually.

Christ has given us power to tread upon these evil forces . . . "Behold, I give unto you power to tread on serpents and scorpions, and over all the power of the enemy; and nothing shall by any means hurt you," (Lk. 10:19).

When facing the enemy, we are over comers . . . never defeated! Yes, Satan is alive but so is Jesus Christ! Only Christians have authority from Jesus to cast out evil spirits. But I will come to you shortly, if the Lord wills, and will know, not the speech of them which are puffed up, but the power. "For the kingdom of God is not in word, but in power," (1 Cor. 4:19).

The Righteous shall stand in Christ's divine power. "We are more than conquerors in Him," (Rom. 8). We are not impressed by the power of Satan and don't give him credit; but rather are wrestling against another kingdom (1Cor. 15:24).
Hebr.11:6.) Believe in your mission in life as a representative of God, (Acts 1:8.) Know your position in Christ, (Eph.2:6). Learn to use the name of Jesus in accordance with the Word of God, (Acts 3:16; 4:12; Jn.14:12-15; 16; 23-26; Col. 3:17; Jn.15: 7-16; 13:35).

CHRIST IS ALREADY SEATED

At His place of Supreme Authority, "Far above all principality, and power, and might, and dominion, and every name that is named, not only in this world, but also in that which is to come; and hath put all things under his feet, and gave him to be the head over all things to the church, which is his body, the fullness of him that filleth all in all, (Eph. 1:21-23).

This book attempts to prevent people from inquiring into those things that God forbids us to do; explaining that the occult is definitely Satan's ballpark; and to arouse and challenge you saints to wield the power of the Holy Spirit; taking your weapons of, high praise, prayer, Bible knowledge, The Name of Jesus, The Blood of Jesus, God's Armor and take back what the enemy has stolen from you and yours! Get him out of your lives and your family's lives and guard against him coming back!

Your part of the Blood Covenant is to walk through the shed blood, coming into partnership with God, accepting His delegated authority and doing some serious damage to the enemy's camp! Jesus never taught his disciples to ask His Father to do their work. He told them, "you go heal the sick, cast out devils, preach and teach and I will confirm my Word with signs and wonders following, etc. Taking communion means taking up your part of the covenant contract, signed in Jesus' Blood, and your part is to take dominion and authority over the enemy, like Jesus spent most of his time teaching them to do!"

Go forth, unashamed, unafraid of the challenge set before you into the battle of the ages. Use the mighty Sword of The Spirit and the power of Jesus' Name, and you will be victorious!

In the New Testament, faith is thought of as an act by which the individual avails himself of the gifts of God, submits himself in obedience to god's commands, and abandons all thought of self, trusting only in God. Faith is confident trust in the unseen power of God. I also pray that this book will change your life and draw you, closer to the cross and the Blood of Jesus - and that you will take your position in the Body of Christ as an active soldier doing whatever He tells you to do until He comes again.

Chapter Thirteen
Witchcraft Voodoo

"And thou shalt not let any of thy seed pass through the fire to mo'lech, neither shalt thou profane the name of thy God. I am the Lord," (Lev. 18:21).

VOODOO ORIGIN

When Haiti established its independence, during the actual ceremony to make it a republic, authorities brought in a pig and it was sacrificed to Satan, and Satan was proclaimed god over Haiti! So from then until now, most leaders have been steeped in Voodoo.

The Bible show how God feels about witchcraft and idolatry. It is an abomination to Him. "For rebellion is as the sin of witchcraft, and stubbornness is as iniquity and idolatry. Because thou hast rejected the word of the LORD, he hath also rejected thee from being king," (1 Sam 15:23).

In the streets of Port-au-Prince, radios blare rhythms of Skah Shah, Taboo-Combo and other popular Haitian songs [Many of their] musicians–live in New York and Boston. The Boat People wanted to follow them and thousands of Haitians have already done so. Outside a factory where hundreds of men and women sit sewing baseballs for America's national pastime, job applicants crowd around a "voodoo reve," a magic pattern of corn grains with a black doll in colored sand, to assure luck for one of them.[105]

Voodoo (from *Vodoun* meaning "Spirit") is a folk religion of mostly African origin and the most distinctive aspect of Haitian

---

[105] "Haiti: A Nation in Agony" Reader's Digest, October, 1981, p. 100.

society. Each village has its Houngans (Male Voodoo Priest) or Mambos (Female Voodoo Priest)?], or Voodoo priest. (One is even listed in the Yellow Pages of the Port-au-Prince Telephone Book!) Voodoo devotees believe that the universe is permeated by spirits (*loa*) whose assistance can be invoked to cure illness, ensure a good harvest, etc. Roman Catholic priests have battled Voodoo, in vain. Voodoo has simply incorporated the Trinity and some Catholic saints into its galaxy of spirits. [106]

Voodoo religion consists primarily in the worship of ancestors and a hierarchy of gods who seek to manifest themselves by taking "possession" of their worshipers during their frenzied dances. These ancestral spirit deities are known collectively as *loa*. During their ceremonies, as they drink blood and dance savagely, the participants fall into a trance and possession takes place by these spirits. In this state the possessing spirit may manifest itself and begin to speak, sing, or curse as well as offer advice, or cure the sick.

VOODOO WIDESPREAD

Voodoo (often called Hoodoo by Negroes) is also practiced in many places in the world today such as South America, Africa, Trinidad, Jamaica, Cuba, and the United States (especially in the South and in Harlem). In many American cities today (New York, Chicago, Los Angeles, Houston, New Orleans) one can purchase a wide assortment of witchcraft and Voodoo supplies . . . including such things as hexing dolls, ingredients for casting magic spells, black candles and charm powers.

---

[106] ibid

The Voodoo cults practice both white and black magic and engage in various forms of Spiritualism and occultism which include trance, divination, magic charming, etc. Their altars are covered with candles and surrounded with statues of some Catholic saints. Hymns are sung to them and the Virgin Mary. [107]

There is a malevolent side to Voodoo as well. One of the most feared spirits is Baron Samedi (Saturday), Lord of the Cemetery. In Voodoo art, he is depicted wearing a black hat and coat and dark eyeglasses. If a Haitian wants to plague an enemy, he entreats the Baron to send a spirit from the cemetery to do the job.

THE SPIRIT OF FEAR

People who are bound by ~~with~~ fear can die from it. It can be shown in test animals that destructive fear and apprehension can destroy the body. To kill a person by Voodoo, all that is needed is to implant the dreaded idea (ouanga-a-mort) into the victim's mind. The person practicing Voodoo uses a SPIRIT OF FEAR and other demonic power to kill. The victim of Voodooism, oppressed by the evil spirits, manifests worry, fear, terror, fear of death, etc; these spirits must be resisted by Jesus' Blood, in the Name of Jesus, by the power of the Holy Spirit and the Word of God. [108]

According to the Bible, the only fear that man should have is the fear of the Lord. Fear of any other kind is from Satan and evil. Fear is an enemy of God and man. The heart that is fully indwelt by Jesus should have no room for fear. Fear cannot exist where God's love is because "perfect love casteth out fear," (1 Jn. 4:18). Fear is a destroyer of hope and faith. Jesus, speaking to the

---

[107] Hobart E. Freeman, Every Wind of Doctrine, (Warsaw, Indiana; Faith Min. & Pub).
[108] Mary Garrison, How to Try the Spirits, (Christ Camp Ministries), p. 16.

disciples: "WHY ARE YE FEARFUL?" The words "Fear not!" and usually spoken by Jesus, are in the Bible three hundred and sixty five times, once for each day of the year!

Dr. John Snell, clinical instructor in psychiatry at Harvard Medical School says: "If people were honest about it, belief in hexing is common in the United States. People who believe strongly enough in a 'hex' can actually die." In fact, Dr. Snell adds: "Those who actually believe in some form of witchcraft are probably in the millions." [109]

VOODOO PRIESTS CONVERTED

Tim Freeman (not real name), a missionary to Haiti once told me of a pastor who had been a voodoo priest: "Francois is a Haitian pastor who lives in a little village possibly 100 miles from Port-au-Prince. It is a very primitive area in the mountains. He was a Voodoo priest for about nineteen years. He had a visitation from the Lord one night in his little mud hut. He was praying, seeking some of his spirits and he was not getting any response from them. The Lord showed up instead, and they had a conversation and Francois said: "You've got the wrong fellow." (This was similar to Paul meeting Jesus on the road to Damascus!)

He was very soundly converted at that time. Since that time, he's been a very powerful man of God. He's been filled with the Holy Ghost since last February. I prayed for him and he spoke with tongues for the first time. He'd never even heard anything about the Holy Ghost! He'd been ministering in this remote area for many years before we came to know him. Now, he's built nine churches there.

---

[109] "Voodoo, Zombies and Satan," Globe News, October 1981.

God has used him to do many supernatural signs and wonders in that area for many years. People had all kinds of curses and diseases operating against and in them. One of the most remarkable miracles involved a woman who had a curse put on her that gave her an elephantitis-type sickness. (Her legs were about three time's normal size. Fluid comes into the belly and arms. This is a common thing in Haiti). She came to his church one night. He told her about the Lord and there were a number of people there that night who had received salvation. That's what he'd been preaching... that's all he knew!

"The Lord instantly healed that woman! It was a profound miracle and a great number of conversions occurred from such miracles the Lord performed for him. He built those nine churches over a period of about two years! The people paid for these churches with their tithes and offerings. No outside help!"

He told me also: "There is an area about eighty-five miles northeast of Port- Au-Prince, way back up in the mountains, where natives have connections with Voodoo.
The native pastor, who oversees about 30 churches in that area, reported to me that this Voodoo practitioner is able to transport both himself and a donkey some twenty miles across the mountains! He transports himself, plus the donkey, to a place where he purchases supplies and food staples.
He can make this trip in about two or three minutes by the help of his demonic powers!"

GOVERNMENTAL INFLUENCES OF HAITIAN HISTORY

Haiti has been troubled by hostilities with the Dominican Republic (formerly Santo Domingo) as well as by domestic political instability, characterized by its presidents' disregard for the constitution and by frequent *coups d'état*. After Francois Duvalier ("Papa Doc") was elected president in 1957, he used a terrorist gang to subdue his opponents and had himself elected president for life. Subsequently, despite an economic decline, continued internal discord, and poor relations with the Dominican Republic, he ruled as a dictator until his death in 1971, when he was succeeded by his son.

"Papa Doc" was one of the most blood-thirsty tyrants the Caribbean had ever seen, and was trained as a physician, but was also an ardent practitioner of Voodoo. He customarily wore the black clothing and heavy eyeglasses of famous Voodoo spirit or *loa*, Baron Samedi, and Haitians say that he kept Voodoo captive spirit of President John F. Kennedy.

His son, Jean-Claude Duvalier, following in "Papa Doc's" footsteps, once released to the world press news that he had placed a curse on (then) President Jimmy Carter.[110]

AMERICAN PASTOR DEFEATS VOODOOISM

Pastor John Jones, an Assembly of God missionary in the Bahamas, also once shared with me some actual experience with Voodoo, dealing with curses: "They make up the dolls to look as much like the person as possible. Then they will put pins into the dolls because they feel that causes hurt and injury to the person they are after. They will put these pins into the areas they want to affect. To frighten the people, they then put these Voodoo dolls in their front of their houses. When the person finds them, it shocks

---

[110] http://www.biography.com/articles/Jean-Claude-Duvalier-9282686

them! The spirit of fear comes in and opens them to the voodoo powers to go into effect.

The voodooist also put explosives in the dolls because so many people, when they find the dolls, would burn them. They believe that when the dolls are burned it breaks the curse or the spell. When these dolls exploded, they cause great injury to people, even killing some.

VOODOO POWERS CAN BE DEFEATED

A young man came to my church. He was working on his Master's degree; his wife was practicing Voodooist. She made a voodoo doll to take him out of the church and draw him into her desired control. She was going to cast a spell on him through the doll that she had prepared when she left the Bahamas and came to the States.

This young man talked to me about the spiritual battle that he was experiencing because of his wife's witchcraft powers. I taught him how to speak the name of Jesus to stop the power of her voodooist. I told him that the Blood of Jesus Christ can break any kind of spell that demonic and satanic worshipers might try to put on him. His wife told him that she had ways of forcing him. However, he was totally set completely free from this evil force through prayer and his dedication to God, the Blood of Christ and the Name of Jesus.

People are very frightened of Voodoo power. On the other hand, many feel that there is really no power there. They believe that there is no strength there, no power in witchcraft or in Voodoo. Yet they'll turn around and say, "The devil has power." They don't realize that voodoo and witchcraft are channels for the devil to use.

THE LIVING DEAD

Zombies, the "living dead" to horror movie fans, are not fictional. They actually do exist! They are people totally controlled by a master or a witch doctor. They do whatever they are told: good or evil. They appear to be the "walking dead," having a blank stare, plastic faces filled with terror and slow, lumbering movements like a puppet. The idea of the Zombies, which was imported from Africa, is the Voodoo belief that a corpse can be re-animated by a spirit who can then be made to obey, mechanically, the wishes of the Voodoo priest.[111]

One Haitian refugee related: "Zombies are created by drugging weak-minded people until they appear dead. They seem to have no heartbeat or blood pressure and a sympathetic doctor will even officially pronounce them dead, and allow them to be buried! When the drug wears off, they are resurrected by the witch doctor, but kept drugged enough so that he or she can completely control them. They are greatly feared by the natives who have seen them."

The young people in *the Walking Dead* book were being drugged in the grave yard and powers were worked by the witches' that turned them into Zombies!

An evangelist friend claims that when a person dies on the Island of Haiti, the Voodooists meet at the grave site and exhume the body the first night. They then call on their demon spirits to enter the body. The dead body will dance under the power of demons. He told me also the Voodooist won't touch a grave that belongs to a Christian!

---

[111] Trevor Dearing, Supernatural Powers, (Plainfield, New Jersey: Logos International) pp. 112-113.

ENGLISH VICAR IS VICTORIOUS

Pastor, Trevor Dearing, Church of England, Vicar, writes: "We can even take command over voodooist in the Name of Jesus, as I did in the case of Maureena. She was a heavily built, West Indian woman who stood rooted to the spot, dazed with shock and terror. She had just discovered an emblem of a black cockerel on a red triangular piece of cotton material. It had been significantly placed on the white sill of the kitchen window in her London home. The terror of that chilling curse made her tremble with fear. She stared, utterly petrified, and fully certain she soon would be dead. She had to escape the spell, but how?"[112]

Dearing goes to tell of her terrors of the curse, "She raced from her home as one demented, seeking refuge among friends, in indescribable ways, quite unable to cope with her job a teacher of handicapped children and to care for herself and small daughter. Finally the Voodoo terrors began to grip her even tighter with no escape from the chilling curse and the frightening hallucinations became worse. Compulsions and fear often drove her to violence. Once she tried to kill her daughter while the child was asleep."[113]

Voodoo works by fear. A voodoo worker will always let the recipient know that a curse has been released. When the receiver sees the evidence from the curse, a spirit of fear will take control of the person because the fear will open them to have a reception to the curse. The Bible does show that fear works in the mind. It causes a person to not be sound in their thinking. It will open a doorway for the devil to enter and cause the curse to work. "For

---

[112] Pastor, Trevor Dearing, Church of England, Vicar, http://www.stpauls-hainault.org.uk/history.asp
[113] http://www.stpauls-hainault.org.uk/history.asp

God hath not given us the spirit of fear; but of power, and of love, and of a sound mind," (2 Tim 1:7).

Dearing continues to describe the voodoo curse, "I first met Maureena at St. Paul's when she came along for help. Five minutes after the service started, Maureena suddenly pitched senselessly to the floor. I immediately sensed a Voodoo curse and knew that there would have to be a fantastic scrap before she could be free. Voodoo is a system of magic worship practiced by West Indies Negroes and Creoles, and once a curse is put on someone it can mean the end of their sanity and even the individual's life.

"... I began to pray for Maureena. She spat at me, growled like an animal, bared her teeth and sprang toward me like a rabid jungle beast. Her hands reached for my throat in an attempt to tear me apart. Stewards came dashing forward and did what they could to restrain her, but it was the power of Jesus that held those hideous demonic forces at bay as I began to cast out the Voodoo spirit. For ten horrifying minutes the battle raged and eventually, as the sweat poured down her ebony face, the evil spirit left her and she was free. Glory be to Jesus![114]

Pastor Dearing makes note of the drastic change over Maurenna."The change that came over Maureena was almost unbelievable. She began to smile, beaming a real love for Jesus towards me and the praising congregation. She had been transformed by Jesus, the great deliverer, but strangely she remembered nothing of the deadly struggle that released her." [115]

---

[114] http://www.stpauls-hainault.org.uk/history.asp
[115] A. Zaldivar, The Miami Herald, 7/18/82, pp. 1B-2B.

VOODOO RISES IN AMERICA

The recent influx of refugees, particularly Haitians, fleeing hunger and poverty, is spreading the power of Voodooist in America. Many have remained in South Florida but others have relocated throughout the country. They bring with them their belief and practice in the power of Voodoo.

A friend of mine in ministry in the Miami are comments: "Mutilated animal bodies are found daily floating in the waterways and human skulls, burned candles and other Voodoo paraphernalia are discovered. Dead animals placed in plastic bags are found on the street curbs every morning from previous nights' sacrifices. This calls for a quick spiritual educational course, because it's beyond anything that we've ever seen before."

AMERICAN POLITICAL ACCEPTANCE

Maurice Ferre, Mayor of Miami, attended a ritual feast of the Santeria Religion in Little Havana. Santeria arrived in Miami with the influx of Cuban people. Santeria is regarded with revulsion by many who object to the sacrifice of animals in the rites. It's an intricate system of animal sacrifice involving the tossing of shells to predict fortunes, week-long "purifications" and Catholic Masses. In Cuba, two Catholic saints are particularly identified with Santeria worship. They are *St. Lazarus*, whose African counterpart is *Babl Aye*, a god of sickness and health: and St. Barbara, whose colors are red and white and who is identified with *Chango*, a god of thunder. As long as people believe in, worship or make sacrifices to these heathen gods, the demons attached to them will give them power to operate.[116]

Metro's Mayor Clark said in an interview that he attends 10 to 12 such parties each Dec. 16th, which is *St. Lazarus' Day*. "When you're in Rome, you do as the Romans do," Clark explained. "This is very close to people's hearts." Clark said he has not been to any feasts at which drums were played.

Ferre said his link to the Santeros is through Emelina Frometa, a long-time political supporter and campaign worker. "Emelina is very important in the Santeria community. Evidently, these Santeros take sides in politics," he observed. Early this year Frometa prevailed upon him to attend the feast. Ferre related how he went on the condition that no animals were to be sacrificed. "If I hadn't gone, those people would have been very angry at me. I went out of courtesy. I'm not a believer. I'm not a practitioner." Ferre was a disbelieving participant, attending for the sake of votes. However, going to these pagan rites, will give the demons power to work against you physically, mentally and spiritually.

Ferre correctly discerns that these voodoo practices are more than a party. However, he does not know what the practices are supposed to accomplish. "There's no way you can convince me it was just a party." As a politician, these rites were being done so that the demons could control him and his decisions while in office! The Bible says, "Ye cannot drink the cup of the Lord, and the cup of devils: ye cannot be partakers of the Lord's table, and of the table of devils," (1 Cor. 10:21).

Ferre goes on to say, "There were drums. People were dressed in red and white, dancing in a circle. During the feast, a man who appeared to be some sort of priest entered the room.

---

[116] ibid

Some of the celebrants embraced him. Others," Ferre said, "prostrated themselves to (worship) greet him."

Ferre makes note that many very influential people were involved with this pagan rite. "I'm frankly amazed at the number of people who are influenced by Santeria, A lot of very prominent doctors, lawyers and businessmen are taken in by it. A lot of people in the political world are very much into it." Religion is a spiritual thing, not an intellectual one. The fact that so many professional, business people and politicians were involved does not sanction voodooist as being good.[117]

Former City Commissioner Armando Lacasa also has a story to recount. The difference in his case is that he had a brush not with Santeria, but with *Brujeria* - or, witchcraft. *Brujeria* is an entirely different practice, of an entirely different sect.[118]

Lacasa reported. "During the campaign, they threw dead animals in front of my headquarters," This meant that the voodooists were working demonic powers against his election. Lacasa said. "On one occasion, he found a dead cat, its legs tied together, at the headquarters door. I didn't give it any importance." This is exactly what the voodooist wants to happen. If a person does not give credence to their released powers, the powers will work. Lacase, it will be remembered, lost the election.[119]

---

[117] ibid
[118] A. Zaldivar, The Miami Herald, 7/18/82, pp. 1B-2B.
[119] ibid

PRESIDENT BILL CLINTON'S AFFAIR WITH VOODOO

Toronto-- When it comes to dabbling in the black arts, former U.S. President Bill Clinton has much in common with deposed Iraqi leader Saddam Hussein.[120]

Saddam reportedly wore a stone around his neck to ward off evil. When he was ensconced in his Iraqi palaces, he summoned up the jinn (genies) to do his bidding.

According to historian Joel A. Ruth, a Voodoo sorcerer, supplied to Clinton by the exiled-by-coup John-Bertrand Aristide, once put a curse on incumbent President George W. Bush, "by manipulating a doll made in the president's image."

Neither Saddam's magic stone, a special talisman meant to keep the Grim Reaper at bay, nor the Voodoo sorcerer's curse against George W. worked. Saddam languishes in prison awaiting trial. Clinton, relegated to the public speaker's tour, was last week paid a $300,000 fee to address a business audience in Bogotá, Colombia.

The long road of destruction Aristide carved through poverty-stricken Haiti was paved in part by one William Jefferson Clinton.

Clinton's friendship with Aristide, a former Catholic priest turned Voodoo practitioner dates back to 1991 when Aristide, ousted in a coup, took up residence in Washington, D.C. joining the cocktail circuit and networking for the political aid needed to help restore his power, he soon found his way within the inner circle of the soon-to-be Democratic presidential hopeful Bill Clinton.

---

[120] http://www.canadafreepress.com/2005/cover062805.htm *by Judi McLeod*, Canada Free Press. Tuesday, June 28, 2005

222

As time would tell, Clinton paid more than a politician's lip service to the practice of Voodoo.

According to the *Haiti Observateur*, "During a March 31, 1995 visit to Haiti under Aristide's restored rule, Clinton took part in a Voodoo initiative ceremony intended to keep him impervious to Republican attacks and to guarantee his re-election."[121]

"Voodoo," Aristide professed in a speech to Congress attendees, "is one of the great religions in the world alongside Christianity, Islam and Judaism".[122]

PAGAN WORSHIP

The Word clearly shows that pagan worship was prevalent in the Old Testament. "And he put down the idolatrous priests, whom the kings of Judah had ordained to burn incense in the high places in the cities of Judah, and in the places round about Jerusalem; them also that burned incense unto Baal, to the sun, and to the moon and to the planets and to all the host of heaven," (2 Ki. 23:5).

Today, the major problem in America is that people do not recognize witchcraft, even when they see it! Actually, many Christians are ending up serving the ancient demons gods that are revealed in the Old Testament. Many do not even believe that Satan is real! In order to be successful against the witchcraft, the Bible does teach that Christians have a spiritual warfare.

Many Christians have departed from the biblical way of serving God and have devised their own attitudes concerning the Devil and how to defeat him. The only way these demonic powers can be canceled is if a stronger power comes to destroy or override the demonic power. The only stronger power is Jesus. You must

---

[121] (*FrontPageMag.com*, Feb. 20,. 2004).
[122] ibid

overcome by binding these voodoo powers in the name of Jesus. You must be a born again Christian to be able to use the name of Jesus in this manner.

The Word says that fasting breaks the yoke, prayer overcomes the powers of darkness and resisting the Devil makes him flee! "Submit yourselves therefore to God. Resist the devil, and he will flee from you. Draw nigh to God, and he will draw nigh to you. Cleanse your hands, ye sinners; and purify your hearts, ye double minded," (Jam. 4:7-8).

Politicians in Boston make the rounds of Irish wakes. In Chicago, they drop in on Polish weddings. In Miami's fractured ethnic politics, office-seekers like Ferre and Metro Mayor Steve Clark have not neglected the Santeros, followers of an African religious practice under a veneer of Catholicism and brought here from Cuba. "It's a major constituency," Ferre said in a recent interview . . . "I can't ignore it." [28]

We see that politicians seeking votes close their eyes to the horror of Satan's kingdom. Since the great influx of the Haitian refugees into Miami, the Voodooists may well be on their way to social status or political power by unscrupulous politicians.

VOODOOISM POWERS OF DARKNESS

Reports of grisly slaughters . . . rituals of witches and Satanists, are growing more and more frequent. After the thrill of sacrificing cattle, dogs and cats wanes; bloodthirsty seekers are driven into darker realms of human sacrifice.

Again, Voodoo, with its strange powers to inflict illness and death is becoming widespread. Zombies and witch doctors do exist! One can go to any major city in the United States, to big towns and small ones take part in serious Voodoo ceremonies, along with businessmen, housewives, doctors, engineers and typists! Many are seeking powers that Voodoo can confer.

Americans are dealing with evil that surpasses anything we've ever known before. And only a great spiritual awakening from Christ can open the eyes of the spiritually blind and weak to set Satan's captives free. Christ purchased mankind's right to freedom with His own Blood. He is Justification for all who believer's charge thereby giving him total peace with God.

Witchcraft has all the resources of Satan behind it, but we have all the resources of heaven at our disposal with the power of God behind, around us, and within us. We have the whole armor of God, loins girt about with truth, the breastplate of righteousness, feet shod with the preparation of the gospel of peace, the shield of faith, the helmet of salvation, and the sword of the Spirit, which is the Word of God.

Let us, therefore, pray with great supplication in the Spirit and fight against the principalities, powers and rulers of the darkness of this world and against the spiritual wickedness in high places.

Chapter Fourteen
Denying Power of Casting out Devils

Now the works of the flesh are manifest, which are these; Adultery, fornication, uncleanness, lasciviousness, 20 Idolatry, witchcraft, hatred, variance, emulations, wrath, strife, seditions, heresies, 21 Envyings, murders, drunkenness, revellings, and such like: of the which I tell you before, as I have also told you in time past, that they which do such things shall not inherit the kingdom of God," (Gal. 5:19-21).

CHRISTIAN MINISTRY

A very important gift in the Christian Church is the ability to discern and cast out evil spirits when they are operating within the Church. We are not supposed to cast out the people, only the evil spirits!

The American church must seek God for the gift of discerning of spirits both, good and bad. It is vital to the church because The Word of God says, "For many have crept in unawares," (Jude 4). Jesus told us that "You shall know the truth and the truth shall make you free," (Jn.. 8:37). Then He explained, "If therefore the Son shall make you free, you shall be free indeed," (Jn. 8:36).

The essence of the Christian ministry is personal service. The earliest ministry of the church was that of the Apostles. As the meaning of the word "apostle" indicates, they were men "sent out" The Bible never told us to cease their beginnings." Jesus was a devil-driving Minister. Jesus set the people free and we must do the same. Casting out demons is a very specialized ministry which, when properly understood, involves unusual qualities of faith, prayer and fasting (Matt. 17:19-20). If we do our part, God will perform His Word.[123]

A prophecy is an incentive to holy living and service to God. We read in (1 Jn. 3:2-3), "Beloved, now are we the sons of God, and it doth not yet appear what we shall be: but we know that, when He shall appear, we shall be like Him; for we shall see Him as He is. And every man that hath this hope [of Christ's coming] in him purifieth himself, even as He is pure." The blessed hope for every believer is a call to godliness and holy living.

SIGNS AND WONDERS

The Lord said signs and wonders should follow them that believe. He gave an example of these signs when He said in (Mk. 16:17), "They shall cast out devils." What happens when you deny the Word? It is most important that we have, in the Body of Christ, the power to discern evil spirits. The Word of God says, "For we wrestle not against flesh and blood, but against principalities, against powers, against the rulers of darkness of this world, against spiritual wickedness . . ." (Eph. 6:12).

Behind problems of the world and every evil which manifest is a hierarchy of evil spirits that are motivated by Satan and his demonic servants. The Apostle Paul teaches about an organized kingdom of principalities and powers that control hierarchy of evil spirits. They rule at various levels of authority, as rulers of this present darkness. These are spirits in high places. Unfortunately Christians are not totally immune to the influences of these powers. Victory comes through Jesus Christ, "Submit yourselves

---

[123] H. A. Maxwell Whyte, Dominion Over Demons (Banner Publishing), p. 175.

therefore to God. Resist the devil, and he will flee from you,"
(Jam. 4:7).

DEMONS AND EVIL SPIRITS

The rise of witchcraft and Satanism can be closely associated
with the outpouring of demons upon the earth. Also it can be
placed at the feet of the multitude of humans who have strayed
away from God. Many in the Church of Jesus Christ have been
blinded to the reality that there is a spiritual warfare between good
and evil. The Body of Christ has not responded to the Lord's
instructions concerning *"casting out devils."*

Clearly the Word of God states that in the last days before
the return of the Lord Jesus Christ sorcery, spiritualism and various
lying wonders of demonism shall prevail. (1 Thess. 2:9-10) says,
"Even him, whose coming is after the working of Satan with all
power and signs and lying wonders, And with all deceivableness of
unrighteousness in them that perish; because they received not the
love of the truth, that they might be saved." While this will come
to its true climax in the [Great] Tribulation nevertheless, such
manifestations of Satan's working will be prevalent in the last
days. This is what we find today. The Devil works as an angel of
light in resenting his powers and signs and lying wonders.
Magazines and books are already in the increase dealing with
psychology, theosophy, fortune telling and foretelling, and all such
crooked thinking results in unrighteous living.

The main idea behind the angels is that they were here to
serve or destroy humans. The holy angels are the messengers of
their Creator, while the fallen angels are the messengers of Satan
who is "the god of this world," (2 Cor. 4:4). (Hebr. 1:14) tells us
of the good angels who minister to man's well-being, while (Eph.

6:12), shows that the evil spirits who war against that in man which is wrought of God.

The Bible clearly exposits or shows or states] that angels dwell in the heavenly spheres. They appear in numbers beyond our count. These powers are gathered in groups which are identified as "thrones," "dominions," "principalities," "powers," "authorities," and "heavenly host" (Col. 1:16; 1 Pet. 3: 22; Lk. 2: 13). Yet, the Bible unmasks the truth that all these authorities are wholly subject to the Lord Jesus Christ. He created the universe and all it contains, including the angelic beings. He created "things . . . visible and invisible," (Col. 1: 16). Peter says that "these beings are subject to Christ," (1 Pet. 3:22). (Jude verse 6) discloses the fact that angels have their own dwelling places. They had an estate given to them.

This host of Satan in the Bible is called 'devils' but the word also means *'demons'*. Demon possession means that the demons enter the body and exercise control over it. Demon influence is set forth as warfare from without (Eph. 6) which is carried on by temptation and influence.

INVISIBLE BUT PERCEPTIBLE

These demons of Satan are bodiless spirits. (Notice Mk. 5:12), "And all the devils (demons) besought Him, saying, Send us into the swine, that we may enter into them." (Read also Matt. 12:43-45). "As they went out, behold, they brought to Him a dumb man possessed with a devil. And when the devil (demon) was cast out, the dumb spake . . ." (Matt. 9:32, 33. Read also Acts 8:6-7; 16: 16; Mk. 5: 1-13).

The Bible also instructs that these demons are wicked and unclean. Let us read (Matt. 8:28), "And when He was come to the other side into the country of the Gergesenes, there met Him two possessed with devils, coming out of the tombs, exceeding fierce, so that no man might pass by that way." (Mk. 9:20), "And they brought him unto Him: and when he saw Him, straightway the spirit tare him; and he fell on the ground, and wallowed foaming." (Read also Matt. 10:1; Mk. 5:2-5).

Jesus taught that these spirits have various spiritual degrees of wickedness. In (Matt. 12:43-45), He says that the demon will return to his house, ". . . taketh with himself seven other spirits more wicked than himself." Now the question comes before us, "Is demon possession possible in our age?" Many missionaries in so-called pagan countries will answer to this question in the affirmative. American ministers are beginning to acknowledge the factuality of demon possessions.

The Word of God confirms that demons can appear as "angels of light" the same as Satan. Christians must have God's Holy Spirit to give us discernment. (2 Cor. 11:14-15), "And no marvel; for Satan himself is transformed into an angel of light. Therefore it is no great thing if his ministers also be transformed as the ministers of righteousness; whose end shall be according to their works."

The target of Satan and his demons is to hinder God's purpose for this age. Satan's intention is to extend his authority to his own kingdom on the earth. His demons are instructed to carry on a definite warfare against all believers according to Ephesians 6.

One technique of the demons is to present a form of godliness but to deny the power thereof. And the multitudes that are withdrawing from the biblically based faith in God, is the best evidence that we have today of the influence of demons. The Bible describes this departure in the following Scriptures. "Now the Spirit speaketh expressly, that in the latter times some shall depart from the faith, giving heed to seducing spirits, and doctrines of devils; Speaking lies in hypocrisy; having their conscience seared with a hot iron," (1 Tim. 4: 1,2). These seducing spirits promote the doctrines of demons. These evil spirits are active in seeking to turn men and women away from the faith. They are in rebellion against God and seek to hinder God and His truth.

DISPOSITION OF THE ENEMY

The ultimate destination of demon spirits is destruction (Great White Throne), (Rev. 21:11-15; Matt. 15:41).

We have, in conflict with the enemy called in angels to wreak havoc on the enemy with their swords, (Psa. 18:37-42). Transference speaks of pursuit of the enemy until he is consumed or destroyed. The root word used in Hebrew (Strong's #3615) means to utterly destroy, consume away, make a clean riddance and quite take away. At the end of the verses it is stated, "beat them fine as dust before the wind; I emptied (cast — KJV) them out as the mire of the streets,). These passages seem to indicate that they can be crushed into virtual nonexistence until the final judgment of God.

In verse 41, "They cried for help, but these were none to save, even to the Lord, but He did not answer them." Perhaps this indicates they can no longer complain to God that they have a legal right to be where they are. Verse 40 states, "That I might destroy them that hate me." Again the word for destroys (Strong's #6789) means to consume, cut off, destroy, vanish.

When the children of Israel were sent into the land they were commanded to "devote" certain things to Him, literally to destroy them (Deut. 13:15, 17; Num. 18:14) and in Deut., God says that if idolatry is proven in another town, its inhabitants must be put to

231

the sword. Since the worship of idols is nothing more than the worship of demons, the order to *"destroy it* (the town) *completely"* (KJV) has a reference to spiritual forces as well. The Hebrew word her (Strong's number 2754) means to make accursed, utterly destroy, etc. (Deut. 13:17), there is a stern warning against holding onto these "devoted" things (Num. 18:14).

Perhaps using the Hebrew word *"Charam"* on the demons could be effective because it means to hand over to the Lord often by utter destruction. See Strong's 3089 translated destroy or "dissolve."

Deliverance workers experiences have, in recent years, have indicated that we can have wide latitude of what to do with the foe once he is vanquished and broken, demons fear the abyss, which is described as full of screaming, tormented beings who all and fall with no help possible, filled with horrible loneliness. The pit and Tartarus are also destinations which fill the enemy with fear and dread. Our advice to workers to just listen to what the Lord says and do this to the enemy.[2]

(Jon. 2:1-6). "Then Jonah prayed unto the LORD his God out of the fish's belly, And said, I cried by reason of mine affliction unto the LORD, and he heard me; out of the belly of hell cried I, and thou heardest my voice. For thou hadst cast me into the deep, in the midst of the seas; and the floods compassed me about: all thy billows and thy waves passed over me. Then I said, I am cast out of thy sight; yet I will look again toward thy holy temple. The waters compassed me about, even to the soul: the depth closed me round about, the weeds were wrapped about my head. I went down to the bottoms of the mountains; the earth with her bars was about me forever: yet hast thou brought up my life from corruption, O LORD my God."

The Bible says that there was a day when the sons of God came before the Lord and Satan came with them. In the discussion that followed between the Lord and Satan, the Lord said, "Have you considered My servant Job? For there is no one like him on the earth, a blameless and upright man? Satan then accursed the Lord of putting a hedge about Job and all that he owned. But put forth thy hand now and touch all that he has; he will surely curse thee to thy face."

The Lord answered, "Behold, all that he has is in your power, only do not put forth your hand on him," (Job 1:12).

Job testimony reveals how a supernatural being works. He never comes out on front stage and says, "Here I am, folks; watch me do my act." He always works in accordance with natural laws or through individuals:

First, Sabeans attacked and took Job's animals, (vs. 15).

Second, fire burned up the sheep and the servants (vs. 16).

Third, Chaldeans raided the camels and killed the servants, (vs. 17).

Fourth, a great wind blew the house down, (vs. 19).

Fifth, boils covered Job's body (vs. 2:7).

While some may attribute these incidents to mere natural phenomena, it is plain that all of these "physical" and "natural" disturbances were done by a supernatural being) Satan.

(Rev. 9:1-3), "And the fifth angel sounded, and I saw a star fall from heaven unto the earth: and to him was given the key of the bottomless pit. And he opened the bottomless pit; and there arose a smoke out of the pit, as the smoke of a great furnace; and the sun and the air were darkened by reason of the smoke of the pit. And there came out of the smoke locusts upon the earth: and unto them was given power, as the scorpions of the earth have power." In the fifth trumpet God loosens demon scorpion horses to string men for six months; these horses come up out of the bottomless pit under the sea", Rev. 9:1-11.

Chapter Fifteen
Signs and Emblems

All signs of the Zodiac - Emblems, symbols, images, all used in the satanic or the occult worship of the gods and goddesses that seek after the lust of Ishtar. Conjuring the spirits of fertility to produce every type of immoral lust after and for the gods of procreation is done through these emblems. The practitioners of the Zodiac are acknowledging their god as Baal, or Lucifer.

The Hexagram - this emblem is one of the most potent of symbols used in the work of the powers of darkness. It produces influences in the rituals for the sacrifices for power, "which is a blood sacrifice." It is the symbol used in the work of magic; this emblem is used in the conjuring of forces, "or entities" that hypnotize or seduce. Evil spirits gather in force at the summons of the person working the hex.

Double Crest - This symbol of a tiny, solid 5-pointed star in the center of a larger 5-pointed star of just lines (single point up), worn and used by the practitioners of the occult, witches, wizards, druids, magicians, astrologers. It is used to summon or conjure the powers of darkness. This crest is used to work divination. The spirits produce every type of influence, powers to manipulate the minds, giving the follower of Satan the power to work every conceivable evil (spells, hexes, curses, insatiable desires).

The Pentagram - This symbol, a five-pointed star of lines, (can also be used with a circle around it, drawn on the floor with the conjurer in the center) is used by fortune tellers, astrologers, psychics, witches, wizards, magicians, and people working divination or conjuring. The pentagram, with a badge around it, is the Insignia for the Masonic Orders Hierarchy.

The Horned Star - Satanists around the world use this emblem to identify themselves as worshipers of the powers of Satan, and the Luciferian Doctrine; this pentagram, upside-down, represents the horns and beard of the goat head, or Satan's head. The emblem is a hex and represents the number of the night of Satan.

Crescent - Symbol used by the worshipers of the Goddess Diana, known as the Queen of heaven and the mother of prostitution, the mother of sexual orgies, and the goddess of fertility. This line-drawn crescent moon (sitting) has a solid 5-pointed small star in the space between the two points. It is typically on the fortune-tellers' booth or turban and used by worshipers of the unknown world: astrologers, psychics, gazers of the crystal ball, spiritualists, fortune tellers and Hindus (Brahma).

Symbols of Hierarchy in the Secret Orders - Symbols worn by the grand Wizards, dragons, Shriners, Egypt Templers, other given honorary degrees by the SECRET ORDER OF THE MASONS OR THE ILLUMINATI.

These symbols declare the wearer as a believer in the Luciferian Doctrine and recognize the **'Ra' as god**. "Reincarnation is the belief of the one who worships **'Ra', the sun god**. The followers of the gods of Mesopotamia, Babylon and Assyria are all worshipers of Baal, the god of every conceivable type of orgy, the creator of insatiable, driving desires. Demonic control and working of curses is given to those that are sold out to the order. "There are measures taken by the satanic world against those that oppose." These emblems are the "earmark "of Satan and HIS ELECT.

(The emblem is a solid black star, single point up, encircled by a crescent moon with the 2 end tips of the moon coming down

236

around the sides to touch the 2 bottom points of the star. At the top point, inside the "moon" is a pharaoh-type face. Behind the top half of the crescent moon is a curved Islamic saber: handle on left, broad tip on the right.

Leprechaun Staff or the **'Italian Horn'** - Often worn as a charm on a neck chain, this "wriggly carrot" is an emblem known in the occult as the Elf or Fairies' wand, introduced by the Lord Druids of Scotland and Ireland, this was used by them as an instrument of pain and torture for castrating humans or animals. It has been hexed and is used for luck and fortune. Satanist Priests wear this emblem for prosperity as a charm about their neck.

Evil Eye of the Pyramid - The pyramid of the eye is the mystic worship of a select order of Liberalists that have built a religion on the mysteries of the Scriptures and who believe they are in control of the "eye of Lucifer" and that they are the "chosen" (of Satan to control the finances of the world). This symbol is one of the most potent in the power of divination. (It can also represent the "third eye" or psychic eye of the gypsies and other divinators). Hexes, curses, psychic control and every corruption conceivable are worked through this emblem. This mark is on the currency of the United States, and declares to the world the eye of Lucifer is over the world's finances. "Behind this is the 'Sun God, Ra'." He gives the wisdom to the financial wizards that control the commercial and financial systems.

Ankh - (alone) - An emblem to identify the wearer as a worshiper of the sun god **'Ra'**, a seeker of the Satanic beliefs, and one who practices the worship to the unknown gods of the supernatural. The wearer acknowledges the sun god Ra, works the voodoo of the unseen world through this hex.

Ankh and Star - This symbol, a fat cross with the top extension being a large oval loop, with a very tiny, solid 5-pointed star just above the left arm of it... is used in the worship of the sun god, Ra, who will give to the wearer the power to produce the insatiable desires of orgies to the worshipers. "The inward (mind) and outward (physical) practice of sex in every form and every type of immorality is a worship to Satan. Practitioners of witchcraft that devise sexual abuse wear this emblem.

Ojo Dios - (God's Eye)-

Created by the American Indians, this emblem or symbol of worship to the heavenly deities: sun, moon, stars, lightning, thunder and the creation of the earth and the things upon it: trees, animals, man, seas, rivers and every creeping thing; also, to the fowls of the air and the fish... looks like a cross of sticks making a "plus sign" then connecting the 4 ends with yarn or cord to form a square, then again, forming a smaller square inside the large border, and symmetrical squares equal distance apart toward the center. There may be little fringe tassels at the four points. Kids bring them home from school as a craft project! With the work of the forces of the spirit world, the worshiper of the deities calls (chants) to the supernatural, and the spirits bring into being the thing or whatever the chanter was seeking from the unknown world... or it will do the reverse, (remove that thing from the natural world).

DEATH SALUTE - Tongue extended (Maori warriors use this, as well as Satanists).

DEVIL'S TRIAD - A salute to the devil made by extending the first three fingers.

IL CORNUTO - A Satanist salute made by the upraised fist with the pinky and index finger extended. (Not to be confused with the Hawaiian hand greeting used to say goodbye or hello, the pinky and the thumb extended.

MYTHOLOGY IS SATANIC

Mythology is idolatrous and satanic. Christians must avoid these fantasy articles. These images can bring powerful spirits into homes. Many Christians believe that these images or statues are just art pieces that they use for decoration. Ignorance is not bliss. Whenever a Christians disobeys the Word of God, they become subject to demonic spiritual attack. These satanic articles are doorways for Satan and his demons to captivate and enslave the minds of people that open the door by accepting these images into their homes.

(Deut. 7:25, 26), gives a clear warning regarding graven images of these creatures. These images includes drawings, imprints, diagrams, engravings, carvings, figurines, paintings, computer print-outs, photographs, trinkets, artwork, jewelry and or any other representation of mythological creatures.

(Deut. 7:25-26), "The graven images of their gods shall ye burn with fire: thou shalt not desire the silver or gold that is on them, nor take it unto thee, lest thou be snared therein: for it is an abomination to the LORD thy God." 26 "Neither shalt thou bring an abomination into thine house, lest thou be a cursed thing like it: but thou shalt utterly detest it, and thou shalt utterly abhor it; for it is a cursed thing."

In verse 25, the Word of God clearly instructs His people to destroy all things related to these fantasy items by burning them with fire. Furthermore, it tells us not to desire any silver or gold that is on them. God commands that the believer is not to desire, or take for personal reasons, or to give to any other individual under any circumstances. In this respect, God was very strict and commanded that there should not be even any "desire" for the item or any part of it. There should also be no emotional attachment to

239

the objects. This includes articles that are inherited from family members, and friends. Of course, these articles also can include objects that are inherited from family members in the Masons, cult religions such as Bibles, religious articles and statutes from the Catholic faith such as, Jesus, Mary, Joseph, and saints.

If a person has a problem destroying the abominable thing, then an ungodly soul tie (demon) with it may be present. The Bible is very specific and commands that there should not be even any "desire" for the item or any part of it. A soul tie can be a linking spirit to the person that gave the article to the believer. It could be a person that is alive or a person that is dead. In any case, the ungodly soul ties with it may be broken after the person repents. Demons are usually shielded by these soul ties and consequently, they should be cast out. These images may cause many problems in a person's life and also anyone that lives in the home. They can cause illnesses of all kinds, nightmares, headaches, physical and spiritual torments and even death.

There is severe danger in being associated in any manner with demonic figures. Look at verse 25. It warns that the mythological creatures are abominations to God. These objects are worshiped by idolatrous people and God will not live alongside them.

The Bible emphatically tells us not to bring these images into our home lest we become accursed like the accursed thing. In other words, the item is already cursed. If we take possession of it, we will bring the curse upon ourselves. We become accursed! Additionally, instead of being amused, intrigued, or charmed by the images, we should utterly detest and hate it.

Unfortunately, millions of Christians are attracted to various demonic creatures of mythology, especially the unicorn. They purchase these items or accept them as gifts thereby bringing a curse upon them and their house (family and possessions). Accordingly, they endanger themselves and others by sharing the doom of the mythological item which is already cursed. As a result, the curse upon the demonic thing automatically comes upon the person and the home.

Christians should unquestionably have no relationship with fantasy figures. Fantasy conditions the mind to ultimately receive the "depths of Satan," (Rev. 2:20-24). It also prepares a pathway into practicing witchcraft.

BIBLICAL PROOF

Moses destroyed the molten calf in such a fashion that the people could not gain access to the gold in it. He burned the idol with fire, melted it, and then ground it into a power. Then he scattered it over the surface of the water and made the people drink it (Ex 32:4, 20). The making and worship of the graven image was a grievous national sin and the people were severely punished for the idolatry involved.

Another Biblical testimony concerns Achan. His entire family and all of his possessions were destroyed because he took "the accursed thing" from Jericho when God demolished the city Joshua. The bodies of the entire family were burned with fire. Notice that the children suffered the death penalty because of the sin of their father. The sin immediately brought an ancestral curse of death upon the children. A curse and reproach were also brought upon the entire nation of Israel. The lost the battle with AI and 36 mighty men of war died. Achan, the father, had been warned along with other Israelites not to take certain items from the city after "the wall fell down flat." This directive by God was very similar to the one in (Deut. 7:25, 26), in which the people were waned not to

241

possess or even desire graven images of heathen gods. The Lord is extremely serious about the relationship of His people with all objects that may be used in any form of idolatry including fantasy, mythological figures such as the unicorn, Pegasus, griffin, mermaids, and many others.

The ministry of Paul at Ephesus, preaching the living God, many peopled were convicted by the Holy Spirit and confessed their sins. They were immediately aware of their sins of practicing magical arts, magic and forms of sorcery. Many collected their books on witchcraft and burned them in the presence of all, (Acts 19:18, 19). It is reasonable to assume that part of the ungodly acts included the use of mythological objects and fantasy figures.

Witchcraft is based solely upon deception, fantasy figures are unreal and are concoctions of human imagination that are inspired and engineered by evil spirits therefore, and they are abomination of God.

UNICORN

Unicorn is defined as "one-horned." It is a mythological animal resembling a horse with a single horn in its forehead as described in ancient Greek and Roman mythologies. It is a symbol of power and is connected with false gods. The unicorn is also associated with the new-age movement in a manner similar to the rainbow. Consisting purely of fantasy, it is demonic and should be avoided. Furthermore, it is a heathen image and should be destroyed.

The unicorn that is shown in our society does not have the hideous appearance described in mythology. There it was said to look much like a horse except that its forehead had a single straight horn with spiral twist. The horn was red at the tip, black in the

242

middle and white at the base. This fantasy animal had a red head and blue eyes. Even though the front half of the body was horse-like, the rear half was a weird demonic mixture. Its hind legs were like an antelope's and its tail was like a lion's. Artists in the middle ages placed a unicorn beside figures of Christ, the Virgin Mary, and Virgin saints as a sign of purity.

COMBATING WITCHCRAFT

The Profession of Faith: All witches will make a profession of faith and say that they are born again. This will obviously be a lie. But one thing they cannot come to say is **"Jesus Christ Son of God who came in the flesh,** died on the cross and three days later arose from the grave and now sits at the right side of the Master."

They can say, "Jesus saves me," but which Jesus do they talk about. You can also ask them if Jesus Christ is Lord to the glory of God and did he come in the flesh as their Savior. They can still say yes and lie, but they cannot verbally make this declaration with their own mouths. Remember, God gave us a test the spirits to see if they are His. So let's use God's Word.

BUILD CREDIBILITY

Witches will build credibility within the churches by volunteering for everything. They will be looked upon as leaders and members who are truly doing the work of the Lord. And they are flawless tithers. This money comes from the Illuminati.

DESTROY THE PRAYER BASE

The single most important weapon that a Christian can use to fight against Satan . . . is prayer, and a witch who has infiltrated the ranks will try to destroy this as soon as possible.

RUMORS

Once the prayer base is destroyed, they will begin rumors. Very few people are strong enough to say, I just don't want to hear it.

TEACH AND CHANGE DOCTRINE

Once the witches have attained teaching positions, they will twist and distort the meanings behind the Holy Scriptures; and while they are doing this, they will recruit as many people as they can into the occult.

BREAK UP FAMILY UNITS:

Witches will do this by constantly having activities that only certain members of the family can attend. They develop programs that only the women of church can attend, or a program that only toddlers can attend. If this is presently going on in your church, it doesn't absolutely mean that witches are there, but if there are no programs that have been developed for the entire family or nothing taught to strengthen the family unit, and then you must take a good look at what's going on around you.

STOP ALL ACCURATE TEACHING ABOUT SATAN:

As long as no accurate teaching about Satan *is* being taught, then he can do his dirty work unhindered. Excuses such as, "We're only giving Satan the glory if we talk about him," or that "It takes your mind off the Lord," or that "might tempt you to Satan" are all Lies. It was God who revealed to us the workings of Satan and wants us to study these things so that we can know how to deal with our adversary, our enemy.

DIRECT ATTACKS AGAINST CHURCH MEMBERS

This is another reason why prayer is so important in the church. Pastors, church leaders and church members, who are really doing the Lord's Work and fighting Satan, are constant under constant attack by witchcraft. If they do not live very close to the Lord, they can and will be afflicted with all sorts of attacks. Many are overcome by physical illnesses, difficulty in concentration, fatigue, and even difficulty in praying.

You must continuously pray to God for protection of these people and for one another.

BINDING RETALIATING SPIRITS

This is what spiritual warfare is about. Jesus must be the center of a person's life. One must know Him from the power of the Word of God, because of His triumph, His people can win their war. The Scripture reveals Him in 'power and authority,' "And what is the exceeding greatness of his power to usward who believe, according to the working of his mighty power, which he wrought in Christ when he raised him from the dead and seet him at His own right hand in the heavenly places," (Eph. 1:10). How wonderful! Nevertheless, look at this. "And hath raised us up together, and made us sit together in heavenly places in Christ Jesus," (Eph. 2:6).

Many of these materialistic false ministers don't like anyone to scripturally to discern and uncover their unscriptural teachings in their ministries. They release curses on those who take time to discern and expose them. They use the scripture, in Isaiah 54:17, "No weapon formed against thee shall prosper; and every tongue that shall rise against thee in judgment, thou shalt condemn This is the heritage of the servants of the Lord and their righteousness is of me."

Well, Jesus talked about the false prophets of His day and there were many. The Apostle Paul pointed false prophets out and called them by name.

Therefore, I hereby bind all the curses that are pronounced upon those Christians who are watchmen on the walls that are placed to warn the sheep that the wolves have come into the flock. Every spoken word against myself and all those, who take the time to see, expose and alert the Body of Christ of the danger of the false teachers are hereby canceled in the name of Jesus. I release the blessings of financial success over every true minister in the Body of Christ in the Name of Jesus.

Praise Your Holy Name Dear Jesus.

Jesus said in (Matt. 12:23-33). Satan is not going to allow anyone to destroy his work without putting up very strong counteraction. His control must first be neutralized before Christians can release his captives.

Jesus asks this penetrating question, "How can anyone enter a strongman's house and carry off his possession unless he first ties up the strongman?" Then Jesus told us that we could enter his house. (Matt. 12:29). The King James Bibles reads, "bind the strongman." Indeed, binding the strong man is the first basic PRINCIPLE of spiritual warfare. In fact, before any warfare opposing powers and principalities and wicked rulers and evil spirits can be won to release the nation, cities, individual, family, the strongman must be defeated, (Matt. 18: 18. 19. 20).

Once Satan's power is bound, Jesus enters freely enters into his house and carries off Satan's possessions. The territory is delivered and Satan loses control.

The Apostle Paul warned, "But I fear lest by any means, as the serpent beguiled Eve through his subtlety, so your minds should be corrupted from the simplicity that is in Christ. For it he that cometh preacheth another Jesus, whom, we have not preached, or if ye receive another spirit, which ye have not accepted, ye might well bear with him." (2 Cor. 11: 3-4).

Do you know what happens to Christians that are having demonic problems? They are falling through the cracks of the church and are being sent to psychologist or psychiatrists. Many ministers believe these people are cursed because they are poor and no one takes time to minister to them. They are being drugged and some even sent to the mental wards. Have mercy Lord Jesus.

Many children of God and sick in bodies, sick in minds, can't seem to serve God, can't read the Word of God, can't go to church, can't pay tithes, gripe about the preacher, their spouse or the people in the church. Meanwhile Christian people delight themselves in riches, swing and dance, sing and eat but many are luke- warm in their commitment to Jesus!

"Now the Spirit speaketh expressly, that in the latter times some shall depart from the faith, giving heed to seducing spirits, and doctrines of devils," (1 Tim. 4:1).

God bless you.

Under these names are countless unclean spirits and each one of them is under the strict control of a commander.

Appendix One

ENTRY POINTS FOR DEMONIZATION

If occult involvement invites demonic invasions, or at least makes it far more likely, it makes great sense to avoid, as one would avoid the plague, such involvement. What sort of activities should be voided? Or put it another way, what is the passageway which spirits from the dark world utilize to move into human lives? What kind of activities and practices create doorways for demonization?

MIND-ALTERING DRUGS

John the apostle writes of a group of people whom he foresees as experiencing the awesome judgments of God. However, rather than changing their lifestyles, they are described as not repenting of "of their murders, their magic arts, their sexual immorality or their thefts. Neither repented they of their murders, nor of their sorceries, nor of their fornication, nor of their thefts," (Rev. 9:21). The word "sorcery" is very significant. It comes from Greek *pharmakeia* which is the word from which we get our English word "pharmacy," or drugstore. It means a drug-related kind of occult worship or black magic.

SATANIC MUSIC

Increasingly over the years, many rock musicians have, both in their music and their proclamations, shown them to be openly satanic. Music is unquestionably, is a major potential entry path for demonization.

SATANIC GAMES AND TOYS

An avalanche of such toys and games has descended upon the shelves of stores today. There are the old standbys such as Ouija boards, tarot cards, Dungeons and Dragons, etc. Added to these video games, computer games are with a high percentage of which has occult and even demonic overtones. These games are addictive. Then there are the numerous truly bizarre figures and toys, ranging from the trolls to grotesque, completely unnatural creations. These occult toys are doorways to witchcraft.

SEANCES AND ASTROLOGY

These "parlor games" are not harmless. They are powerful doorways to demonization. These practices deliberately open invitation to spirit beings to manifest themselves. Astrology is seeking personal guidance by applying the use of horoscopes.

OCCULT BOOKS, MAGAZINES AND COMICS

Included in this group the reader finds "sacred scriptures" of Eastern religions, such as *The Tibetan Book of the Dead, the Bhagavid-Gita, Three Ways of Asian Wisdom* and Hinduism, etc.

MOVIES

Horror Movies, Rosemarie's Baby and The Exorcist were some of the early movies produced that focused on demonization and the paranormal. A flood of TV programs, movies which pleasantly present the occult, the spirit world and the New Age as harmless entertainment. These are avenues of overt Satanism, witchcraft or New Age/Eastern religions.

FILLING AMERICA AND CANADA WITH NEW GODS

Researcher McCandlish Phillips is most instructive: Canada and the United States are filling up with . . . new gods . . . coming in from the East as fast as Satan can import them . . . The satanic forces of darkness are not deployed uniformly among the nations, and demonic activity is by no means equal in all areas of the world. Some nations are under far heavier demonic occupation than others, and in those areas the activity of evil spirits is far more pronounced.

There are places in which Satan and his demons have had great influence, precisely because of the extent of idolatry, false religion and occultism in those places . . . The rising indulgence in idolatry, false Eastern religions, occultism, spiritualism and immorality gives Satan the occasion he needs to release more and more demons upon our population.

Any involvement with witchcraft (whether it is called "white" or "black," Satanism or Eastern religions, in which demonization invariably plays, a role, opens one to the possibility of demonic attack or demon possession.

WITCHCRAFT

ASTROLOGY ~ (Deut. 4:19; Dan. 1:20, 2:2, 10, 27; 5:57, Ch. 11, 15; Isa. 47:13).
CHARMING ~ (Deut. 18:11; Psa. 58:5; Is. 19:3; Jer. 8:17; Ezek. 13:18-20).
CHILD SACRIFICE ~ (Deut. 18:10; Lev. 18:21; 20:2-5; I Ki. 11:7; 2 Ki. 17:17; 23:10; Jer. 32:35).

DIVINATION ~ (Gen. 44:5; Lev. 19:26; Num. 22:7; 23:23; Deut. 18:10, 14; 2; Ki.17:17; 21:6; Jer. 14:14; 27:9; 29:8; Ezek. 12:24; 13:6, 7, 19, 23, 29; 21:21; Acts 16:16).

ENCHANTMENTS ~ (Deut. 18:10; Ex. 7:11, 22; 8:7, 18; Num. 23:23; 24:1; Lev. 19:26; 2 Ki. 17:17; 21:6; II Chron. 33:6; Eccel. 10:11; Is. 47:9, 12; Jer. 27:9).

FALSE INTERPRETERS OF DREAMS ~ (Jer. 27:9).

MAGICIANS ~ (Genesis 41:8,24; Ex. 7:11,22; 8:7,18; 9:11; 13:23; 19:11; Dan. 1:20; 2:2,10,27; 4:7,9; 5:11; Ezek. 21:29; and Acts 19:19).

MEDIUMS ~ (Deut. 18:11; 2 Ki. 21:6; Is. 19:3; Jer. 29:8).

NECROMANCY Talking to the Dead ~ (Deut. 18:11; Is. 8:19).

OBSERVING TIMES ~ (Lev. 19:26; Deut. 18:10, 14; 2 Ki. 21:6; 2 Chron. 33:6).

PROGNOSTICATORS ~ (Is. 47:13, 14; Lev. 19:26).

PSYCHICS ~ (Deut. 18:11; 2 Ki. 21:6; Is. 19:3).

SATANISTS ~ Modern-day versions of worshipers of demons, Baal and other false gods/goddesses, (in Bible times people didn't realize what Satan was propagating); the practice of sacrificing children and infants live and screaming into the fire to the 'god of Molech' and other demon gods; today, Satanic ritual abuse, infant/adult sacrifices.

SOOTHSAYING/FORTUNE TELLING ~ (Deut.18:10; Lev. 19:26; Joshua 13:22; Dan. 2:27; 4:7; 5:7, 11; Is. 2:6; Mic. 5:12; Acts 16:16).

SORCERY (Pharmakia - the root of our word, pharmacy, or drugs) ~ Ex. 7:11, 22:18; Lev. 19:26; Nu. 23:23; 24:1; Deut. 18:10, 14; 2 Ki...21:6; 2 Chron. 33:6; Is. 47:9; 12; 57:3; Jer. 27:9; Dan. 2:2; Mal. 3:5; Acts 8:9,11; 13:6,8; Gal. 5:20; Rev. 9:21; 18:23; 21:8; 22:15).

SPIRITISTS ~ (Deut. 18:10, 11; Is. 19:3).

WITCH/WIZARD ~ (Lev. 19:31; 20:6,27; Deut. 18:11; I Sam. 28:3,9; 2 Ki.. 21:6; 23:24; 2 Chron. 33:6; Isa. 8:19; 19:3; 28:18).

WITCHCRAFT ~ (Deut. 18:10; Lev. 19:26; 1 Sam. 15:23; 2 Ki. 9:22; 2 Chron. 33:6; Mic. 5:12; Nah. 3:4; Gal.5: 20).

Appendix Two ~ Glossary Of The Occult

AMULET ~ Ornament inscribed with a magic spell or sign, usually worn around the neck or wrist to ward off evil and to 'help' the wearer.

ANIMISM ~ Belief that inanimate objects, such as rocks, trees, the wind, are alive and has souls.

ASTROLOGY ~ Study of the position of the stars in order to understand and predict their influence on human affairs and world events such as floods, earthquakes, etc.

AUGURY ~ Practice of omen, sign, portent.

BEWITCH ~ To influence, especially harmfully, by witchcraft; to cast a spell.

BLACK MAGIC ~ Witchcraft. Sometimes called 'black arts'.

CHARM ~ Act of spell having magic power; something worn by a person to ward off evil.

CLAIRVOYANCE ~ Ability to discern things that are not yet present to the senses.

CONJURE ~ To summon a departed spirit or a devil - often by incantation.

COVEN ~An assembly of thirteen witches/warlocks.

CRYSTAL GAZER ~ Person who uses a crystal ball to look into the future.

CURSE ~ To call harm or injury upon a person; or the injury that comes in response to the invocation.

DEMON ~ Evil attendant power or spirit, subservient to Satan.

DIVINATION ~ Practice of seeking to foretell or foresee the future and discover hidden knowledge, often by means of omens, augury or other occult means. (Including 'water-witching' with sticks or a rod)

EFFIGY ~ In voodoo, an object that's usually a doll made of clay, straw, rags, etc. to represent the intended victim of the doll-maker's curses, spells and evil.

EXORCISM ~ Catholic Ritual used to drive away an evil spirit. Jesus cast devils out. Christians cast devils out.

ESP ~ Abbreviation for extra-sensory perception.

EXTRA-SENSORY PERCEPTION ~ Ability to gain insights or knowledge without the use of ordinary senses (sight, hearing, smell, etc)...

FAMILIAR SPIRIT ~ Spirit embodied in an animal which attends, serves and guards a person.

FETISH ~ Object regarded as magical or sacred by primitive people, for use in avoiding evil and attracting good for the owner.

FORTUNE TELLER ~ One who tells future events, usually for individuals.

HEX ~ To affect by an evil spell; or the sign used by believers in the occult realm to ward off evil spirits.

HOROSCOPE - Diagram showing position of planets and stars with their signs of the zodiac... used by astrologers to foretell 'supposed' events of a person's life and give related guidance.

INCANTATION ~ Charm or spell that is spoken or sung as part of a witchcraft ritual.

MAGICK ~ Supernatural power over natural forces, by use of charms, spells, etc. (Not to be confused with sleight of hand tricks often performed on stage: 'magic').

MEDIUM ~ Individual who acts as a means of communication between this world and the spirit world, with ability to talk to and call up the dead.

NECROMANCY ~ Conjuring spirits for the purpose of revealing the future or influencing future events.

OCCULT ~ Secret, mysterious, relating to supernatural agencies or forces.

OUIJA BOARD ~ Flat wooden surface with the alphabet and other signs used to obtain spiritualistic knowledge. This is sometimes considered a game.

PALMISTRY ~ Reading a person's character or future by the lines on his palms.

PHRENOLOGY ~ Reading a person's character by the conformation of the skull.

POLTERGEIST ~ noisy, mischievous ghost (a demon) who is said to be responsible for strange noises such as rapping or knocking, or movement of inanimate objects. These Poltergeists seem to be especially ready to perform around young girls.

PRECOGNITION ~ Discernment about an event not yet experienced, achieved by means beyond the ordinary physical senses.

PREMONITION ~ Uneasy anticipation of an event without any conscious reason for anxiety.

PRESENTIMENT ~ Feeling that something is about to happen.

PSYCHIC ~ Person who is sensitive to non-physical forces and their significance in the material world.

PSYCHIC PHENOMENA ~ Events that cannot be explained by physical reference, so are attributed to non-physical forces.

REINCARNATION ~ Rebirth of a soul into a new human body or other form of life. A false teaching of the devil: his substitution for resurrection life. An element of the Hindu religion and belief of many "new-agers."

SATANIST ~ Devil worship, usually involving a travesty of Christian rites.

SEANCE ~ Group meeting to receive communication from spirits. A medium usually presides at a séance.

SEER ~ One who predicts future events or developments.

SORCERY ~ Use of power obtained from control of, or the help of, evil spirits... especially for divination or necromancy.

SOOTHSAYING ~ Act of foretelling future events.

SPELL ~ Spoken word or pattern of words with magical power.

SPIRITISM or SPIRITUALISM ~ Belief that departed spirits commune with living people usually through a medium but sometimes through other psychic phenomena.

TAROT CARDS ~ Set of 22 picture playing cards used in fortune telling.

TELEPATHY or, MENTAL TELEPATHY ~ Communication from one mind to another without use of the ordinary physical channels of hearing, seeing, touching, etc.

TRANCE ~ State of partially suspended animation.

VOODOO ~ Religion derived from African ancestor worship practiced by Natives of West Indies, African and other Americans, especially Jamaica, Haiti, Central America, New Orleans, N.Y.C., and just about everywhere they've migrated to - involving spells, necromancy and communication with animistic gods. Effigies and other cursed objects are used to bring harm to the intended victims.

WARLOCK ~ One who works black magic; obs; a male witch

WITCH ~ A woman or man, who practices the black arts; one who has supernatural powers because of a pact with the devil.

WITCHCRAFT ~ Communion with the devil for purposes of working evil.

WITCHES' SABBATH or SABBAT ~ Midnight assembly of coven of witches for performing rites.

WIZARD ~ Skilled magician; sorcerer

ZODIAC ~ Imaginary belt of planets and constellations in twelve 'houses' which supposedly affect human experience ...represented by astrological signs.

Bibliography

Arnold, Clinton E Ephesians: Power and Magic (Cambridge, England, Cambridge University Press, 1989, p. 27.

Bayly, Joseph, What about Horoscopes? Arthur Lyons; the Second Coming; Satanism in America.

Barnhouse, Donald Grey. The Invisible War, Zondervan Publications pg. Grand Rapid Mi., 180,

Basham, Don; Can a Christian Have a Demon? 1971: Whitaker Books. Deliver Us From Evil, 1972, Chosen Books.

Bjornstad and Shildes Johnson; Stars, Signs, and Salvation in the Age of Aquarius,

Bethany Fellowship, Inc. Minn.

Brooks, Pat; Occult Experimentation, (tract) 1972: Moody Press, Chicago.

Chafer, Lewis S. Systematic Theology, Vol. 2, copyright 1947 by Dallas Seminary, Dallas Tx.

Christensen, Larry; the Christian Family, 1970: Bethany Fellowship, Minn.

Charisma Magazine, Lake Helen, Orlando, Fl.

Clark's Commentary, Vol., 5, p 370, "LUKE".

Corrie Ten Boom, Defeated Enemies, Christian Literature Crusade, Fort Washington, Pennsylvania, 19034,

Demonbusters www.blood of Jesus.demonbusters.com Stan & Elizabeth Madrak

1Doreen Irvine, Freed From Witchcraft, (Thomas Nelson Publishers) p. 102. 2. "Deadly Horror of the Devil Cults" Weekly World News, October 20, 1981.

http://www.divinerevelations.info/dreams_and_visions/Diliv ered_from_the_powers_of_Darkness_by_Emmanuel_Eni.htm

http://en.wikipedia.org/wiki/Earth_in_the_Balance

Expelling demons by Derek Prince Publication. Ft. Lauderdale, Fl. 33302

Encyclopedia Britannica, art, "Easter.

Ernest, Victor H.; I Talked with Spirits, Tyndale House Publishers, Wheaton, Illinois.

Hammand, Frank & Ida Mae Pigs in the Parlor, Impact Books, Kirwood Mo. 36322.

Freeman, Dr. Hobart E.; Angels of Light, 1969: Logos International Publishing Co., Plainfield, New Jersey.

Great People and the Bible, the Reader's Digest Association, Inc. 1974.

Frazer, the Golden Bough, p. 471. Frazer, the Golden Bough, p. 471.

Gasson, Raphael; the Challenging Counterfeit, Logos International, Plainfield, New

Louise Heubner, 'Official Witch of Southern California'. Eugene Debs, Jersey.

Irene A. Park with Jeffrey Park, the Witch That Switched (Charlotte, N.C). p. 76.

H. A. Maxwell Whyte, Dominion Over Demons (Banner Publishing), p. 175.

Hislop, the Two Babylons, p. 103.

Holliday, Dr. Pat; the Walking Dead; Be Free; Born Anew; Solitary Satanist; Witch

Doctor and the Man-Fourth Generation Witchdoctor finds Christ, Signs and Wonders and

Reactions; Spirit of Idolatry Transference of Spirits, Miracle Outreach Ministry, San

Jose Blvd., 2804, Jacksonville, Fl. 32257.

Jarman, Ray; Pseudo Christians, Logos International; Plainfield, New Jersey. Koch Dr

Jessie Penn-Lewis, War On the Saints (Christian Literature Cursade) p. 21.

C.S. Lewis, the Screwtape Letters (New York: The Macmillan Co., 1969), p. 3.

Kurt; Between Christ and Satan, 1962: Occult Bondage and Deliverance, Kregel

Publications; Grand Rapids, Michigan.

Erica Joseph of Breakthrough Missions (address unknown) in a booklet titled "Sex with Demons - Nightmares, Incubus and Succubus"

Layman's Bible Encyclopedia, Cleveland Tenn. Pg `95

Mel Tari, Like A Mighty Wind, (Harrison, Ar. - New Leaf Press), p. 56.

http://www.amazon.com/Beautiful-Side-Evil-Johanna-Michaelsen/dp/0890813221

Manuel, Francis D.; Though a Host Should Encamp, 1971: Christian Literature

Mary Garrison, How To Conduct Spiritual Warfare, As I See It, (Hudson, Florida: Christ Camp Ministries, Inc). p. 65.

Crusade; Fort Washington, Pennsylvania.

Martin, Walter; the Kingdom of the Cults, Bethany Fellowship, Inc.; Minn. Minn.

The Gene and Earline Moody Deliverance Manual, WWW.blood of jesus.Demonbuster.

Com

Irene Park, "The Witch That Switched" "Halloween & Pagan High Masses .Tampa, Fla.

Penn-Lewis, Jessie, and Robetts Evan; War on the Saints, Christian Literature Crusade;

Fort Washington, Pennsylvania.

Petersen, William L; Those Curious New Cults, Keats Publishing, New Canaan,

Connecticut.

Expelling demons by Derek Prince Publication. Ft. Lauderdale, Fl. 33302

A. Rex Shanks, CROWN OF LIFE MINISTRIES, Eyes of Understanding.

Merrill F. Unger, *Demons in the World Today* (Tyndale House Publishers). Why a second work on the subject of demonism, while the first, *Biblical Demonology,* is still in print?

The Encyclopedia Americana, Vol. 6, p. 623.

Philips; the Bible, the Supernatural and the Jews, World Publishing Company; New

York, NY

"Haiti: A Nation in Agony" Reader's Digest, October, 1981, p. 100.

What's Your Question? On the Holy Spirit, Fasting, Healing, Glossolalia, and Demons,

Ken Sumrall, Whitaker Books 607 Laurel Drive, Monroevill, Pennsylvania 15145

Hobart E. Freeman, Every Wind of Doctrine, (Warsaw, Indiana; Faith Min. & Pub)

http://www.sermonindex.net/modules/mydownloads/viewcat .php?cid=521&min=20&orderby=titleA&show=20 Rev. Milton Green, Sermons.

Schwarze, C.T.; the Program of Satan Good News Publishing Co. Weschester, 111.

The Eerdmans Bible Dictionary,"

The Church that Jesus Built, by Eugene Goodman, Turner's Creek Baptist Church, Yadkinville, N.C.

The Complete Guide to the Bible, Reader's Digest, Pleasantville, New York/Montreal

Thomas, F. W.; Kingdom of Darkness, Logos International; Plainfield, New Jersey.

[Thomas Ice and Robert Dean, Jr., *Overrun By Demons*, (Eugene, OR: Harvest House, 1990), p. 116].Robison's "Absolutes" are nothing but mainstream American civic values: "People Matter Most," "Greed Destroys," "Character Counts," etc

Unger's (From the New Unger's Bible Dictionary. Originally published by Moody Press of Chicago, Illinois. Copyright (c) 1988.)

Wilburn, Gary A.; the Fortune Sellers, Regal; Glendale, CA.

Williams, Charles; Witchcraft, 1959; World Publishing Co. Cleveland.

Upham, Charles W.; Salem Witchcraft, 1867: Wiggin and Lunt, Pulling Down Strongholds, 1971;

Hidden Spirits, 1970; Return to the Pattern, 1977; Fear Destroys, 1978; (booklets)

Scarborough, Ontario; 2 Delbert Drive.

World Book Encyclopedia

Worley, Win; Diary of An Exorcist; Battling the Hosts of Hell, .B.C. Publications; P.O. Box 626, Lansing, 111. 60438

Wilkerson, Ralph; ESP or HSP? Melodyland Publishers; P.O. Box 6000, Anaheim, California, 92806

Whyte, Rev. H.A.M.; the Power of the Blood, 1972; Dominion Over Demons, 1979;

A. Zaldivar, The Miami Herald, 7/18/82, pp. 1B-2B.

http://www.exposingsatanism.org/signs2.htm

http://www.nazarite.net/satanic-symbols.html

http://www.secularhumanism.org/library/fi/cohen_24_4.htm

http://www.divinerevelations.info/dreams_and_visions/Diliv ered_from_the_powers_of_Darkness_by_Emmanuel_Eni.htm

A. Zaldivar, the Miami Herald, 7/18/82, pp. 1B-2B.

[1] http://www.canadafreepress.com/2005/cover062805.htm *by Judi McLeod,*

Canada Free Press. **Tuesday, June 28, 2005**

(FrontPageMag.com, Feb. 20, 2004).

96830981R00147

Made in the USA
Columbia, SC
06 June 2018